Trustworthy AI

Damian Okaibedi Eke · Kutoma Wakunuma ·
Simisola Akintoye · George Ogoh
Editors

Trustworthy AI

African Perspectives

palgrave
macmillan

Editors
Damian Okaibedi Eke
School of Computer Science
University of Nottingham
Nottingham, UK

Simisola Akintoye
Northumbria Law School
Northumbria University
Newcastle upon Tyne, UK

Kutoma Wakunuma
De Montfort University
Leicester, UK

George Ogoh
School of Computer Science
University of Nottingham
Nottingham, UK

ISBN 978-3-031-75673-3 ISBN 978-3-031-75674-0 (eBook)
https://doi.org/10.1007/978-3-031-75674-0

This work was supported by the Engineering and Physical Sciences Research Council [grant number EP/Y009800/1] and Faculty of Computing, Engineering and Media, School of Computer Science and Informatics, DMU

This Palgrave Macmillan imprint is published by the registered company Springer Nature Switzerland AG
The registered company address is: Gewerbestrasse 11, 6330 Cham, Switzerland

Foreword: Exploring the African AI Ecosystem

The progress of artificial intelligence (AI) currently appears irresistible. AI tools and technologies continue to become better, faster, more widely available and at the same time get applied to an ever-increasing number of tasks, questions and problems. It is therefore not surprising that much activity is undertaken to better understand and steer AI use across technologies, applications, cultures, jurisdictions, etc. This book is a welcome contribution to this discussion, looking primarily at the African context and how we can ensure that the development and use of AI in Africa can be promoted in ways that bestow benefits on the local population while avoiding downsides, problems, ethical and other concerns.

The focus on Africa sharpens awareness of some aspects of technology use. One prominent aspect is that of Africa's colonial history and the danger of the intended or inadvertent use of AI to establish new colonial dependencies. The lens of colonialism and decolonisation sensitises us to the underlying assumptions of AI that are worthy of broader discussion. Where AI systems are based on machine learning that utilises large data sets, a key question is where those datasets originate and what they represent. In the case of medical data, for example, datasets including biomarkers or signs of diseases, a key question is whether the machine learning model is applicable to populations who differ significantly from those represented in the original dataset. Given that some diseases have different prevalence in different populations, a key question could be whether a machine learning model and AI systems based on it, for example an automated pathology identification system, that is built on data from European individuals is applicable to African populations.

This is a pertinent question to ask, given that much medical data is collected in industrialised countries and that less affluent countries, including many African countries, have fewer resources to dedicate to the collection of medical data and therefore contribute less to medical datasets. This is an example of an issue that may preclude the successful deployment of AI in Africa and thus harm local populations by depriving them of potential benefit. However, to some extent this is also an 'easy' problem in that it is subject to scientific evaluation where studies can help understand the limits of the applicability of models across populations and, where there is a problem of applicability, this can in principle be solved by providing missing data from the populations that are not covered. In practice, this may well be a significant undertaking calling for data collection from many individuals and require unavailable resources, but in principle it is a solvable problem.

This points to the broader social, economic, and political questions that drive AI policy and thus research and eventual use. While it may be possible to scientifically investigate the applicability of an AI system to specific applications, as in the example of a medical diagnosis system as indicated above, these systems are always embedded in broader contexts that have significant implications for their use and the broader consequences of this use. This points to problems that do not have their origin in AI but that have potentially fundamental implications for AI. One of these is the problem of justice and distributions of resources. As with most other technologies, AI has the potential to alleviate this sort of problem, for example by facilitating better access to education, offering new business opportunities, or providing novel means of expression. However, it can also be used for the opposite purpose by reducing choice, creating monopolies or oligopolies and using AI for control. Prominent voices suggest that current AI structures are more geared towards the latter than the former (Zuboff, 2019).

At this point we do not know what the eventual outcomes of the wider use of AI will be for Africa, nor for the world at large. It is probably safe to say that some people will benefit, but probably not all will. Some will suffer disadvantages, some of which will be new, but many will build on existing inequalities and injustices, for example where well-established problems of digital divides, both within and between countries, lead to unequal access to potential AI benefits.

One can read the chapters of this book as pointing to key aspects of this debate. We need to look at different application sectors such as healthcare or transport to understand possible implications. Similarly, we should explore how AI will affect the many different roles and activities that we all inhabit, from professional work as IT specialists to the implications for our gender roles. Elsewhere I have suggested that a useful concept to think through the implications of AI is the concept of flourishing (Stahl, 2021). Flourishing is a concept with a long history in moral philosophy, often linked to ideas of virtue. I believe that it is fairly uncontentious to say that human activity, including the use of AI should aim to foster and promote the flourishing of humans but also of the social and natural environment that we need to flourish. But how would we know whether a use of AI promotes flourishing? How can we make decisions on which applications to support, which technical design options to implement?

There are no simple answers to such questions, which call for detailed technical knowledge, empirical understanding of the sociotechnical environment of technologies and a careful exploration of possible and desirable futures. I believe that one theoretical position that can offer a vantage point for exploring possible configurations that allow flourishing is the idea of interpreting AI as part of and embedded in social, technical, economic, and political ecosystems (Stahl, 2022, 2023). One advantage of this perspective is that it helps us look beyond the technical artefact and understand why an identical AI system may have very different consequences in different environments. It can help explain why a traffic management system used in Nairobi may work perfectly well, whereas it fails when implemented in Copenhagen.

One reason why I have introduced this idea of AI as an ecosystem in this foreword to a book that looks at AI in Africa is that it can help shed light on how we position and frame the research questions we explore. The book sets the reference ecosystem as that of Africa. By seeing Africa as an example of an AI ecosystem, we can immediately see the interconnected nature of ecosystems. The African AI ecosystem forms part of the global ecosystem, which is obvious, not least from the fact that much AI is driven by the big Tech companies which have global influence. At the same time, the geographical borders of the African AI ecosystem can be divided further, following large regions, such as east, central, or west Africa, by using national borders as dividing lines, cultural, ethnic, or language borders. It seems likely to me that there will be commonalities across Africa but also important differences which we need to be aware of when looking at the implications of AI use. What works in Cairo may not work in Lagos or Johannesburg, and what is successful in a rural area reliant on subsistence farming may fail in an urban area. The point here is that we need to actively reflect on and be critical of the boundaries we draw, often implicitly, around the ecosystem we are interested in.

Engaging in active boundary critique of the ecosystem under investigation means that researchers interested in AI need to reflect on and be explicit about the assumptions and decisions. This is often difficult, not least because many of our assumptions are tacit and implicit. Engaging in the sort of active reflection that allows us to surface these assumptions is important because it allows us to better understand the limitations of our insights and recommendations.

I believe that this ecosystem view may help understand the strengths and weaknesses of the research positions we take and thus help us interpret the chapters in this book. It is also important because it helps us see that the African context is a specific one that requires specific attention but that it is part of the global AI ecosystem. By reflecting on the boundaries of our subject matter we can better see which aspects of it are unique, but also where insights may be transferable and of interest elsewhere. This, in turn, can help ensure that the work presented in this book can unfold its uses in Africa, but can also be relevant in other AI ecosystems and thereby increase its reach and impact.

Prof. Bernd Carsten Stahl
Director
University of Nottingham
Nottingham, UK

Responsible Digital Futures
https://www.nottingham.ac.uk/computerscience/research/responsible-digital-futures.aspx

References

Stahl, B. C. (2021). *Artificial Intelligence for a Better Future: An Ecosystem Perspective on the Ethics of AI and Emerging Digital Technologies*. Springer International Publishing. https://doi.org/10.1007/978-3-030-69978-9

Stahl, B. C. (2022). Responsible innovation ecosystems: Ethical implications of the application of the ecosystem concept to artificial intelligence. *International Journal of Information Management*, *62*, 102441. https://doi.org/10.1016/j.ijinfomgt.2021.102441

Stahl, B. C. (2023). Embedding responsibility in intelligent systems: From AI ethics to responsible AI ecosystems. *Scientific Reports*, *13*(1), Article 1. https://doi.org/10.1038/s41598-023-34622-w

Zuboff, S. (2019). *The Age of Surveillance Capitalism: The Fight for a Human Future at the New Frontier of Power* (1st edition). Profile Books.

The original version of the book has been revised. A correction to this book can be found at https://doi.org/10.1007/978-3-031-75674-0_13

Acknowledgements

We would like to thank everyone who has provided support and assistance towards the successful publication of this book. In a special way, we want to express our thanks to our respective members of our research groups - the Responsible Digital Futures (RDF) group of the School of Computer Science, University of Nottingham, UK, and the Centre for Computing and Social Responsibility, UK who provided stimulating conversations that helped the formulation of the initial ideas of this book. We are also indebted to our colleagues and collaborators from the Responsible AI UK (RAIUK) project and a special mentor to all of us Prof Bernd Carsten Stahl. We are also grateful to Rachael Ballard who expertly supported this work from MacMillan Palgrave as well as all the chapter contributors.

Also, **Damian Okaibedi Eke** thanks his family; Wife—Linda and children; Chizitere, Chidimma, Chizurumoke, and Nnabuihe who continue to provide Daddy the conducive environment to work.

Kutoma Wakunuma thanks her family, particularly her beloved daughter Angelica who is always loving, patient, supportive, and understanding of Mummy's sometimes busy schedule.

Simisola Akintoye thanks her family for the love and support provided during the process. She is particularly thankful to her children—Enoch, Ethan, and Elias who have been nothing but loving boys to mum during this time.

George Ogoh thanks his family including Halima his dear wife and children Zazzau, Zaltana, and Zaire for their constant support and understanding during this period.

Contents

Notes on Contributors

Muhammad Adamu is a Research Fellow in Responsible AI for Health at the University of Nottingham, UK. His current research focuses on establishing "AI in/from Africa" theme via responsible research and innovation, health data governance, and responsible digital futures. He is strongly associated with the "African perspective" in Human-computer interaction and he received his Ph.D. from Lancaster University, UK.

Simisola Akintoye is an Associate Professor of Law at Northumbria University School of Law. She is interested in multidisciplinary research around legal and ethical regulation of Emerging Technologies and Corporate Sustainability. Her research covers critical issues at the intersection of law and technology including Data Governance, Privacy and Data Protection, Ethics of Emerging Technologies and Responsible Research and Innovation (RRI). Simi is an International Privacy Practitioner and was the Data Protection Officer for the European Union Future and Emerging Technologies Human Brain Project (HBP). She is involved in multi-disciplinary Policy Expert Reports on the future implications of AI and societal benefit. Over the years, Simi has formed consortia that contributes to the furtherance of knowledge, practice and public policy in applied contexts of research, teaching, consultancy and business. Her current research investigates the legal, ethical and socio-cultural implications of AI in Africa towards developing an inclusive, equitable and sustainable AI ecosystem for Africa.

Joseph Damilola Akinyemi obtained his B.Sc. in Computer Science from the University of Ilorin, Ilorin, Nigeria and obtained both his Masters and Doctorate degrees from the University of Ibadan, Ibadan, Nigeria. He is currently a lecturer at the Department of Computer Science, University of York, Heslington, UK. His research interest is in Computer Vision, Pattern Recognition, and Machine Learning.

Eugeniah Arthur holds a Ph.D. in Statistics from Bowling Green State University, specialising in high-dimensional data reduction, machine learning, and data visualisation. Currently, she works as a data scientist at First Solar.

Kehinde Aruleba is a lecturer in Computer Science at the University of Leicester, UK. His research mainly focuses on improving computer science education through technology, pedagogy, and content. He is also interested in AI and its application, focusing on responsible AI.

Abiola Joseph Azeez is a Ph.D. candidate in AI Ethics at the University of Ottawa, domiciled in the Philosophy Department and affiliated with the Canadian Robotics and AI Ethical Design Laboratory (CRAiEDL) and the Canadian Society for the Study of Practical Ethics (CSSPE). A distinguished contributor to the CAIDP's AI Policy Clinic and MILA's Responsible AI and Human Rights programme. Abiola has contributed to significant projects such as the Interpol-UNICRI Responsible AI Toolkit for Law Enforcement and CAIDP's AI and Democratic Value Index (AIDV). His current research focuses on developing an AI Data Context Index to enhance data security in the Global South, particularly regarding facial recognition technologies as digital surveillance tools. Notably, Abiola has presented his work on "Trust Norms for Generative AI Data Gathering in the African Context" at the Data for Policy 2024 Conference at Imperial College London, with the paper forthcoming from Cambridge University Press.

Dr. Yemisi Babalola is a professor of Information Management with nearly 20 years of experience in higher education. She holds a degree in Linguistics, Information Science with a Ph.D. in Information Resources Management from Babcock University. Since joining Babcock University, Dr. Babalola has been a professor of Information Resources Management.

Damian Okaibedi Eke is Assistant Professor at the School of Computer Science, University of Nottingham, UK. His research in ethics of emerging technology, particularly AI, spans across several previous and ongoing projects such as UKRI's Responsible AI UK (RAI-UK) and Responsible Generative AI in the UK and Africa (RAISE) projects, EU's Sustainable eThics Reviews of digital heAlth Technology dEsiGn In sub saharan africa (STRATEGIC) and the Future and Emerging Technologies Human Brain Project (HBP) as well as the Wellcome Trust funded project BRIDGE. His research interests cover critical philosophical issues at the intersection of Technology, Data and Society including; Data Ethics and Governance, Responsible Innovation and ICT4D.

Ayodeji Olusegun Ibitoye is a distinguished Ph.D. holder in Computer Science and a lecturer at the University of Greenwich, London, UK where he brings a wealth of expertise in data science, natural language processing (NLP), and machine learning engineering. With a robust career spanning academy and industrial domains, he specialises in leveraging AI-driven technologies to advance business intelligence and healthcare predictive solutions. Renowned for his consultancy works, Ayodeji is celebrated for his ability to foster trust and credibility in complex research, and cutting-edge solutions, ensuring that organisations can confidently navigate the intricacies of AI integration and innovation.

Memunat A. Ibrahim is a software engineer and a Ph.D. student at the School of Cybernetics, the Australian National University. Her Ph.D. research explores the design of trustworthy and socially acceptable autonomous ground vehicles (AGVs) for African societies, using Nigeria as a case study. With academic backgrounds in computer science and cybernetics, Memunat has worked in software development, user experience research, AI ethics, and data governance in Africa. Memunat's areas of interest are in the design, engineering, and governance of safe and trustworthy (AI or data-driven) systems and decolonial AI ethics.

Maha Jouini is programme officer at African union development Agency (AUDA-NEPAD) and Visitor researcher at Witwatersrand University based in Johannesburg South Africa. Maha Jouini worked as an AI policy researcher at Global Index on Responsible AI in Senegal. She served as ambassador in Google's Women Techmakers initiative where she advocated for Woman inclusion and AI responsible use in Francophone Africa namely in Senegal, Mauritania, and Tunisia. Currently she is the vice president of Agence Africaine et francophone de l'intelligence artificielle. Maha believes in AI impact on Business development, She delivered Mentoring sessions to women and youth in Africa. She was part of Women Innovators Programme (WIP) launched by UNDP Arab region states and Now she is Mentor at Incubateur Paris 2024 launched by L' Agence française de développement. She participated at the Global responsible AI hackathon 2023 launched by Woman in AI Ethics Initiative in 2022 UNESCO and the Asfari Institute for Civil Society and Citizenship at AUB consider Maha Jouini among top 20 woman changemakers pioneers in MENA, thanks to her commitments to woman digital rights and economic inclusion.

Dr. Tope Ladi-Akinyemi holds a medical degree from Olabisi Onabanjo University and completed her residency training in Public Health at the same institution's teaching hospital. Her research interests encompass preventing and controlling STIs and HIV, Adolescent Health, Maternal and Child Health, Mental Health, Health Economics, and Health Informatics. She is a senior lecturer in the Department of Community Health and Primary Care at the College of Medicine, University of Lagos, Lagos State, Nigeria.

Dr. Khadijat Tope Ladoja received her B.Sc. degree in Computer Science from the University of Ilorin, Nigeria, in 2010. She then completed her M.Sc. and Ph.D. degrees in Computer Science at the University of Ibadan, Nigeria, in 2014 and 2021, respectively. Currently, she is a faculty member in the Department of Computer Science at the University of Ibadan, with over five years of teaching and research experience. Her research focuses on Natural Language Processing, specifically targeting language models for low-resource Nigerian languages and computer vision. Dr. Ladoja's dedication to teaching and research has earned her the fellowship of the "Empowering the Teachers" programme at MIT, USA, and recognition as one of the Top 200 young researchers by the Heidelberg Laureate Foundation (HLF).

Dr. Eucabeth B. O. Majiwa has a Ph.D. in agricultural economics earned in 2017 from Queensland University of Technology [QUT], Australia and a master of International Development Studies (Development Economics) from the National Graduate Institute of Policy Studies, Japan in 2007. Currently, Eucabeth is a lecturer in the Department of Agricultural and Resource Economics at Jomo Kenyatta University of Agriculture and Technology [JKUAT] where she teaches and supervises students in Agribusiness and Agricultural Economics. Dr. Majiwa has fifteen years' experience in research administration & extension, and community development, and seven years teaching experience. Her research interests focus on Agriculture/Agribusiness and rural economic issues including food systems, farm-level efficiency, and technology evaluation and transfer. The researcher focuses on work that will help identify programmes and policies to improve productivity and efficiency in farming and agri-business systems. Her current project is AI adoption and use by smallholder women farmers and traders in Kenya and the upscaling of African Indigenous vegetables. Other research includes circular economy practices, mapping of land degradation and economics of it in Narok County. She has played as a Mentor and Coach and Member of the Technical Committee on SME Mentoring and Coaching, of the Jomo Kenyatta University of Agriculture and Technology College of Agriculture which involves mentoring of SMEs in the Agribusiness Value Chain in Kiambu, Nairobi, and Machakos Counties of Kenya under a collaborative project of Jomo Kenyatta University of Agriculture and Technology and the Food and Agriculture Organization of the United Nations.

Dennis Munetsi holds a B.A. in International Migration and Ethnic Relations and an M.A. in Political Science, with a major in Global Political Studies, both from Malmö University. He also earned an M.Sc. in Global Sexual Reproductive and Perinatal Health from Dalarna University. Dennis is a doctoral researcher and lecturer in social sciences at Malmö University's Department of Global Political Studies in Sweden, where he teaches Political Science and International Relations courses. His research, funded by the Wallenberg AI, Autonomous Systems and Software Program—Humanity and Society (WASP-HS), primarily focuses on the transnational transfer and geo-technological implications of AI-infused digital healthcare interventions for women in peripheral communities. Through his research, Dennis aims to contribute to how AI-infused digital technologies can be leveraged to improve healthcare access and outcomes in Africa, particularly enhancing marginalised women's access to reproductive healthcare.

Dr. Angella K. Ndaka is a national consultant on Gender and Youth Integration in Agriculture Digitization at the Food and Agriculture organisation of the UN(FAO). She is also a critical AI researcher at and Co-founder of the Centre for Epistemic Justice Foundation. She holds a Ph.D. in sociology and Gender studies from the Centre for

Sustainability (CSAFE), University of Otago, New Zealand. Her other qualifications include a Master of Public Policy from Crawford School of Public Policy, Australian National University, Australia, and Education degree from Kenyatta University, Kenya. Her research interests focus on Critical scholarship on AI and emerging technologies, and wider AI sociotechnical systems. Her most recent publications have focused on epistemic justice in technology knowledge co-production, decolonial perspectives in AI sociotechnical systems, gender perspectives in AI, as well as emerging AI and digital policy landscape. In the past she has worked as a consultant with different international development organisations and an Academic with Kenyatta University department of Public Policy. She is a multi-award winner for her thought leadership in the critical AI space.

Dr. Seydina Moussa Ndiaye is senior lecturer at Cheikh Hamidou Kane Digital University (Senegal). He also supports the Ministry of Higher Education, Research and Innovation, steering the digital transformation of Senegal's higher education system. Seydina coordinated the acquisition of Senegal's supercomputer, TAOUEY. At national level, he is a member of several bodies, including National Digital Council, National Cryptology Commission, Steering Committee of the Digital Technology Park Project (PTN), Board of Directors of SENUM SA, and President of the Senegalese Association for AI. Seydina has supported the Senegalese government in the conceptualization of national AI and data strategies. Seydina is an expert to the African Union for the drafting of the Pan African Strategy on AI and to the Global Partnership on Artificial Intelligence (GPAI). He is also a member of the UN SG's High-Level AI Advisory Body. Seydina holds a Ph.D. in Computer Science, specialising in Artificial Intelligence (Paul Sabatier University), and an MBA (IAE Paris Sorbonne).

Makuochi Samuel Nkwo is a lecturer and Human-Centred AI researcher at the University of Greenwich, London, UK. He has a Ph.D. in Computer Science. While his current research focuses on responsible designs and innovations, he works at the intersection of human-computer interaction, artificial intelligence, digital ethics and governance, and their application to digital health, education, ecommerce, and sustainable future.

George Ogoh is a Senior Research Fellow in the School of Computer Science, University of Nottingham. His research covers a wide range of themes in emerging technology ethics and social responsibility and include topics on Responsible Research and Innovation (RRI), Responsible Innovation, diversity and equality, data governance, and data protection. He has been involved in several EU funded projects including the Responsible Innovation Compass project, the Human Brain Project (HBP), environMENTAL project and the iRECS Project. His publications cover a variety of topics on responsible development and the use of emerging technologies such as Artificial Intelligence, Brain Research Infrastructures, Virtual reality, Contact Tracing Apps, Additive Manufacturing etc.

Abigail Oppong is a consultant, independent researcher, and research associate at the Center for Human-Inspired AI (CHIA), focusing on natural language processing to create an impact in marginalised communities. With a background in science, computing, and community engagement, her research involves collaborating with interdisciplinary teams to explore how emerging technologies, like AI, can better serve marginalised communities. Her research interests include Gender in AI/Language Technologies, Neurolinguistics, AI and Art, and Health Technologies.

Ayomide Owoyemi has a background in Medicine, public health, and product management. He has had experience working as a clinician and public health physician in Nigeria. He was a global fund project consultant for HIV care and management. He has also built digital health products for Nigeria and other African countries. He led the team that built the first COVID-19 triage tool in Africa and the first AI-based recommendation system for health insurance in Nigeria. He also worked with Boston Consulting Group as a Product Manager. He just earned a Ph.D. in health informatics at the University of Illinois Chicago, focusing on AI/ML applications in healthcare.

Harriet A. M. Ratemo is a devoted and skilled research scientist with a strong desire to advance knowledge in the field of computing. With more than a decade of expertise in higher education teaching, research, and publication, Harriet has established herself as a leader in the fields of information security, artificial intelligence, and cyber security. They have a track record of obtaining research grants, engaging with multidisciplinary teams, and successfully presenting their findings. Harriet is a dedicated computer science researcher, actively seeking new research opportunities and collaborations, demonstrating a strong commitment to furthering knowledge and tackling complex challenges that drive innovation and foster scientific discovery. Harriet is currently a Ph.D. Student at United States International University studying Information Systems and Technology (IST) with an M.Sc. Information Science and a B.Sc. in Computer Technology. Her research interests are in Artificial Intelligence, Information and Computer security, Cyber Security, Project Planning, and Technology Implementation.

Emma Ruttkamp-Bloem is a philosopher of science and technology, an AI ethics policy advisor, and a machine ethics researcher. Emma is a member of the UN Secretary General's AI Advisory Body. She is the Chairperson of the UNESCO World Commission on the Ethics of Scientific Knowledge and Technology (COMEST). Currently, she is the Head of the Department of Philosophy, University of Pretoria, and leads the AI ethics group at the South African Centre for AI Research (CAIR). Emma led the UNESCO Ad Hoc Expert Group that prepared the draft of the 2021 UNESCO Recommendation on the Ethics of AI and contributed to development of its implementation instruments. She is a member of the Global Academic Network, Centre for AI and Digital Policy, Washington DC and has worked on projects related to AI ethics with the African Union Development Agency (AUDA)-NEPAD and the African Commission on Human and People's Rights (ACHPR). She is a member of various international AI ethics advisory boards ranging from academia (e.g. the Wallenberg AI, Autonomous Systems and Software Programme Human Sciences), the inter-governmental sector (e.g. as member of UNESCO' AI Ethics without Borders and Women4EthicalAI initiatives), to the private sector (e.g. SAP SE). She is an associate editor for the *Journal of Science and Engineering Ethics*, and a member of the editorial board of the *Journal for AI Law and Regulation* and the *Cambridge Forum on AI: Law and Regulation.*

Elnathan Tiokou is a Ph.D. student and researcher in cutting-edge Artificial Intelligence. He is dedicated and determined to help change the narrative of Africa through trustworthy, inclusive, and responsible AI. In addition to his research, he is the founder of the young African technology company CHRONEXIS. In his spare time, he creates content on social media to inform, educate, and inspire people with his knowledge, stories, experiences, and achievements. His mission is to inspire young people and provide them with the resources to achieve their meaning of greatness beneficial to society.

Edmund Terem Ugar is a philosopher of Medicine, Public Health, and the Ethics of Artificial Intelligence (AI), Robotics, and Big Data. He is a Ph.D. candidate in the Department of Philosophy at the University of Johannesburg. Edmund is a researcher at the Centre for African-China Studies. He was a research fellow at the Digital Medical Ethics Network (2023), an affiliate of the Faculty of Medicine at the University of Tübingen and Potsdam in Germany. Additionally, Edmund is a recipient of the University of Johannesburg Commonwealth Scholarship. Finally, he is a recipient of the Notre Dame—IBM Technology Ethics Lab Grant ($60,000) with the project entitled "Technology Transfer and Culture in Africa: Large Scale Models in Focus".

Kutoma Wakunuma is Associate Professor in Information Systems at De Montfort University where she works within the Centre for Computing and Social Responsibility (CCSR). She also serves as interim Co-Director for the Centre. Her research interests are in understanding the social and ethical implications of digital technologies and the role that emerging technologies such as AI play in both the Global South and the Global North. In particular, her research work has focussed on Responsible Innovation, AI governance, computing ethics, digital innovation and digital technologies for development including gender. In addition to projects funded by other agencies, she has also been involved in several EU funded projects focussed on emerging technologies, ethics and Responsible Innovation. She also acts as a European Commission Ethics Expert and Project Evaluator. Dr Wakunuma is also Subject Group Leader for the Information Systems group within the School of Computer Science and Informatics.

Elizabeth Williams is an associate professor in the School of Engineering at the ANU. Her Ph.D. was in nuclear physics, from Yale University, and she worked in fundamental and applied nuclear sciences before transitioning to research focusing on cyber-physical systems. Her current work explores the design of technologies for safety-critical systems, with a focus on maximising safety (as defined contextually) in diverse settings. She is creator, co-host, and producer of the Algorithmic Futures Podcast, which investigates how complex technologies, including AI, are shaping—and being shaped by—our world.

Michael Zimba is the executive dean of the Malawi Institute of Technology, Founding Lead of the Center for Artificial Intelligence and STEAM (CAIST), and associate professor of Artificial Intelligence (AI) & Data Science at the Malawi University of Science and Technology. He is a 2024 Selectee to the AI Connect II by the US Department of State; Oxford University Press' Unit Editor for AI in Society Series; Nature-certified Review Editor of the Cambridge Journal of AI; 2024 EDSAFE AI Catalyst Fellow on Safe AI in Education and Member of the Global Academic Network of the Center for Artificial Intelligence and Digital Policy (CAIDP). He is an African Union (AU) Commission's Contributing Expert to Science, Technology, and Innovation Strategy for Africa (STISA 2024 & 2034) and AU High-Level Panel on Emerging Technologies' (APET's) Contributing Expert on AI. Among other publications, Michael co-authored the AU Technical Report on AI titled "AI for Africa: Artificial Intelligence for Africa's Socioeconomic Development"; AU White Paper on AI titled "Regulation and Responsible Adoption of AI for Africa towards Achievement of AU Agenda 2063" and AU's "Artificial Intelligence Continental Roadmap for Africa", a roadmap towards the development of the AU AI Continental Strategy. Michael consults for several top international and local organisations, universities, research institutions, journals, and conferences.

List of Figures

List of Tables

CHAPTER 1

African Perspectives of Trustworthy AI: An Introduction

Damian Okaibedi Eke, Kutoma Wakunuma, Simisola Akintoye, and George Ogoh

Background

In 2024, the EU AI Act became the first-ever comprehensive legal framework on AI in the world as *Regulation (EU) 2024/1689 of the European Parliament and of the Council.* The fundamental aim of this Act and other policy measures such as EU AI innovation Package and

D. O. Eke (✉) · G. Ogoh
School of Computer Science, University of Nottingham, Nottingham, UK
e-mail: damian.eke@nottingham.ac.uk

G. Ogoh
e-mail: George.Ogoh@nottingham.ac.uk

K. Wakunuma
Centre for Computing and Social Responsibility, De Montfort University, Leicester, UK
e-mail: kutoma@dmu.ac.uk

S. Akintoye
Northumbria Law School, Northumbria University, Newcastle Upon Tyne, UK
e-mail: simi.akintoye@northumbria.ac.uk

D. O. Eke et al. (eds.), *Trustworthy AI*,
https://doi.org/10.1007/978-3-031-75674-0_1

the Coordinated Plan on AI, is to foster Trustworthy AI in Europe and beyond; to ensure that Europeans can trust what AI can offer. This is in keeping with the integration of ethics into digital technologies (Eke and Stahl, 2024) and stems from the idea that some AI systems create risks that need to be addressed on the basis of well-crafted principles of Trustworthy AI. These principles were developed by the independent High-Level Expert Group on AI set up by the European Commission in 2018 (HLEG, 2019). The Ethics Guidelines for Trustworthy AI developed by this group opined that AI needs to be ethical (respecting ethical values and principles), lawful (respecting all applicable laws and regulations), and robust (from a technical perspective while taking into account its social environment). It also proposed seven key requirements that a system should meet to be considered trustworthy AI in the EU and these include; *Human agency and oversight, Technical Robustness and safety, Privacy and data governance, Transparency Diversity, non-discrimination and fairness, Environmental and Social well-being, and accountability.* As this framework is predominantly shaped by the socio-cultural values and perspectives of the European Union, it raises an important question and point of consideration with respect to whether these principles can be directly applied in Africa given the varying interpretations and potential understandings that the components and requirements of the framework may demand. For instance, differences arise in understanding human autonomy and personhood between European and African cultures leading to distinct considerations when applying concepts related to human agency and oversight. Similarly, the principle of privacy and data governance may encounter differences in expectations and arrangements between Europe and Africa.

As such, this book explores African interpretations of Trustworthy AI and its component requirements. These interpretations will provide reasoned African understandings of how to consider Trustworthy AI systems in African contexts. The aim is to provide practical and theoretical insights that can allow the operationalisation of African values and principles in AI design and deployment. It will provide stakeholders (policymakers, industry players, civil society, and citizens) with an African-centric approach to AI governance. The effect European Regulations can have on other regions, often called the *Brussels effect* (Bradford, 2020) was evident from the GDPR. To avoid blind adoption of the provisions of this Act in Africa, it is important to understand how African values and principles align with the European interpretations of the trustworthy

AI principles. The way we understand AI, AI ethics, and governance can only be through our meanings, our stories and our narratives. This is an opportunity to understand Trustworthy AI from African stories, meanings, narratives, contexts and realities.

This is a follow-up publication to our book on *Responsible AI in Africa: Challenges and Opportunities* (Eke et al., 2023b). Having highlighted the foundational approaches for Responsible AI in Africa, there is a need to provide practical analysis that can lead to actionable steps for human-centred AI systems that align with African values and concerns. This book offers African perspectives as a counter to an AI governance model developed in the EU and other more advanced countries in the Global North. It introduces *decoloniality* as the missing principle that aligns with African perspectives of Trustworthy AI.

Trustworthy AI: The Current Discourse

The European Union (EU) has positioned itself at the forefront of the global discourse on AI, striving to balance innovation with ethical responsibility. The EU's approach to trustworthy AI is multifaceted, incorporating ethical guidelines, regulatory measures, and strategic initiatives. It aims to ensure that AI technologies are developed and deployed in ways that are beneficial to society while embedding European values at their core.

Thus, European values are central to the European Union's approach to trustworthy AI, serving as the foundation upon which strategic initiatives, guidelines, and regulatory frameworks are built. The values outlined in Article 2 of the Treaty on the European Union form the basis of the rights enjoyed by residents of the Union. However, values that have influenced the EU's approach are highlighted in the Guidelines for Trustworthy AI (HLEG, 2019) where the Commission set out the family of values that are particularly apt for AI systems. These include respect for human dignity; freedom of the individual; respect for democracy, justice and the rule of law; equality, non-discrimination and solidarity; and citizens' rights. Instances of this focus on European values can be seen in many of the trustworthy AI initiatives promoted by the European Commission (Eke & Stahl, 2024). For example, in the Communication on Artificial Intelligence for Europe (European Commission, 2018a), the Commission acknowledges that technologies are based on values. As with any transformative technology, AI technologies raise new ethical and legal questions; therefore, to ensure that AI is developed and applied appropriately in ways that promotes innovation, respects the Union's values, fundamental rights and ethical principles such as accountability and transparency are emphasised.

The Coordinated Plan on Artificial Intelligence stresses that AI needs vast amounts of data and a well-functioning data ecosystem built on trust, and the General Data Protection Regulation (GDPR) is the anchor of trust for the collection and use of data in the Union (European Commission, 2018b). With the GDPR, the EU has set a new global standard by placing a strong emphasis on individual rights, which reflects core European values. This approach has been pivotal in building and maintaining public trust in AI technologies. By prioritising the protection of personal freedoms, privacy, and ethical considerations, the EU aims to ensure that AI systems are not only innovative but also align with the principles of human dignity, equality, and the rule of law.

Furthermore, in its white paper on the European Approach to Excellence and Trust in Artificial Intelligence, the European Commission has maintained that there is a need for a common European approach. This is because "the introduction of national initiatives risks to endanger legal certainty, weaken citizens' trust and to prevent the emergence of a dynamic European industry" (Kilian, 2020). This indicates that the Commission favours a common European approach to AI as this ensures uniform standards of trustworthiness which is vital for strengthening public trust. National initiatives with varying standards and regulations could confuse citizens about the safety and reliability of AI systems. Inconsistent protections and varying levels of oversight might erode public trust. On the other hand, a unified strategy ensures that all AI systems meet the same stringent criteria, reinforcing public confidence in their use. By uniting member states under a shared vision, the EU can effectively harness the transformative potential of AI while upholding its core values.

In the light of this, the EU AI Act (European Parliament, 2024) was established to provide a clear harmonised legal framework for trustworthy AI across the EU, ensuring legal certainty for developers, providers, and users of AI technologies and systems. The Act adopted a risk-based approach that explicitly categorises certain AI systems as high-risk (e.g. AI applications in areas like law enforcement, critical infrastructure, and biometric identification), requiring them to undergo a rigorous assessment to ensure they do not infringe on fundamental rights such as privacy, non-discrimination and protection from harm. Also, the Act bans AI practices that are not trustworthy and are deemed contrary to European values, such as social scoring by governments and mass surveillance. This prohibition helps protect individual freedoms and democratic values by preventing the misuse of AI in ways that could undermine trust and democratic institutions.

Beyond the EU's perspectives on Trustworthy AI, a number of Ethical AI initiatives or projects are based on the idea of Trustworthiness. Nvidia (a company whose contributions to AI span from hardware innovations to software platforms and ecosystem development) has four guiding principles of Trustworthy AI; *privacy, safety and security, transparency* and *non-discrimination* (Nvidia, 2024). Microsoft's Trustworthy AI initiative promises to make AI more explainable, fair, robust, private, and transparent (Microsoft, 2024). Deloitte, a global professional services firm that provides audit, consulting, tax, and advisory services to a wide range of clients across various industries, is another company that has adopted a Trustworthy AI framework (Deloitte, 2024). This framework has seven dimensions of making AI—transparent and explainable, fair and impartial, robust and reliable, respectful of privacy, safe and secure, and responsible and accountable. These are similar to the EU trustworthy AI principles. In the UK, the UKRI (UK Research and Innovation) has committed over £33 million (through the Strategic Priorities Fund) in a Trustworthy Autonomous Systems (TAS) fund to Trustworthy AI (UKRI, 2020). This is to enable the development of socially beneficial autonomous systems that are both trustworthy in principle and trusted in practice by individuals, society and government.

The reason for highlighting these initiatives is to show the relevance governments and commercial entities are putting on trustworthiness of AI systems. Trustworthy AI principles fosters public trust and acceptance. By adhering to principles of trustworthy AI, organisations can harness the full potential of AI technologies, minimising identifiable risks and maximising benefits for society. But how different are trustworthy AI discussions from responsible AI?

Responsible AI *vs* or/*and* Trustworthy AI

In our first book, the emphasis was on *Responsible AI,* while in this book our focus is on *Trustworthy AI.* The shift from Responsible AI to Trustworthy AI evident in policies and practice represents an evolution in how organisations and governments conceptualise and implement AI technologies. The critical question here is, how similar or different are these two concepts? In our view, these are two distinct but related concepts. Responsible AI provides a fundamental theoretical approach on how everyone involved in the AI lifecycle understands and acknowledges their roles in creating ethical, fair, inclusive, explainable, and accountable AI systems while trustworthy AI focuses on the practical aspects of ensuring trust *in AI* and that AI systems are trusted *by* users and the society at large. Responsible AI establishes and defines principles and values fundamental to ethical AI. Responsibility here does not refer to the AI as an artefact but to the responsibility of the individuals or institutions involved in the AI design, development, and deployment to the users, society and the environment. How to make the whole AI lifecycle from design, development, and deployment responsible and sensitive to human and environmental needs and interests. Trustworthy AI on the other hand encompasses practices, principles, and approaches to ensure trust in and by users and relevant stakeholders. While Responsible AI provides the ethical foundation, Trustworthy AI deals with the technical and operational implementation of these principles to build and maintain trust in AI technologies. There is an emphasis on building trust between AI designers, developers, users, and stakeholders through reliability and adherence to ethical standards. Trustworthy AI seeks to answer the question, what can make AI systems to be trustworthy in a particular ecosystem or context? In this book therefore, we are asking the question of what can make AI systems developed in and for Africa to be trustworthy? It is important to note that we are not making an argument for one concept over another, both *Responsible AI and Trustworthy AI* discussions and approaches are critical in making AI applications more tailored to relevant contexts, and needs as well as more effective for human flourishing. For us, it is not Responsible AI *vs* Trustworthy AI. Trustworthy AI approaches build on the theoretical foundations laid down by Responsible AI. Therefore, it is Responsible AI *and* Trustworthy AI.

Trustworthiness in African Contexts

Trust plays a pivotal role in the acceptability of AI systems. Trust influences attitudes towards AI. From the above, the European commission has conceptualised their perspectives on trust in the requirements set out by the HLEG. However, as Ewuoso (2023) pointed out, trust and trustworthiness tend to differ among social groups. The underlying conditions that shape these concepts are fundamentally different in different regions. That means that African perspectives of trust are likely different from European perspectives. Thus, it is important to explore some African perspectives of trust and trustworthiness and how these can influence the role AI can or is allowed to play in Africa. How the parameters of trustworthiness are defined for AI will likely differ between the two regions.

Eke et al. (2023a, 2023b) observed that many African societies are characterised by values and moral principles based on communitarianism. Conceptualised slightly differently in many African cultures, the idea of communality and interconnectedness are deeply embedded in various aspects of African life, including social structures, decision-making processes, and cultural practices. From *Ubuntu* in South Africa, *Ujamaa* in Swahili, and *Umunna* in Igbo tribe of Nigeria, belief that an individual's identity and well-being are inextricably linked to the community's welfare is emphasised. This manifests in many ways such as mutual support and cooperation, shared values and norms, communal approaches to conflict resolution—community cohesion and more importantly, interdependence. African societies are therefore an ecosystem where humans, spirits (often represented in animate and inanimate objects) are deeply interdependent. Central to this holistic cultural ecosystem is trust.

The different meanings attributed to trust in African languages highlight the centrality of trust in the communality of African societies. Some of these meanings include 'dependence', 'hope', 'expectation', 'faith', and 'confidence' (Idemudia and Olawa, 2021). See Table 1.1.

The above connotations of trust hint at the criticality of trust in the inherently relational values and norms in African societies. As Ewuoso (2023) pointed out; "trust is both necessary to foster relationships and, at the same time, it is the reason for the existence of the relationship". This is the concept of trust as relational. However, in these communities, faith, hope, confidence, or dependence is reposed in someone or something that is in harmony with the community; someone or something that

Table 1.1 Different meanings of trust in some African Languages

#	*African word for Trust*	*Meaning*
1	*'ìgbẹ̀kẹ̀le—Yoruba Nigeria*	Dependence
2	*Ithemba—Zulu—South Africa*	Trust, hope, expectation, faith, and dependence
3	*Imuentinýan/iyegbekọ/Ọmwan imuentinýan—Edo, Nigeria*	To depend or rely on someone
4	*Dogara*	Faith or dependency (on God)
5	*ntụkwasị obi—Igbo, Nigeria*	Reliance or dependence (or literarily placing one's heart or confidence in something or someone)
6	*ho tšepa ha—Sesotho, South Africa*	Confidence
7	*Tshêpa—Setwana, Botwana*	Confidence in someone
8	*Imani—Swahili, Eastern Africa*	"faith" or "belief",
9	*Ahoto*	Reliance, confidence, or assurance in someone or something

can be trusted or that has demonstrated trustworthiness. Requirements for trustworthiness are therefore determined by the essentiality of maintaining social cohesion and mutual support and benefits. One of these requirements is consistency and reliability. Others are respect and reciprocity, transparency and openness, accountability and justice. These are similar to the 7 requirements of trustworthiness in AI explained above. For instance, 'transparency' is critical to the idea of interdependence. Explainable AI or less opaque AI will therefore help to enhance trust (Ewuoso, 2023). However, the difference is that in the European perspective, individuals are emphasised more than the collective: 'autonomy' and 'individual privacy' over 'collective privacy'. In Africa, the principle of solidarity, shared responsibility and collective privacy will take precedence over privacy of the individual. In that sense, the perspectives are dissimilar.

Furthermore, the willingness to maintain harmony and work towards the benefit of society, while refraining from actions that could harm the group, is fundamental to building and sustaining trust in African cultures. This collective ethos fosters social cohesion and mutual support. As individuals see themselves as integral parts of the community, there is a strong sense of collective responsibility where all actions are expected to contribute to the common good. Trust underpins this ethos and forms the basis for all social relationships. Applied in AI, the question will be: Does the AI system operate in a way that maintains the harmony of the community? The collective benefit rather than personal benefits will be the focal point.

Additionally, spiritual and ancestral beliefs play a significant role in cultivating trust within African cultures. Trust in spiritual authorities, ancestral guidance, and the supernatural realm helps to reinforce a sense of interconnectedness and collective responsibility within the community. These beliefs often emphasise the importance of human connection, consciousness, and natural order. In AI this may bring about scepticism or even fear. Some may view AI as a disruption to the natural order or as a challenge to human uniqueness and spiritual beliefs about the soul or consciousness. This means that in cultures where there's a strong emphasis on trust in spiritual or ancestral entities, people may be more hesitant to trust AI systems, particularly if they perceive them as separate from or in conflict with their spiritual beliefs. In this instance, dispelling relevant misconceptions becomes a key part of cultivating trust in the AI systems. Another way of doing this is to align the AI systems with spiritual or ancestral values - for example, by promoting harmony, interconnectedness, or social well-being. This may improve the acceptability of such systems and how they are integrated into daily life.

Fundamental to this discussion is the influence of colonialism to the central dynamics of African communality. Colonialism disrupted traditional social structures (e.g. social hierarchies and systems of governance), undermining cultural practices, and eroding trust within communities (Kingston, 2015). Colonialism brought Western values, norms, and institutions that were often at odds with traditional African cultural practices. They exploited ethnic, tribal, and religious divisions, creating artificial boundaries and fostering inter-group rivalries that undermined solidarity and trust within communities. Together with the economic, and labour exploitations that characterised the colonial era, effects of the damage done to social structures are still evident till date. Today, the legacies of the colonial era are evident in AI systems in what is often referred to as *coloniality*. Therefore, AI will need to prove that it has no colonial tendencies (or that it is in harmony with African contextual needs and values) to be trusted in many parts of Africa. In this book, we introduce decoloniality as an essential requirement for trustworthiness in AI. This means that AI systems designed, developed or deployed in and for Africa need to ensure that they have no colonial tendencies; what datasets inform them, who is making critical decisions in the design and development process, and who effectively controls the data and the algorithm? These are questions decoloniality as a requirement can help us answer.

Our argument here is that trustworthiness of AI in Africa will include achieving the principles proposed by the EU HLEG such as human agency and oversight, technical robustness and safety, privacy and data governance, transparency, diversity, non-discrimination, and fairness, societal and environmental well-being and accountability. But most importantly, it will encompass aspects such as usability (considering African contexts), accessibility and affordability, decoloniality, and demonstration of adaptability of AI to local contexts. These are concepts or principles that were not highlighted by the EU but that are necessary requirements to achieve trustworthiness in the African concept.

Structure of the Volume

Through twelve chapters, this book presents perspectives of trustworthy AI in Africa, addressing the need for an equitable AI ecosystem that prioritises African societal and communal benefits over the interests of global tech giants. It challenges African AI stakeholders to take collective ownership of the ethics and governance of the design, development, and deployment of AI, for the benefit of African communities.

In the introductory chapter, the editors set the stage by unpacking the concept of trustworthiness of AI in Africa, focussing on the current global discourse around trustworthiness including the EU HLEG and EU AI Act. The chapter further explores the notion of Responsible AI and Trustworthy AI as related but distinct concepts. While Responsible AI provides the theoretical ethical framework for design, development, and deployment of AI systems, ensuring that they are inclusive and equitable, trustworthy AI focuses on how to practically ensure that AI systems are trusted within specific ecosystems. Both concepts complement each other and are not mutually exclusive. The editors further examine the concept of trustworthiness in African contexts, enumerating the different meanings attributed to trust in African languages, highlighting the centrality of trust in the communality of African societies. To conclude, the chapter argues that the concept of trustworthy AI in Africa goes beyond the principles highlighted by the EU HLEG to include core concepts that are peculiar to African contexts including decoloniality, accessibility, and local adaptation.

Following this, Munetsi focuses on the intricate relationship between technology, society, and power, highlighting Africa's vital contribution to global technological innovation while challenging the perception of technology as inherently neutral. He posits that technology often serves as a political instrument for dominant groups, influenced by historical contexts that have perpetuated Africa's subjugation. To counter this, he advocates for a prefigurative Afrocentric approach to AI development, integrating African epistemologies to reflect African politics and power within global socio-technological frameworks. This contribution highlights the need for innovation in Africa's traditionally peripheral technological status, urging substantial reforms in the continent's tech sector. The chapter discusses the complexities of evolving state governance in Africa, where traditional power dynamics are disrupted by globalisation and regional integration, resulting in hybrid governance models of shared sovereignty. It proposes a three-tiered governance model for scalable AI solutions, emphasising inclusivity and adaptability to Africa's unique conditions. This participatory model, extending beyond elite circles, aims to harness local, national, and regional diversities for a unified African AI strategy that promotes collective progress and equitable technological benefits distribution.

In Chapter 3, Seydina examines trustworthiness as a requirement for AI in Africa. He discusses existing AI use cases in agriculture, education, and finance, highlighting that AI faces challenges from both foreign and local perspectives. The chapter unpacks the trust issues associated with the adoption of foreign technologies, and the dynamics of developing homegrown AI. Externally developed AI often neglects African values and cultures, leading to mistrust and reinforcing biases. While there is a push for African-developed AI to address local needs, issues like underdeveloped infrastructure, scarce data, and limited expertise hinder progress. This creates a question about the trustworthiness of AI solutions developed entirely within Africa. The chapter advocates for a sovereign approach to AI that incorporates local values, manages biases, and involves diverse stakeholders, balancing technological independence with international cooperation to build a trustworthy AI ecosystem.

Chapter 4 explores trustworthy AI in Africa as a distributed concern. Makuochi and Adamu examine how the normative framing of AI in Africa, particularly ethics, responsibility, and trustworthiness, can be better understood through Bruno Latour's concept of "Distributed Concern". By reconceptualising "matters of facts" as "matters of concerns", the authors argue that trustworthy AI, seen as a distributed concern encompassing ethical, socio-cultural, geopolitical, economic, pedagogical, and technical dimensions, requires a continual process of reconciling values. The authors engage in sustained discursive argumentation to demonstrate how analysing trust as a spectrum can clarify the processes that normalise trustworthy AI as ethical, lawful, or robust, highlighting the scalable nature of trustworthiness in AI research and design.

In Chapter 5, Ibitoye et al. advocates for an Afrocentric framework tailored to African healthcare, integrating AI with cultural values and ethical considerations. This chapter stresses the necessity of AI systems that are culturally sensitive and adaptable to diverse African settings, infrastructure, and health norms. Key elements include incorporating African values into AI principles, fostering collaboration among stakeholders, and prioritising user-centric design to build trust and meet local healthcare needs.

Chapter 6 investigates the impact of funding disparities on developing and implementing trustworthy AI frameworks in Africa. Drawing on global AI projects, Azeez et al. examine resource allocation challenges, highlighting concerns about Western-biased AI technologies and the historical impact of colonialism, which perpetuate technological colonialism. To counter this, they propose an ideal trustworthy AI model aligned with African ontology, emphasising relationality and human-centeredness. By addressing the funding deficit to prioritise trustworthy AI research in Africa, the authors offer insights on effectively channelling financial resources, including utilising dormant funds, corporate social responsibility, partnerships, and community-driven initiatives, to foster a trustworthy AI framework rooted in the African ethos.

In Chapter 7, Zimba et al. highlight the transformative impact of artificial intelligence as a general-purpose technology on global socio-economic and political systems, emphasising the strategic advantage for those who invest in AI. They highlight the uneven distribution of AI technologies and skills, with the global north leading and Africa significantly lagging. Unlike previous industrial revolutions, Africa must shift this narrative by developing context-aware, responsible AI technologies reflective of its socio-cultural context. The chapter argues for proactive measures by African governments, universities, and institutions to enhance local AI capacity, emphasising skill development, infrastructure, and market potential. It advocates for ethical AI-by-design, co-created by diverse stakeholders, to ensure fair and representative AI development.

Chapter 8 addresses the crucial issue of AI safety from an African perspective, focusing on Nigerian road traffic as a case study. It critiques the dominance of Western-developed trustworthy AI principles, which may not adequately address the unique challenges faced in African contexts, potentially causing disproportionate harm. The chapter examines AI safety definitions and practical safety concerns in the Nigerian road traffic system, identifying key socio-technical and environmental factors essential for safe AI adoption. The authors conclude with recommendations to prioritise safety in AI systems, emphasising research and stakeholder engagement, empowering African researchers, respecting African values in global AI discussions, and fostering public awareness and community involvement in AI safety.

In chapter nine, Owoyemi et al. examine trustworthy AI in healthcare in Nigeria. Healthcare systems in many African countries face significant challenges, including insufficient infrastructure, outdated and poorly maintained facilities, and a severe shortage of essential medical supplies and medications, which collectively undermine their ability to provide adequate care. However, digital health technologies, particularly AI, hold promises for addressing these challenges by improving access to medical services, providing health education, and enabling remote monitoring of chronic conditions. Despite the potential benefits, ethical considerations in the design, development, and deployment of these technologies are crucial to ensuring their equitable and beneficial impact. This chapter explores how Nigerian digital health startups address ethical concerns through a web-based cross-sectional survey, focusing on data processing activities and the application of ethical principles in the rapidly evolving digital health landscape. Their findings highlight the current state of ethical considerations and the implications for designers, developers, policymakers, and academics.

Chapter 10 examines the differential impact of AI on various populations, particularly highlighting how biased gender norms affect women, especially women of colour, in STEM. Using Kenya and Ghana as case studies, the authors employ methods like informal sessions, participant observation, digital content analysis, and AI model character analysis to explore how AI shapes and is shaped by gender norms. The study discusses how these norms, or "onto-norms", influence AI design, training, and usage, perpetuating certain gender practices in digital spaces.

It argues that onto-norms affect how AI interacts with content related to women, often leading to misrepresentation or exclusion. To combat these biases, the chapter proposes a framework for building AI systems with intentionality to ensure women's original intentions for data are respected, thereby reducing the perpetuation of gender biases.

In Chapter 11, Ruttkamp-Bleom explores what is necessary to ensure trustworthy AI practices in Africa, emphasising social justice. She advocates for developing a sustainable and equitable AI ecosystem that prioritises social justice. Introducing the concept of 'AI justice', the chapter asserts that AI should serve every African inhabitant by embedding principles of relational ethics and combining data and design justice approaches. Trustworthy AI practices are defined as those that protect the rights and benefits of the communities whose data they use. The chapter challenges African AI stakeholders—researchers, designers, developers, deployers, and users to take collective ownership of AI and build resilience against the exploitative Big Tech business model.

In the last chapter, the editors propose decoloniality as an essential trustworthy AI requirement in Africa. The editors explore colonial tendencies embedded within AI that perpetuate biases, inequalities, and systemic discrimination rooted in coloniality. The chapter introduces decoloniality as a critical requirement for AI systems, especially in regions with continued scar of coloniality, emphasising the need for a decolonial approach to AI development and deployment by showcasing how AI technologies often reflect and reinforce colonial legacies. It further explores the concept of trustworthy AI in the African context, addressing how AI can be designed to respect African values, foster transparency, and build trust. The editors advocate for rethinking of AI from a perspective that values local knowledge systems, promotes inclusive participation, and ensures equitable benefits for African communities. Finally, they provide practical insights for policymakers, designers, and developers to implement decolonial AI systems that protect cultural identities, promotes fairness, and address the real needs of African communities.

Conclusion

Overall, this book highlights unique dimensions of trustworthy AI in Africa, emphasising the need for an AI ecosystem that intentionally challenges and addresses issues such as coloniality in all stages of the AI lifecycle. Current discourse on trustworthy AI neglects the issues relevant to Africa such as the impact of coloniality on AI design and use. We argue that trustworthiness cannot be achieved without a reasoned effort to consider African socio-cultural expectations, needs, and values. The book argues that while achieving globally proposed principles of trustworthiness is essential, additional requirements such as decoloniality, usability, accessibility, affordability, and adaptability to local contexts are necessary for AI to be truly trustworthy in Africa. The book stresses that African perspectives, deeply rooted in communitarianism, spiritual beliefs, and the legacy of colonialism, necessitate unique considerations for trustworthiness in AI. The book uniquely introduces decoloniality as a crucial principle for trustworthy AI in Africa, ensuring that AI systems are free from colonial tendencies and are adaptable to local contexts. By prioritising local values, managing biases, and fostering collaboration among diverse stakeholders, Africa can overcome current challenges and subsequently position its AI ecosystem as a model for inclusive, sustainable, and ethical development of AI on a global scale. The book provides practical and theoretical insights on operationalisation of African principles in AI systems, offering a roadmap for trustworthy AI that emphasises on technological sovereignty, international cooperation, and the integration of local values. The book challenges policymakers, designers, developers, and researchers to ensure that AI systems in Africa align with the continent's unique needs, realities, and contexts.

References

Bradford, A. (2020). The Brussels effect: How the European Union rules the world. *Faculty Books* [Online]. https://scholarship.law.columbia.edu/books/232

Deloitte. (2024). *Trustworthy Artificial Intelligence (AI)™* [Online]. Deloitte United States. https://www2.deloitte.com/us/en/pages/deloitte-analytics/solutions/ethics-of-ai-framework.html. Accessed 6 August 2024.

Eke, D., & Stahl, B. (2024). Ethics in the governance of data and digital technology: An analysis of European data regulations and policies. *Digital Society, 3*(1), 11.

Eke, D.O., Chintu, S.S., & Wakunuma, K. (2023a). Towards shaping the future of responsible AI in Africa. In *Responsible AI in Africa: Challenges and opportunities* (pp. 169–193). Springer International Publishing.

Eke, D.O., Wakunuma, K., & Akintoye, S. (2023b). *Responsible AI in Africa: Challenges and opportunities*. Springer International Publishing.

Commission, European. (2018). *Communication artificial intelligence for Europe*.

Commission, European. (2018). *Coordinated plan on artificial intelligence*. European Commission.

Parliament, European. (2024). *Regulation (EU) 2024/1689 of the European parliament and of the council*. The European Parliament and the Council of the European Union.

Ewuoso, C. (2023). Black box problem and African views of trust. *Humanities and Social Sciences Communications, 10*(1), 1–11.

HLEG. (2019). High-level expert group on artificial intelligence. *Ethics guidelines for trustworthy AI*, 6. https://www.aepd.es/sites/default/files/2019-09/ai-definition.pdf. Accessed 6 August 2024.

Idemudia, E. S., & Olawa, B. D. (2021). Once bitten, twice shy: Trust and trustworthiness from an african perspective. In C. T. Kwantes & B. C. H. Kuo (Eds.), *Trust and trustworthiness across cultures: Implications for societies and workplaces* (pp. 33–51). Springer International Publishing.

Kilian, G. (2020). *WHITE PAPER. On artificial intelligence-a European approach to excellence and trust* [Online]. https://policycommons.net/artifacts/3457112/white-paper-on-artificial-intelligence/4257573/. Accessed 6 August 2024.

Kingston, L. (2015). The destruction of identity: Cultural genocide and indigenous peoples. *Journal of Human Rights, 14*(1), 63–83.

Microsoft, M. (2024). *Trustworthy and responsible AI network expands to help European healthcare organizations enhance the quality, safety and trustworthiness of AI in health* [Online] Stories. https://news.microsoft.com/2024/06/16/trustworthy-and-responsible-ai-network-expands-to-help-european-healthcare-organizations-enhance-the-quality-safety-and-trustworthiness-of-ai-in-health/. Accessed 6 August 2024.

Nvidia. (2024). *NVIDIA trustworthy AI* [Online] NVIDIA. https://www.nvidia.com/en-gb/ai-data-science/trustworthy-ai/. Accessed 6 August 2024.

UKRI. (2020). *New trustworthy autonomous systems projects launched*. https://www.ukri.org/news/new-trustworthy-autonomous-systems-projects-launched/. Accessed 6 August 2024.

CHAPTER 2

Prefiguring Afro-Centric and Inclusive AI Digital Commons: A Normative African Perspective to AI Development, Deployment, and Governance

Dennis Munetsi

Introduction

Technologies are not neutral; they are the embodiment of social constructs imbued with political meanings and implications. As Lucy Suchman insightfully observes in Birhane (2020), "technology is not merely about the design of physical objects; it is about the design of practices and possibilities". Societies and their actors mould these technologies, and in turn, technologies mould societies. They serve as both an expression and a tool of power for dominant social groups, a concept explored by Coeckelbergh (2022). Such expressions of power are not new; they are the continuation of historical systems of exploitation,

D. Munetsi (✉)
Department of Global Politics, Malmö University, Malmö, Sweden
e-mail: dennis.munetsi@mau.se

Wallenberg AI, Autonomous Systems and Software Program-Humanity and Society, Malmö, Sweden

D. O. Eke et al. (eds.), *Trustworthy AI*,
https://doi.org/10.1007/978-3-031-75674-0_2

marginalisation, and oppression of marginalised groups for the benefit of dominant ones (Burnette et al., 2019). Within this intricate web of relationships, the creators and proprietors of technology profoundly influence the lifestyles and knowledge systems of users. This symbiosis between technology and society underscores the significant impact that technologies have on our daily social practices.

This chapter focuses on the African continent, examining the significance of artificial intelligence (AI) in relation to Africa's position within the global context of technological innovation. It proposes a strategy for crafting technologies that are deeply rooted in African values, norms, and cultural identities. Furthermore, this strategy advocates for the creation of algorithms that are infused with African political thought, cultural practices, and prospects. In the light of this historical context, the chapter turns to the potentialities of AI as a beacon of change both in terms of technological innovation and global politics. The strategy outlined here is not just about developing new technologies; it is about embedding African values, norms, and identities into these innovations.

This chapter introduces a prefigurative Afro-centric approach to the development of AI and associated digital resources. It acknowledges the technology's potential to transform positively and disrupt the existing global power dynamics in technological innovation, advocating for a "just and equal" redistribution of global and social power. The proposal examines these power dynamics through a social scientific perspective, offering critical insights into the role of technology in societal structures. The chapter provides an overview of AI, highlighting its historical milestones, and sets the stage for a discussion on prefigurative politics. It contrasts two perspectives on technological advancement: incremental and radical change approaches. The discussion then shifts to Africa's contribution to and position within the historical narrative of technological evolution. In conclusion, the chapter outlines a preliminary framework for the governance of the envisioned prefigurative Afro-centric AI, emphasising the need for inclusive and equitable policies.

Background

AI's influence on society is undeniable, with its applications spanning healthcare, where it aids in early disease detection and crafting personalised treatment plans, to transportation, where it contributes to the development of autonomous vehicles that enhance safety and efficiency;

and to education, where it facilitates personalised learning experiences (Albarrán Lozano et al., 2021). However, despite the broad spectrum of its applications and its potential for positive impact, it is crucial to recognise that AI technologies can also be misused, posing risks to humanity, the environment, and other species (Olhede & Wolfe, 2018). Moreover, systems designed to streamline and automate social services can inadvertently become inflexible, excluding marginalised groups from essential services (Litman et al., 2021).

Amidst the challenges previously outlined, AI's evolution presents a beacon of hope for societal benefit. It empowers communities to forge shared resources, solutions, and tools collaboratively, tackling both local and global social issues, as Huang and Siddarth (2023) have observed. An illustration of AI's potential for communal upliftment is the collective aspiration to co-create, co-own, and share the fruits of African AI and digital resources. This vision, championed in this chapter and echoed by African scholars like Oubibi et al. (2022) and Ade-Ibijola and Okonkwo (2023), envisions what can be termed as Afro-centric AI digital commons. These are collective assets that are conceived, used, shared, and governed by a broad coalition of stakeholders through participatory and democratic processes. Such an approach highlights the critical need to incorporate African perspectives and stakeholders in the creation and management of technological solutions—"for Africans, by Africans, and under African conditions". This paradigm exemplifies how the rise of AI can be strategically leveraged to challenge and reshape global disparities and injustices.

History of AI

Contemporary AI developments are the fruit of extensive research and development efforts that span decades, tracing back to pivotal moments such as the Dartmouth Conference in 1956 and the AI boom of the 1960s (Anyoha, 2017). These advancements have not only kept pace with sociocultural evolution but have also, in some cases, been a catalyst for it, leading to a growing demand for advanced devices with high processing power and internet access. This demand has necessitated the creation of regulatory frameworks like the EU AI Act and the Brazilian AI Bill (Munetsi, 2022), illustrating the complex interplay between technological innovation, sociocultural shifts, and political action.

The transformative and disruptive potential of AI, whether perceived as hype or reality, has sparked extensive debates across various disciplines. Nevertheless, the impact of these transformations on groups historically excluded from technological progress is often neglected. Hence, there is a need for a comprehensive understanding of the historical factors that have left certain social groups and geographies behind in the technological race (Mabawonku, 2003). Moreover, discussions must extend to how these historically marginalised communities can engage with emerging technologies in a way that allows them to influence and contribute to future technological advancements.

Despite notable instances of innovation, Africa's current state of AI preparedness is not sufficient to redefine the continent as a key player in the global arena of science and technology (Oxford Insights, 2022; UNCTAD, 2023). I contend that Africa and its constituent states require a radical transformation that prioritises action-oriented, experimental, and multifaceted change processes over theoretical and utopian approaches. This chapter introduces a solution-oriented dialogue based on prefigurative politics, advocating for Afro-centric technological change processes that lead to the creation of Afro-centric AI and digital commons.

Prefigurative Afro-Centric Technological Change: Pluralism and the Role of the "Publics"

Prefigurative politics are inherently proactive and anarchist in nature, advocating for a society that reflects the collective aspirations of its members through everyday actions. Such politics challenge the status quo and strive to correct undesirable conditions that hinder collective progress (Lederman, 2015). The goal is to ensure that the outcomes of these actions align with the means employed and the collective desires of the community (Boggs, 1977). In the African context, this means critically reflecting on the current state of living conditions and the scientific and technological culture as a starting point for developing technologies that are truly Afro-centric.

This community-driven approach to politics of change emphasises the importance of a participatory process where the visions and methods for actualization are collectively determined by society's members (Leach, 2013). The relationships among diverse stakeholders are crucial, as they collectively demand better living conditions, which are essential for fostering the creativity necessary for scientific advancement (Mabawonku, 2003).

In this vision of prefiguration, the public's demands for technological change are directed not only at scientists but also at all members of society, including industries responsible for producing accessible goods and political systems that create environments conducive to social interaction and creativity (Mabawonku, 2003). A prefiguring society also pressures itself to engage in dynamic and critical discourses, where ideas are debated and passed on (Leach, 2013). Thus, the call for technological change is accompanied by demands for a democratic society where individuals are free to fulfil their constitutional roles, leading to an evolution of knowledge systems that embrace new ideas and discoveries. As Teng-Zeng (2006, p. 1) posits, "science and technology are integral to human development, and the growing importance of indigenous knowledge and its preservation underscores the relevance of knowledge in all civilizations."

Therefore, the demand for Afro-centric technologies encompasses not only the technical aspects but also calls for a comprehensive cultural co-evolution. Afro-centric imaginaries should envision a transition from Africa's peripheral status in global technological innovation to becoming a hub for Afro-centric technological advancements that embody the Pan-African goals of emancipation and improving the lives of African peoples (Edo & Olanrewaju, 2012). To realise these goals, the embodiment of change must reflect a commitment to a vision of prefigurative struggle through local, intimate structures that anticipate a future liberated society and state (Boggs, 1977). At its heart, this struggle is built on three pillars: punctuated ness, embodiment, and situatedness. Thus, Africa and its states must employ strategies that utilise this moment of AI disruption to develop technological systems that are deeply rooted in African localities and cultures, with epistemological conceptions that are intrinsically linked to indigenous knowledge.

Incremental Nature of Technological Innovation

The emergence of AI is not a result of random occurrences but stems from a series of incremental changes in technology, investment, policy, and sociocultural practices. These changes are not isolated events but are deeply rooted in the historical capacities and momentum that different entities have accumulated, shaping their current roles and positions in contemporary AI innovation. Fialho et al. (2009) liken technological change to a speciation process, where existing technologies evolve into new forms through gradual modifications. This incrementalist perspective posits that technological advancements are the culmination of minor yet significant alterations to existing technologies rather than monumental leaps.

As technologies are exposed to varying conditions and undergo selection processes, they diverge cumulatively from their origins, creating distinct technological species and domains, as Levinthal (1998) notes. This evolutionary journey begins with either convergence—where technologies from different application domains merge to form a new technology related to a previous domain—or fusion, as described by Fialho et al. (2009), which involves the amalgamation of technologies from existing domains to create new technologies for an entirely new domain.

This view of incrementalism underscores the integral role of technological change in the broader narrative of economic and social transformation throughout human history. The increasing significance of indigenous knowledge, its application, and preservation, as highlighted by Teng-Zeng (2006), affirms the enduring importance of situated and contextual knowledge in all civilizations' social change processes. Moreover, technological change is not an isolated phenomenon; it co-evolves with society, responding to existing or emerging social challenges that necessitate new scientific knowledge and technological capabilities to forge novel interventions.

For such change to materialise, a conducive environment is essential, comprising a "right public" with specific technological needs that inspire scientific creativity for improved living conditions, as Mabawonku (2003) articulates. Additionally, supportive policy frameworks (Cowhey & Aronson, 2017) and the industrial capacity to fulfil new demands (Fialho et al., 2009) are critical. The public's demand for new technological innovations is thus a relational, situated, and punctuated phenomenon deeply embedded in socio-technological evolutionary processes. By situating technological changes within the larger tapestry of sociocultural dynamics, we foster an ecosystem of interconnected social drivers that facilitate the conception, development, and ethical governance of "moral" technologies.

Radical Technological Change as a Starting Point for Incremental Changes

The narrative on technological change presents a dichotomy: while incremental innovation is the norm, radical technological shifts are sometimes necessary, especially for countries with limited participation in prior technological developments. Mabawonku (2003) notes that African states, often sidelined from "modern" scientific advancements, may opt for drastic changes to bridge the gap and compete globally. South Korea's transformation from an agrarian society under Japanese rule to a leader in information and communication technologies exemplifies this, as Cowhey and Aronson (2017) detail. The nation's success hinged on systemic reforms and robust investments, fostering a high R&D intensity within a "top-down" innovation system that encouraged collaboration among government, industry, and academia. This environment nurtured the growth of chaebols like LG and Samsung, propelling them into new industries through significant R&D investments and protection from competition.

Similarly, China's metamorphosis from an agrarian state to a technological behemoth within 35 years, as described by Zheng and Wang (2012), showcases the impact of radical technological change. Initially, China's development was fuelled by a 'brute-force imitation' strategy, which involved assimilating modern manufacturing techniques through extensive labour-intensive production. This approach enabled China to rapidly catch up with advanced manufacturing technologies, as Xie, Ni, and Ren (2006) observed.

These examples illustrate how radical technological changes can catalyse the rise of new actors on the global stage, particularly when there is an absence of a dominant design or solution addressing their specific problems and needs. Fialho et al. (2009) discuss how such conditions foster product innovation, allowing countries traditionally excluded from the technological forefront to become significant players. However, this requires robust public support and a heightened technological awareness—a public with distinct technological needs that spurs scientific creativity for improved living standards, as Mabawonku (2003) argues. The "right public" is thus essential for fostering an environment conducive to significant technological advancements and innovations.

History of Technological Innovation in Africa

This section outlines three interconnected perspectives on Africa's technological history. Firstly, the continent's technological development deficit is attributed not to an absence of potential or capability but to historical and systemic obstacles such as colonialism and the extraction and exploitation of natural resources. These factors have historically marginalised Africa within global production, supply, and value chains. Secondly, Africa has made significant yet often unrecognised contributions to global technological innovations and has not been adequately compensated for these contributions. Lastly, the disruption of Africa's indigenous science and technology by colonial regimes has had enduring impacts, impeding the continent's capacity to compete and excel in the development and advancement of its technological innovations. Together, these points offer a nuanced understanding of the complex challenges and potential opportunities that Africa faces in asserting its role and influence within the global arena of technological innovation.

An Erased History

Historical narratives about global developments and technological advancements often omit the role played by the African continent in success stories despite its significant and crucial contributions. In analysing Africa's technological history, Teng-Zeng (2006) contended that the continent and its states have always "form(ed) part of a broader pattern of (global) change in what can be called scientific development and management". Acemoglu et al. (2002) and Dumett (1985) have long argued that the continent's raw materials, such as copper, gold, cobalt lithium, and many other precious metals, have been the backbone of many physical infrastructures underlying several technologies. These contributions through the supply of natural resources are significant to the incremental momentum that has led to contemporary technological advancements of which AI is a part (Table 2.1).

For instance, Africa became significant during the years leading up to the War when Britain lost control of most of its rubber sources, leading to the need to identify new sources (Wendt, 1947). In a historical analysis of the role of Africa in the Second World War, Wendt (1947, p. 3) noted that,

Table 2.1 US natural rubber and latex supply between 1940 and 1945 (in long tons) (Wendt, 1947)

IMPORTS	1940	1941	1942	1943	1944	1945
Latin American	11.1	10.8	14.5	26.2	32.8	37.6
Far East	799.8	1,007.6	255.5	20.1	60.3	69.9
African	7.3	10.6	12.6	13.6	19.0	35.7
Subtotal	818.2	1,029.0	282.6	59.9	112.1	143.2
U. K. Transf.	—	—	—	—	1.5	1.7
Salvage	—	—	0.1	0.4	0.3	[a]
Total Imports	818.2	1,029.0	282.7	60.3	113.9	144.9
Less Shrinkage	—	—	—	5.3	6.2	9.8
After Shrinkage	818.2	1,029.0	282.7	55.0	107.7	135.1
U. S. Guayule Production	—	—	—	0.3	0.1	0.6
Total New Supp. After Shrinkage	818.2	1,029.0	282.7	55.3	107.8	135.7

[a] 28 long tons.

Source: Facts for Industry, Tables 3, 4. Civilian Production Administration, Rubber Division, Bureau of Census Series 26-1-1.

> The military success of the "United Nations" in World War II was threatened by a rubber shortage. Japanese capture of the principal rubber producing areas of the Far East in 1942 eliminated the sources of 90% of the world's natural rubber production.

African territories emerged as pivotal sources of raw materials following Britain's diminished access to Scandinavian iron and other valuable metals, as well as the loss of rubber supplies from Malaya and the Dutch East Indies (Dumett, 1985). Although Africa's geopolitical significance increased, its minerals played a disproportionately large role in the Allied powers' rearmament and wartime munitions production, overshadowing the continent's political stature and economic development level (Dumett, 1985, p. 382). This historical context raises a pertinent question for envisioning an Afro-centric technological future: Have global interactions with Africa, particularly in terms of supply, production, and value chains, evolved?

In today's landscape, marked by AI advancements, colonial legacies persist through the extraction and exploitation of minerals crucial for AI technology infrastructure. Despite Africa's considerable share of global mineral reserves, the processing of these resources predominantly occurs abroad. For example, China, holding a mere 30% of the world's mineral reserves, processes significant quantities of global minerals: 73% of cobalt, 40% of copper, 59% of lithium, and 67% of nickel. Additionally, China manufactures over 80% of the world's solar panels and more than 70% of lithium-ion battery cells (SAIIA, 2022). Such external processing diminishes the value African nations derive from their minerals, perpetuating historical economic disparities. Nonetheless, the rise of AI and technological shifts offer Africa a chance to chart a new course. By capitalising on these developments, Africa has the potential to ascend as a frontrunner in technological innovation.

Cultural Erasure and Monopoly

The history of Africa's technological innovation—or the absence thereof—stems from a systematic obliteration of the colonised peoples' ways of being and knowing, coupled with the disruption of their indigenous technological evolution. Acemoglu et al. (2000) contend that colonial regimes distorted and interrupted the natural trajectory of socio-technological advancement and indigenous knowledge systems within the territories they occupied. They posit that the type of institutions established by colonial powers was influenced by the viability of European settlement, which in turn was largely determined by the local disease environment. In regions where high mortality rates precluded settlement, colonial powers were inclined to set up extractive institutions designed to syphon resources and wealth, thereby derailing the territories' inherent social and technological development (Acemoglu, Johnson, & Robinson, 2002). This had a profound effect on indigenous epistemologies and practices.

The narrative of Africa's overlooked scientific and technological heritage is not a series of random oversights but rather a manifestation of systemic issues rooted in the legacy of colonialism and the consequent cultural erasure. Scholars like Horton, cited by Mabawonku, have characterised African culture as an exemplar of 'unscientific cultures' with inheritors who generally possess "uncritical minds" (Mabawonku, 2003, p. 122). Furthermore, it has been argued that there was "little pre-colonial science, despite fairly advanced numerological and other speculative activities" (Teng-Zeng, 2006, p. 3). John Paul Nyuykongi also addresses the challenge of epistemic bias against African epistemology, suggesting that the bias favouring the Western cultural paradigm is among the most pervasive globally (Nyuykonge, 2020). Such perspectives often downplay or disregard the importance of pre-colonial African legacies. Notably, in pre-colonial times, institutions like the Library of Alexandria and the University of Timbuktu were pivotal in managing the production, storage, and dissemination of knowledge (Teng-Zeng, 2006). However, these institutions and processes were disrupted by colonial interventions, stripping African societies of the foundational elements necessary for sustained progress in science and technology through successive generations.

The absence of a knowledge base and material foundation upon which to build a continuum of indigenous African technologies remains a significant concern, particularly in relation to their role in modern technologies. Economies, technologies, and knowledge should be viewed not merely as accumulations of capital, materials, and human skills but also as repositories of information, learning, and adaptability. Understanding why African states have struggled to build upon these foundations is crucial for fostering improvement (Mabawonku, 2003, p. 117). Mabawonku further elucidates that varying cultural objectives and the tools they engender will yield distinct cultural products, leading to disparate states and levels of economic and social development. The erasure and supplanting of African histories of pre-colonial progress have yielded outcomes aligned with the objectives of colonial systems on the continent, thus depriving it of an autonomous and self-directed socio-technological evolution.

Prefiguration: Towards Afro-Centric AI Commons

The introduction posited that emerging technologies have the potential to alter various facets of societal norms and behaviours significantly. The extent and nature of these changes, however, are influenced by historical contexts, colonial legacies, and the roles that different societies and groups assume within the technology lifecycle. Cultural tools developed within specific societies instigate shifts in the organisation of social life. Nevertheless, as Mabawonku (2003, p. 119) notes, "the different cultural purposes and the corresponding cultural tools will produce different cultural products or a different state and level of economic and social development". Consequently, the cultural aftermath of colonialism—the erasure of indigenous ways of being and knowing—has shaped Africa's current position in the realm of technological innovation.

The exclusion of colonised peoples from actively participating in the development of their societal structures means that their social issues often remain unaddressed, lacking relevance and importance to the dominant groups that drive technological advancement (Basu, 2022; Russell, 1986). Nevertheless, competition among established social groups creates opportunities for marginalised groups to rise and vie for influence (Cowhey & Aronson, 2017). According to Fialho et al., such competitive dynamics offer moments of opportunity during technological upheavals, allowing oppressed groups to challenge the status quo and devise solutions tailored to their unique social challenges.

Two intersecting conditions drive Africa's emergence as a contender in global technological innovation. On the one hand, intense competition among technological alternatives leads to the selection of dominant designs and subsequent periods of stability (Fialho et al., 2009, p. 312). The most robust models and innovations prevail, while others fall by the wayside. On the other hand, historically oppressed and sidelined social groups seize moments of disruption and turmoil resulting from this competition to subvert the extractive and exploitative systems established by dominant groups. These competitive conditions generate an abundance of digital resources, which hold potential value for peripheral societies and can be harnessed for the initial development of Afro-centric AI. This approach mirrors strategies employed in China, where extractable excess from the core has been utilised to foster technological growth (Baslandze et al., 2021).

From Imitation to Afro-Centric Speciation Events

Afro-centrism in AI development is not about reinventing technology but rather about actively engaging in the production process and meaningfully participating in the evolution of technology. This approach involves utilising readily available resources from the global core, tailoring them to local needs, and integrating them with indigenous knowledge systems—a concept known as the lock-in effect. Although China and Africa differ significantly in culture, history, and politics, China's strategies for technological imitation could inform the development of Afro-centric AI. This strategy would enable African nations to catch up with and compete alongside other global powers (Xie et al., 2006).

The "foreign excess" referred to by Xie et al. consists of surplus digital resources that emerge from intense competition in developed regions, which Fialho et al. have discussed. Baslandze et al. (2021) suggest that such technological spillovers enable less technologically advanced contexts to absorb and cultivate homegrown innovations. In crafting Afro-centric AI, the speciation process might involve subtle modifications of these external digital resources, resulting in minimal divergence from the original sources. This deliberate and incremental adaptation, driven by unique selection pressures and genetic drift within the African context, could set off a distinct evolutionary trajectory, culminating in the creation of African AI and a digital commons (Levinthal, 1998).

NEPAD, the African Union's Agency for Science and Technology, posits that Africa must strategically engage with AI, choosing to either adopt or disregard certain aspects as the technological landscape evolves (AUDA-NEPAD, 2022). By investing in, utilising, and shaping the deployment of AI technologies, Africa can enhance cost-effectiveness and conduct framework assessments, thereby fostering socioeconomic development.

Therefore, in the realm of prefigurative Afro-centrism, the entire sequence—from imitation to the initiation of speciation, through the incubation of separate reproductive processes, to the application of repurposed digital resources within African settings—is a series of intentional steps. These steps are designed to instigate a divergent evolutionary path that yields an African AI tailored to the continent's unique conditions and timelines.

Characteristics and Challenges of a Prefigurative Afro-Centric AI

One critique of prefigurative movements is that their sustainability, in the long run, is threatened by a lack of clarity on how this form of participatory democracy will look (Lederman, 2015), consequently replacing their predecessor systems and declining. This decline occurs because of the following:

> Jacobinism, "in which popular forums are repressed or their sovereignty usurped by a centralised revolutionary authority"; spontaneism, a strategic paralysis caused when parochial or anti political inclinations inhibit the creation of broader structures of effective coordination; corporatism, which occurs when an oligarchic stratum of activists is co-opted, leading them to abandon the movement's originally radical goals in order to serve their own interests in maintaining power. (Leach, 2013, p. 2)

Cognizant of these challenges to prefigurative movements, this chapter calls for a sustained course of action over time that gradually shapes a new culture of science while leveraging indigenous ways of coexisting. Indigenous ways of life, such as the Nhimbe concept, which emphasises collaborative community participation, offering free services to help members of the community complete tasks such as tilling the land, building homes, clearing the fields, and harvesting, among other homestead chores in return for convivial moments around food, songs, folklore, and alcohol can be instrumental (Mahohoma & Muzambi, 2021). Borrowed local epistemologies allow prefiguration strategies to be sustainable in creating local digital resources that mirror the inputs and efforts of community members. The characteristics of this prefigurative process should be inclusive and participatory, foster mutual spaces for co-ownership of resources and ideas, that the ideas and strategies are situated in local issues, that the algorithms embed local indigenous values in their local and or regional endeavours, that the responses should be rapid and timely to seize the opportunities presented by disruptions, that

"African publics" in their plurality and diversity should be at the centre of the prefiguration.

Pluralism, Scalability, and Challenges to Traditional Governance

The development of African AI and its associated digital commons should be predicated on the understanding that the complexities of globalisation and regional integration are increasingly challenging traditional state systems and their governance monopolies. This shift has led to the emergence of complex hybrid African state identities, with sovereign prerogatives being ceded to regional bodies in the quest for regional prosperity and security (Babones & Aberg, 2019; Jalloh & Abass, 2014). Such dynamics have transformed the political landscape both within and across states.

A key challenge in this evolving context is the non-exclusivity of regional integration frameworks. The existence of "multiple and overlapping multilateralismus" without a single, undisputed regional forum for norm custodianship, conflict management, and dispute arbitration complicates the governance landscape (Byiers, 2017). The absence of a regional "moral police" also poses significant implications for the initiatives discussed in this chapter.

When considering the scalability, interoperability, resource allocation, implementation, and monitoring of AI, these political complexities must be addressed. It is essential to develop scalable solutions that can adapt to growing regional demands, implement effective resource management strategies, devise robust implementation plans tailored to each region's specific challenges and opportunities, and establish comprehensive monitoring and evaluation frameworks. The issue of overlapping memberships in intra-regional and sub-regional bodies can be mitigated by defining clear roles and responsibilities and creating coordination mechanisms to prevent duplication of efforts and ensure efficient resource utilisation.

Furthermore, the process of producing and deliberating on AI should extend beyond the structuralist conceptions of participation in technological developments that often refer to the scientists, elites, and governments to include a broader range of stakeholders, particularly those directly impacted by AI technologies. Ensuring the inclusion of the "right public", whose needs drive the development of Afro-centric AI, is crucial. This pluralistic approach to governance guarantees that the technologies developed are attuned to local issues and necessities.

This chapter outlines three tiers of governance for prefigurative Afro-centric AI and digital commons:

Micro-level: This level focuses on dispersed, local, small-scale initiatives. Communities and groups identify their specific needs, engage in lock-in strategies, and commence domain-specific speciation processes. This grassroots approach aligns with the principles of speciation and natural selection, as AI resources are crafted to address local challenges by those who are intimately familiar with the issues.

Meso-level: At this intermediate stage, domain-specific and local commons are amalgamated into larger communal, institutional, and national endeavours. States and institutions are empowered to customise the AI transformation process to meet national objectives.

Macro-level: The highest level involves the regional integration of digital commons, with transnational and regional governance entities orchestrating continent- and region-wide initiatives for the collective benefit. Here, differences and similarities among states, transnational actors, communities, and developers are not seen as competitive factors but as means for broader integration, eliminating redundancies, and fostering synergy. National AI strategies should not be viewed as competitive assets but rather as part of a deliberate strategy for labour division and specialisation.

Conclusion

The chapter has highlighted the unique opportunity AI disruptions offer Africa to redefine its role in global technological developments. These disruptions could be a catalyst for Africa to assert its technological sovereignty by developing innovations that embody African values and identities. However, the continent faces a critical decision: seize this moment to chart a new course or risk further marginalisation in the global political and production systems.

Historically, colonialism disrupted Africa's natural, technological evolution, leaving it unprepared for the unfolding AI revolution. Despite this, Africa does not need to start from scratch. By strategically embracing and adapting global technological advancements, Africa can create distinctive technologies that resonate with its own norms and values. This process involves reclaiming indigenous knowledge systems and integrating them with global technological trends, positioning Africa as an active contributor to the global technological narrative.

This approach is proactive, aligning with African priorities to initiate a divergent evolution of digital resources. It treats technological disruptions as tools for empowerment, enabling Africa to reverse historical exploitation patterns. It repositions Africa not as a mere recipient of global technologies but as an active participant, shaping its own scientific and technological culture amidst significant AI-driven changes and ultimately fostering a distinct African science and technology culture that thrives on its terms during this transformative era.

References

Acemoglu, D., Johnson, S., & Robinson, J. A. (2000). *The colonial origins of comparative development: An empirical investigation*. https://doi.org/10.3386/W7771

Acemoglu, D., Johnson, S., & Robinson, J. A. (2002). Reversal of fortune: Geography and institutions in the making of the modern world income distribution. *The Quarterly Journal of Economics, 117*(4), 1231–1294. https://doi.org/10.1162/003355302320935025

Ade-Ibijola, A., & Okonkwo, C. (2023). Artificial intelligence in Africa: Emerging challenges (pp. 101–117). https://doi.org/10.1007/978-3-031-08215-3_5

Albarrán Lozano, I., Molina, J. M., & Gijón, C. (2021). Perception of artificial intelligence in Spain. *Telematics and Informatics*, 63. https://doi.org/10.1016/J.TELE.2021.101672

Anyoha, R. (2017). *The history of artificial intelligence: Can machines think?*, *Havard Kenneth C.Griffin Graduate School of Arts and Sciences*. Available at: The History of Artificial Intelligence. Accessed 13 March 2024.

AUDA-NEPAD. (2022). *Artificial intelligence is at the core of discussions in Rwanda as the AU high-level panel on emerging technologies convenes experts to draft the AU-AI continental strategy, African Union Development Agency (AUDA-NEPAD)*. https://www.nepad.org/news/artificial-intelligence-core-of-discussions-rwanda-au-high-level-panel-emerging. Accessed 13 March 2024.

Babones, S., & Aberg, J. H. S. (2019). *Globalization and the rise of integrated world society: Deterritorialization, structural power, and the endogenization of international society. International Theory*, 11(3), 293–317. https://doi.org/10.1017/S1752971919000125

Baslandze, S., Han, P., & Saffie, F. (2021). Imitation, innovation, and technological complexity: Foreign knowledge Spillovers in China. *SSRN Electronic Journal* [Preprint]. https://doi.org/10.2139/SSRN.3806435

Basu, S. (2022). Three decades of social construction of technology: Dynamic yet Fuzzy? The methodological conundrum. *Social Epistemology, 37*(3), 259–275. https://doi.org/10.1080/02691728.2022.2120783

BBC News. (2023). *AI and data labelling: 'I felt like my life ended'*. BBC.

Birhane, A. (2020). Algorithmic Colonisation of Africa. *SCRIPTed, 17*(2), 389–409. https://doi.org/10.2966/SCRIP.170220.389

Boggs, C. (1977). Revolutionary process, political strategy, and the dilemma of power. *Theory and Society, 4*(3), 359–393. https://doi.org/10.1007/BF00206985.

Burnette, C. E., Renner, L. M., & Figley, C. R. (2019). The framework of historical oppression, resilience and transcendence to understand disparities in depression amongst indigenous peoples. *British journal of social work, 49*(4), 943–962. https://doi.org/10.1093/bjsw/bcz041.

Byiers, B. (2017). *Regional organisations in Africa - Mapping multiple memberships, ECDPM.* https://ecdpm.org/work/regional-organisations-in-africa-mapping-multiple-memberships. Accessed 15 January 2024.

Coeckelbergh, M. (2022) *The political philosophy of AI an introduction.* 1st edn. Polity Press. https://www.wiley.com/en-us/The+Political+Philosophy+of+AI%3A+An+Introduction-p-9781509548552. Accessed 11 January 2023.

Cowhey, P. F., & Aronson, J. D. (2017). *Digital DNA: disruption and the challenges of global governance.*

Deokule, T. (2018) *Machine learning approaches for menstrual cycle tracking.* https://dataspace.princeton.edu/handle/88435/dsp01pz50gz849. Accessed 23 November 2022.

Dumett, R. (1985). Africa's strategic minerals during the Second World War. *The Journal of African History, 26*(4), 381–408. https://www.jstor.org/stable/181656. Accessed 28 December 2023.

Edo, V. O., & Olanrewaju, M. A. (2012). An Assessment of the Transition of the Organization of African Unity (OAU) to the African Union (AU), 1963–2007. *Journal of the Historical Society of Nigeria, 21*(2012), 41–69. https://www.jstor.org/stable/41857189. Accessed 13 March 2024.

Fialho, B. de C., Hasenclever, L., & Hemais, C. A. (2009). Punctuated equilibrium and technological innovation in the polymer industry. *Revista Brasileira de Inovação, 2*(2), 309–328. https://doi.org/10.20396/rbi.v2i2.8648875.

Hassan, A. (2023, December 14). *35 Poorest countries in Africa based on 2023 GDP per capita.* Yahoo Finance. https://finance.yahoo.com/news/35-poorest-countries-africa-based-215136678.html?guccounter=1&guce_referrer=aHR0cHM6Ly93d3cuZ29vZ2xlLmNvbS8&guce_referrer_sig=AQAAAFmL4xecYDvOJP1xacQWSi4X49I9-EBu6BakO4PNvuZrC9tm3X8wA4zIfrkNI-2Gc3zVNv1TkICU-66QrTIuluiVndsY5-Qc3bVGECdhd8-SKauRQybrBOf8xUPxtQq4kD_JrT-Uy62hjNeEq4oncPgmg13z_gnih71g3JLZL0sr. Accessed 10 January 2024.

Huang, S., & Siddarth, D. (2023). Generative AI and the Digital Commons. ArXiv. https://arxiv.org/abs/2303.11074v1

Jalloh, C. C., & Abass, A. (2014). Regional integration in Africa. *African Journal of Legal Studies, 7*(1), 1–5. https://doi.org/10.1163/17087384-12342038.

Kirmayer, L. J., et al. (2011). Rethinking resilience from indigenous perspectives. *Canadian Journal of Psychiatry, 56*(2), 84–91. https://doi.org/10.1177/070674371105600203.

Leach, D. K. (2013). Prefigurative Politics. *The Wiley-Blackwell Encyclopedia of Social and Political Movements* [Preprint]. https://doi.org/10.1002/9780470674871.WBESPM167

Lederman, S. (2015). Councils and revolution: Participatory Democracy in anarchist thought and the new social movements. *Science & Society, 79*(2), 243–263. https://www.jstor.org/stable/24583897. Accessed 11 January 2024.

Levinthal, D. A. (1998). The slow pace of rapid technological change: Gradualism and punctuation in technological change. *Industrial and Corporate Change*, 7(2), 217–247. https://doi.org/10.1093/ICC/7.2.217.

Litman, M. L., et al. (2021) *Gathering strength, gathering storms: The one hundred year study on artificial intelligence (AI100) 2021 Study Panel Report.* Stanford, CA. https://ai100.stanford.edu/gathering-strength-gathering-storms-one-hundred-year-study-artificial-intelligence-ai100-2021-1-0. Accessed 14 March 2024.

Lupton, D. (2020). Australian women's use of health and fitness apps and wearable devices: a feminist new materialism analysis. *Feminist Media Studies, 20*(7), 983–998. https://doi.org/10.1080/14680777.2019.1637916.

Lützelschwab, C. (2013). *Settler colonialism in Africa.* Brill. https://brill.com/display/book/9789004232655/B9789004232655-s007.xml. Accessed 13 March 2024.

Mabawonku, A. O. (2003). Cultural framework for the development of science and technology in Africa. *Science and Public Policy, 30*(2), 117–125. https://doi.org/10.3152/147154303781780588.

Mahohoma, T., & Muzambi, P. (2021). Nhimbe as a model for re-invigorating sustainable socio-economic development in Zimbabwe and Africa. *Theologia Viatorum, 45*(1). https://theologiaviatorum.org/index.php/tv/article/view/51/241. Accessed 5 March 2024.

Moor, J. (2006). The Dartmouth college artificial intelligence conference: The next fifty years. *AI Magazine, 27*(4).

Munetsi, D. (2022). Rethinking governance for resilient AI futures. In M. Thörnkvist (Ed.), *If only the lake could talk: Futures of AI for sustainability* (pp. 35–48). Media Evolution. https://www.mediaevolution.se/if-only-the-lake-could-talk/. Accessed 26 January 2023.

Nyuykonge, J. P. (2020). African epistemology and the challenge of epistemic bias. *Humanitatis Theoreticus, 4*(1). https://www.integhumanitatis.com/product/african-epistemology-and-the-challenge-of-epistemic-bias-by-john-paul-nyuykongi/. Accessed 13 March 2024.

Olhede, S. C., & Wolfe, P. J. (2018). The growing ubiquity of algorithms in society: Implications, impacts and innovations. *Philosophical Transactions of the Royal Society A: Mathematical, Physical and Engineering Sciences, 376*(2128). https://doi.org/10.1098/rsta.2017.0364

Osborn, E. L. (2004). "Rubber fever", Commerce and French Colonial Rule in Upper Guinée, 1890–1913. *The Journal of African History, 45*(3), 445–465. https://www.jstor.org/stable/4100754. Accessed 9 January 2024.

Oubibi, M., et al. (2022). The Challenges and opportunities for developing the use of data and Artificial Intelligence (AI) in North Africa: Case of Morocco. *Lecture Notes in Networks and Systems (LNNS), 455*, 80–90. https://doi.org/10.1007/978-3-031-02447-4_9.

Oxford Insights (2022) *Government AI Readiness Index 2022*. Malvern. https://oxfordinsights.com/ai-readiness/ai-readiness-index/. Accessed 8 January 2024.

Russell, S. (1986). The social construction of artefacts: A response to Pinch and Bijker. *Social Studies of Science, 16*(2), 331–346. https://doi.org/10.1177/030631278601600200 8/ASSET/030631278601600200 8.FP.PNG_V03.

SAIIA. (2022). *Africa's mineral resources are critical for the green energy transition, South African Institute of International Affairs (SAIIA).* https://saiia.org.za/research/africas-mineral-resources-are-critical-for-the-green-energy-transition/. Accessed 29 December 2023.

Statista. (2023). *Global internet penetration rate as of October 2023, by region*. https://www.statista.com/statistics/269329/penetration-rate-of-the-internet-by-region/. Accessed 8 January 2024.

Teng-Zeng, F. K. (2006). Science, technology and institutional cooperation in Africa: From pre-colonial to colonial science. *Eastern Africa Social Science Research Review, 22*(1), 1–37. https://doi.org/10.1353/eas.2006.0001.

UNCTAD. (2021). *Economic Development in Africa Report 2021: Reaping the Potential Benefits of the African Continental Free Trade Area for Inclusive Growth*. Geneva. https://unctad.org/system/files/official-document/aldcafrica2021_en.pdf. Accessed 8 January 2024.

UNCTAD. (2023). *Economic Development in Africa Report 2023*. Geneva. https://unctad.org/publication/economic-development-africa-report-2023. Accessed 19 October 2023.

WeForum. (2020). *This region will be worth $5.6 trillion within 5 years—But only if it accelerates its policy reforms*. World Economic Forum. https://www.weforum.org/agenda/2020/02/africa-global-growth-economics-worldwide-gdp/. Accessed 8 January 2024.

Wendt, P. (1947). The control of rubber in World War II. *Southern Economic Journal, 13*(3), 203. https://doi.org/10.2307/1053336

WIPO. (2022). *GII 2022 at a glance: The Global Innovation Index 2022 captures the innovation ecosystem performance of 132 economies and tracks the most recent global innovation trends*. Geneva. https://www.wipo.int/edocs/pubdocs/en/wipo-pub-2000-2022-section1-en-gii-2022-at-a-glance-global-innovation-index-2022-15th-edition.pdf. Accessed 8 January 2024.

Xie, G., Ni, J., & Ren, L. (2006). Imitation innovation in China: A case study of the software industry. *2006 Technology Management for the Global Future - PICMET 2006 Conference, 2*, 988–991. https://doi.org/10.1109/PICMET.2006.296630

Zheng, C., & Wang, B. X. (2012). Innovative or imitative? Technology firms in China. *Prometheus, 30*(2), 169–178. https://doi.org/10.1080/08109028.2012.668304

CHAPTER 3

Building Trustworthiness as a Requirement for AI in Africa: Challenges, Stakeholders and Perspectives

Seydina Moussa Ndiaye

Introduction

Artificial Intelligence (AI) continues to have an impact on a variety of sectors and is becoming more widespread in everyday life, both in the workplace and in the private sphere. Moreover, AI is increasingly used in complex fields and critical situations. In this context, the notion of trusted AI is becoming very crucial. The focus on Trustworthy AI aims to mitigate risks and increase user acceptance of the technology. The main aspect of Trustworthy AI is to emphasise the importance of developing systems that are legally and ethically compliant, and robust throughout their lifecycle. However, it is not simply a question of promoting responsible AI by essentially addressing solution designers or developers so that they incorporate responsible principles and methods. In fact, when it comes to trusted AI, the focus is more on the user of the technology to ensure

S. M. Ndiaye (✉)
Science, Technology and Digital Department, Cheikh Hamidou Kane Digital University, Dakar, Senegal
e-mail: seydina.ndiaye@unchk.edu.sn

D. O. Eke et al. (eds.), *Trustworthy AI*,
https://doi.org/10.1007/978-3-031-75674-0_3

that it is used reliably and in accordance with their values. Various computational techniques have been developed to meet these requirements, such as improving security, guaranteeing non-discrimination, increasing transparency and protecting privacy. Implementing trusted AI also involves validation and verification strategies and standardisation efforts. This implies a certain visibility over the entire lifecycle of AI solutions and a certain ability to act throughout the process to guarantee compliance with requirements, whether ethical, regulatory or technical. To ensure trust, it is therefore important to develop solutions that are not only technically sound but also culturally sensitive and ethically aligned, particularly in diverse contexts such as Africa.

In the African context, the notion of trusted AI can be analysed from two points of view. As the technology is mostly a foreign one in Africa, many uses are based on solutions that have been totally or partially developed outside the African context. From this point of view, solutions developed in the West often fail to take into account African values, realities and cultures, which can lead to mistrust. This situation is reminiscent of the exploitation of colonial times, with Western technology monopolies dominating the AI landscape in Africa. Although AI offers potential benefits for African development in various sectors, there are challenges related to technology transfer, infrastructure and adaptation to local needs. Ethical considerations are crucial, as AI systems can perpetuate biases and fail to incorporate African perspectives on the individual and humanity. Human biases are very real and a number of studies[1] have been carried out in this area. The real problem with human bias is that we introduce it into the programming of algorithms, sometimes without being aware of it, thereby creating algorithmic bias (Awan, 2023). To ensure trusted AI, from this point of view where the technological solution had not, at the outset, integrated the context of its application, several elements need to be taken into account.

In addition, several countries on the continent have set up national strategies, and we even have a pan-African dynamic with the African Union, which launched its strategy document[2] in February 2024

[1] Bertrand, Marianne and Sendhil Mullainathan. "Are Emily and Greg More Employable Than Lakisha and Jamal? A Field Experiment on Labor Market Discrimination," *American Economic Review*, 2004, v94 (4, Sep), 991–1013.

[2] https://onedrive.live.com/?authkey=%21AKJcwcnXeRGANKQ&id=14DDAD979C3656DF%2145404&cid=14DDAD979C3656DF.

(AUDA-NEPAD, 2024). What all these strategy documents have in common is the interest in promoting AI made in Africa to meet the needs of the continent and the world. So, a second angle of analysis is that in this context, where technological infrastructures are not developed, data is scarce, people who master the technology are very rare and there are no regulations mature enough to govern the design, deployment and use of the technology, how can we trust AI solutions developed entirely in Africa?

The first section of this chapter presents an overview, without being exhaustive, of existing use cases across Africa. In the second section, we will look at the problem of using AI solutions designed outside Africa in Africa and the trust issues that arise from this. The third section will examine the dynamics of the development of African AI and the different stakeholders involved. The notion of trust will also be discussed, and what it means for each stakeholder. A fourth section will conclude this chapter.

AI Adoption in Africa

AI is revolutionising many sectors around the world, and Africa is no exception. Despite demographic and economic challenges, AI is seen as a powerful enabler to overcome major obstacles and drive growth on the continent. Areas such as healthcare, agriculture, education and finance are already benefiting from innovative solutions thanks to AI (Gikunda, 2023; Nibigira et al., 2024). However, Africa faces challenges such as lack of adequate digital infrastructure, lack of expertise and ethical concerns related to AI. Despite these obstacles, the enthusiasm and determination of African players is palpable, with promising initiatives[3] driven by visionary governments, bold entrepreneurs and talented researchers (Azaroual, 2024).

A Nascent but Dynamic Ecosystem

AI is transforming various sectors in Africa. In healthcare, it is being used for medical diagnosis, image analysis and patient records management, with notable initiatives in Kenya, Rwanda, South Africa, Nigeria and

[3] https://idrc-crdi.ca/en/stories/artificial-intelligence-african-style.

Ghana (Kinyua Gikunda, 2023). In agriculture, AI is optimising production, managing water resources and controlling pests, with examples of use in Kenya, Nigeria, Tunisia and Senegal (Gwagwa et al., 2021). In education, AI is personalising learning, automating administrative tasks and supporting distance learning, with pilot projects in Rwanda, Kenya and South Africa (Onyebuchi Nneamaka Chisom et al., 2024). In finance, AI is automating banking processes, assessing customer creditworthiness and combating fraud, with applications in Kenya, Nigeria, South Africa and Ghana (Oriji et al., 2023).

Despite many challenges, 69.16% of African businesses are implementing information security strategies, 45% of which are using AI-based technologies (Nibigira et al., 2024). The African startup scene is witnessing a surge in AI innovation. Companies such as Intron Health[4] in Nigéria, minoHealth AI Labs[5] in Ghana, iCog Labs[6] in Ethiopia, Lelapa AI[7] in South Africa and Kera[8] in Senegal are at the forefront of developing AI solutions tailored to African needs. From healthcare to language technologies, these startups demonstrate the continent's growing AI capabilities. However, adoption rates among small and medium-sized enterprises remain low due to fears of losing control of critical business processes and a perceived lack of IT maturity (Schoeman & Seymour, 2023). For AI to drive socio-economic inclusion in Africa, policymakers need to consider key dimensions such as gender equity, cultural and linguistic diversity, and labour market developments (Gwagwa et al., 2020). A vibrant ecosystem of grassroots communities is driving the development of AI talent in Africa. Initiatives such as Deep Learning Indaba,[9] AI Saturdays Lagos[10] and others promote knowledge sharing, training and research collaboration. Through their efforts, Africa is rapidly building a solid foundation for AI excellence on the global stage.

[4] https://www.intron.io/.

[5] https://www.minohealth.ai/.

[6] https://icog-labs.com/.

[7] https://lelapa.ai/.

[8] https://kera.health/.

[9] https://deeplearningindaba.com/.

[10] https://www.aisaturdayslagos.com/.

Perspectives and Challenges

Africa faces many challenges in adopting AI. The lack of sufficient quality data is a major obstacle. Inadequate digital infrastructure is holding back the adoption of AI, particularly due to the high cost of Internet access. The continent also suffers from a shortage of AI skills and insufficient investment in research and development (Eke et al., 2023). Ethical and regulatory issues also pose challenges, requiring clear frameworks for the responsible use of AI. Lastly, the lack of incentive-based public policies, structural inequalities and the digital divide are significant obstacles, making equitable access to AI technologies difficult (Amankwah-Amoah & Lu, 2022; Nibigira et al., 2024).

Some recent studies explore the adoption and implications of generative AI in Africa. While these technologies hold promise in various sectors such as journalism, finance and marketing (Gondwe, 2023; Jaldi, 2023; Katterbauer et al., 2024; Okolo, 2023), they also present challenges. Concerns include potential misinformation, plagiarism and bias due to unrepresentative datasets (Gondwe, 2023). In Nigeria, interest in generative AI tools such as ChatGPT does not correlate with literacy levels or socio-economic factors, suggesting widespread curiosity across various demographics (Ahiara et al., 2023). The financial technology sector in Africa could particularly benefit from generative AI, despite regulatory and economic barriers (Katterbauer et al., 2024). However, the limited African corpus of learning data for AI raises concerns about effectiveness and equity in local contexts (Gondwe, 2023). These studies highlight the need for responsible development and use of generative AI in African contexts, taking into account local needs and potential risks (Gondwe, 2023; Okolo, 2023).

Despite this, the adoption of AI in Africa offers an immense potential to stimulate economic growth and improve quality of life. By overcoming the challenges mentioned and exploiting the opportunities offered by AI, Africa can position itself as a major player in the AI revolution. This requires increased investment in digital infrastructure, professional training and research and development. Visionary government policies and strategic partnerships between the public, private and civil society sectors are essential to create an enabling environment for AI-enabled innovation and economic growth (Arakpogun et al., 2021; Deo Shao et al., 2023).

However, the integration of AI in Africa is not homogeneous. While some African countries are making progress in their adoption of AI, others face obstacles such as structural inequalities and the digital divide. An inclusive and holistic approach is needed to ensure that all African countries can reap the benefits of AI and close the gap with the rest of the world. To realise the full potential of AI in Africa, it is crucial to increase investment in digital infrastructure, professional training and research and development. By working together, African countries can turn today's challenges into opportunities and pave the way for a future where AI makes a significant contribution to sustainable development and improved quality of life for all Africans (Mbuvha et al., 2024).

Yet some research indicates that most AI solutions used in Africa are based on technologies developed outside the continent, which poses problems of local adoption and relevance (Birhane, 2020; Arakpogun et al., 2021). This "algorithmic colonisation" often does not meet the specific needs of Africa and can hamper local innovation (Birhane, 2020).

Trustworthiness of External AI Solutions in Africa

The rapid progress of AI and its increasingly widespread application to achieve sustainable development goals and stimulate economic growth make mastery of this technology increasingly vital for every nation. This mastery is essential to ensure technological, economic, social and political sovereignty. However, current trends in AI, in particular the rise of generative AI as one of the most powerful approaches, require access to vast amounts of data and significant computing power that most companies and even countries lack. As a result, we are witnessing a polarisation of control over AI between the USA and China, with large US technology companies virtually monopolising the power of generative AI.

Against this backdrop, many countries have become aware of the need for a specific strategy to master AI technologies, and are making substantial investments in this area in order to exploit the full potential of AI. This is to enable their companies to benefit from the opportunities it offers, to take advantage of this technological revolution and to remain competitive in the global economy. However, these investments are not feasible in all countries. Indeed, the least technologically and economically advanced countries are very limited in terms of the financial efforts they can devote to the development of AI. Nevertheless, despite these limitations, more and more emerging or developing countries are formulating their AI development strategies, given the importance of the subject and the stakes of this technology in today's world. This is the case in Africa, where these strategies also propose extensive use of the technology and its appropriation in all sectors of activity. To achieve this, despite medium- and long-term policies to develop local talent and technological infrastructures, it is sometimes necessary to take certain shortcuts to use or adapt solutions developed outside Africa. What's more, the consumer AI solutions available worldwide are also being appropriated by Africans. But what is the risk when such solutions developed elsewhere are used in an African context? Can African users trust such AI solutions?

The General Public

Although we do not have a precise estimate of the level of use of AI technologies by the general public in Africa, the development of generative AI leads us to believe that the African population is increasingly interested in using these technologies. The growing interest of African populations in AI technologies is accompanied by concerns about their suitability for local contexts. AI solutions developed by the West often fail to take into account African values, realities and cultures, which can lead to mistrust (Okolo, 2023). This echoes the exploitation of the colonial era, with Western technology monopolies dominating the AI landscape in Africa (Birhane, 2020).

One of the main characteristics of artificial intelligence, and machine learning in particular, is that it is strongly linked to the data used to learn the underlying model. Consequently, when it comes to implementing solutions that have an impact on humans, if the data is not diversified, the model that will be used to make decisions runs the risk of being biased and unable to take into account certain characteristics specific to a category of people. Among the African users of these AI solutions, there may be unconditional users who believe that everything the AI says is an absolute truth and who therefore do not take the precaution of critically examining what is generated. Indeed, the concern about hardcore AI users in Africa highlights a deeper problem in the adoption of AI technologies on the continent.

Indeed, algorithmic biases in data-driven innovation and AI systems are a growing concern and stem from three main sources: data biases, societal biases and algorithmic design biases (Akter et al., 2021). These biases can lead to unfair outcomes and discrimination in a variety of areas, including personal finance, healthcare and employment (Hajian et al., 2016).

The lack of data in African contexts is a major factor contributing to data bias.[11,12] Many AI systems are built from datasets that do not adequately represent African populations or their unique challenges. AI tools can therefore provide misleading or harmful information, which hardcore users may accept without question. For example, inaccuracies have been identified in medical applications of AI, where results may not match the realities faced by African users due to a lack of localised data.[13]

Furthermore, societal biases are very real and numerous studies[14] have been carried out in this area. The real problem with societal bias is that we also introduce it into the programming of algorithms without being aware of it. This bias often stems from training data reflecting existing social inequalities, which risks exacerbating discrimination (Islam, 2024). Ethical considerations are crucial, as AI systems may perpetuate biases and fail to incorporate African perspectives on personhood and humanity (Kohnert, 2022; Nwankwo & Sonna, 2019). These ethical implications of AI systems that perpetuate societal biases are a growing concern.

Algorithmic design biases, on the other hand, can emerge from seemingly innocuous information processing patterns, making them difficult to identify and mitigate (Johnson, 2020). They may, however, be conscious, i.e. voluntarily incorporated by solution designers in order to have specific behaviours according to certain targets (Fabi & Hagendorff, 2022). Thus, it is interesting to note that some researchers advocate the intentional implementation of certain biases in AI systems. These algorithmic design biases could improve decision-making in complex environments or promote desirable social behaviour (Fabi & Hagendorff, 2022). However, finding a balance between mitigating biases and maintaining the accuracy of judgements remains challenging, as attempts

[11] https://www.afrilabs.com/harnessing-ai-for-africas-future-intel-empowering-builders-across-the-continent-2/.

[12] https://african.business/2024/04/technology-information/ai-the-african-opportunity.

[13] Ibid.

[14] Bertrand, Marianne and Sendhil Mullainathan. "Are Emily and Greg More Employable Than Lakisha and Jamal? A Field Experiment on Labor Market Discrimination," *American Economic Review*, 2004, v94 (4,Sep), 991–1013.

to remove surrogate attributes can compromise system performance (Johnson, 2020). Ultimately, promoting the ethical and transparent development of AI requires constant vigilance and a holistic approach. To address these issues, a multidimensional approach involving diverse perspectives in both datasets and development teams is essential (Ribeiro Fernandes & Vieira Graglia, 2024).

Beyond the biases, the issue of AI use also raises concerns about trust with the general public. There is a real risk that AI technologies could be misused by malicious actors to manipulate and exploit people. AI systems are already being used for fraudulent activities, human rights abuses and the creation of harmful content (Anderljung & Hazell, 2023). The rise of AI-powered language models and chatbots presents risks of misinformation and manipulation of human decisions (Williamson & Prybutok, 2024). These technologies threaten privacy, autonomy and democratic processes by enabling detailed behavioural profiling and voter manipulation (Manheim & Kaplan, 2018). Cyber-attacks on the banking sector and attempts to manipulate public opinion using advanced technologies are on the increase (Pantserev, 2021).

In this context, to strengthen AI Trustworthiness, it is therefore important to raise awareness among the general public in Africa of these potential biases, malicious uses and the operating principles of the most widespread AI solutions, to enable them to have a better insight to appreciate the quality of the results obtained and the information offered to them.

Professional Deployment

While AI has potential benefits for Africa's development in various sectors, there are challenges related to technology transfer, infrastructure and adaptation to local needs (Kohnert, 2022). Most AI solutions deployed in Africa in many sectors are applications using models developed outside Africa. In healthcare, AI systems have been used to improve patient-worker interactions, detect eye conditions and analyse health data for disease diagnosis and monitoring (Akpanudo, 2022; Mbunge & Batani, 2023). AI is also being applied to climate change adaptation, making predictions about weather patterns, floods, droughts and human migration (Rutenberg et al., 2020).

From the point of view of solution designers in Africa who use models pre-trained in other contexts as a basis, it is important to carefully consider the approach to be taken in adapting models to the local context. Indeed, studies highlight the need to consider colonial history, country of origin and national income level as potential sources of bias in AI systems (Asiedu et al., 2024). Challenges related to mitigating bias in learning data and developing culturally sensitive AI governance frameworks are also noted (Oluka, 2024). For example, to ensure fairness and mitigate bias in AI applications for global health, researchers propose evaluating systems based on suitability, bias and fairness criteria (Fletcher et al., 2021). These studies highlight the importance of incorporating local values, ethical considerations and socio-cultural diversity in the development of AI for Africa, while addressing potential biases and equity issues in order to improve healthcare outcomes in the region. The adoption of AI in Africa raises questions about technology transfer, local needs and the development of endogenous AI solutions (Kohnert, 2022).

The adaptation of AI models to new contexts calls for several methods to guarantee robust performance and ensure greater confidence. Domain adaptation techniques modify a model trained in one domain so that it performs well in a different but related domain, using supervised, unsupervised or adversarial methods. Data augmentation allows the training dataset to be enriched with synthetic data or transformations to improve generalisation. Model ensemble methods combine several models to improve performance, while active learning makes iterative use of human expertise to label uncertain predictions (Osborne & Baldridge, 2004). "Few-shot" and "Zero-shot" learning methods enable models to recognise new classes with minimal or no examples, taking advantage of meta-learning or integration-based methods. Multi-task learning (Caruana, 1996) trains a model on several related tasks simultaneously for better generalisation, and fine-tuning hyperparameters (Liu et al., 2022) specifically for the new context optimises model performance. Regularisation techniques, such as L1/L2 regularisation and dropout, prevent overfitting and improve generalisation (Rezaeezade & Batina, 2022). Finally, explainable AI (XAI) methods, such as feature importance and model interpretation tools, ensure that the model fits correctly by providing information about its decision-making process (Tiwari, 2023; Zodage et al., 2024). Below, we look in more detail at some of the methods we consider interesting in the African context.

- Transfer learning is the most widely used method. It is a machine learning technique that exploits knowledge from one task to improve the performance of another, related task (Ahmed Ali et al., 2023). It is particularly useful when the labelled data available for the target task is limited, overcoming overfitting and improving model generalisation (Ahmed Ali et al., 2023; Sreerama & Sistla, 2023). In natural language processing, transfer learning methods have significantly improved state-of-the-art performance on various tasks (Ruder et al., 2019). The approach typically involves refining a pre-trained model using new data relevant to the new context (Sreerama & Sistla, 2023). Transfer learning has also been applied to predictive model control, where it reduces the amount of data required for learning and improves the performance of target systems (Arce Munoz et al., 2023). This technique has shown promise in a variety of fields, including computer vision, healthcare and process automation (Sreerama & Sistla, 2023; Arce Munoz et al., 2023).

- Another method is domain adaptation techniques, which apply models trained in one domain to a different but related domain. Unsupervised domain adaptation, where labels are only available in the source domain, has received particular attention (Farahani et al., 2020). Various approaches have been developed, including divergence-based, adversarial discriminative, adversarial generative and self-supervision-based methods (Zhao et al., 2020). These techniques aim to align disparities between domains, enabling the model to be generalised to the target domain (Farahani et al., 2020). Deep learning has been combined with domain adaptation to take advantage of powerful hierarchical representations while reducing dependence on target data labels (Wilson & Cook, 2018). One innovative approach uses generative adversarial networks (GANs) to learn unsupervised pixel-level transformations from source to target domain, outperforming state-of-the-art methods in a variety of scenarios (Bousmalis et al., 2016). This diverse range of techniques demonstrates ongoing efforts to address the challenges of domain adaptation in visual tasks and machine learning applications.
- A method particularly suited to the African context is data augmentation, which is a powerful technique for improving the generalisation and performance of machine learning models, particularly when training data is limited. It involves creating synthetic samples through transformations in the data space or feature space (Devries & Taylor, 2017; Wong et al., 2016). While data space augmentation is most effective when plausible transformations

are known, feature space augmentation offers a domain-agnostic approach (Devries & Taylor, 2017; Wong et al., 2016). In theory, data augmentation acts as a regulator, preventing overfitting and improving model robustness (Kumar et al., 2019). It also influences the optimisation landscape and convergence behaviour of deep learning algorithms (Kumar et al., 2019). When combined with transfer learning, data augmentation can significantly improve model performance on classification tasks, especially in scenarios with limited target domain data (Su et al., 2024). This synergistic approach has been experimentally validated on various datasets, demonstrating its effectiveness in improving model generalisation and adaptability to real-world applications. However, synthetic data do not represent real-world data, and so in contexts where cultural or historical specificities need to be taken into account, it is important to reconsider such choices.

- Few-shot and zero-shot learning enable models to recognise new classes with minimal or no examples, taking advantage of meta-learning or embedding-based methods. Relationship networks learn a deep distance metric to compare query images with a few examples of new classes (Sung et al., 2017). Another approach uses class models embedded in a higher-dimensional space, enabling shot-free learning and achieving peak performance on few-shot benchmarks (Ravichandran et al., 2019). For zero-shot learning, a generative framework based on exponential family distributions can predict unseen classes using attribute-linked conditional class distributions (Verma & Rai, 2017). This method extends to few-shot learning by updating distributions with additional labelled examples. Different approaches to few-shot learning include shallow models, Bayesian networks and neural networks, with various training methods such as domain adaptation and transfer learning (Kadam & Vaidya, 2018). These techniques aim to address the challenge of limited training data in machine learning applications.
- To address problematic biases and measure the diversity in the dataset, researchers have developed many methods. For example, there are tools like D-BIAS, which uses causal models and human-in-the-loop approaches to detect and mitigate social biases in datasets (Ghai & Mueller, 2022). Guha Balakrishnan et al. (2020) proposed an experimental approach using synthetic image grids to reveal causal links between attribute variations and performance changes in face

analysis algorithms. Alexander Amini et al. (2019) introduced a tunable algorithm that uses variational autoencoders to learn latent structures in datasets and re-weight data points to address racial and gender bias in facial detection systems. Runshan Fu et al. (2020) provided a comprehensive overview of algorithmic bias, discussing its definition, detection methods, sources and correction techniques. The Vendi Score, introduced as a similarity-based diversity metric for machine learning, extends the Hill number concept from ecology (Friedman & Dieng, 2022). It addresses limitations in existing diversity measures by incorporating user-defined similarity functions without requiring reference datasets (Friedman & Dieng, 2022). Pasarkar and Dieng (2023) further expanded this concept, creating a family of Vendi scores with varying sensitivities to item prevalence. These metrics have been applied to molecular simulations and image-generative models (Pasarkar & Dieng, 2023). These studies collectively contribute to the growing body of research aimed at understanding, detecting and mitigating algorithmic bias in various AI applications.

When the solutions deployed are based on models developed outside the continent, these methods can be applied individually or in combination, depending on the specific requirements and constraints of the new context. However, there has been growing interest in developing AI applications made in Africa in recent years (Wairegi et al., 2021; Arakpogun et al., 2021; Gikunda, 2023; Kiemde & Kora, 2020). But in a context where the lack of data, talent and computing infrastructure is still real, how do we establish trust for such AI solutions?

Building African AI Trustworthiness

African countries have resolutely turned their attention to appropriating AI, mastering it and adopting it in all sectors of activity. With the launch of its national AI strategy in 2018[15] Mauritius was the first African country to clearly show its ambition in the field. It has been joined by several African countries that have published their AI strategy or are in

[15] https://ncb.govmu.org/ncb/strategicplans/MauritiusAIStrategy2018.pdf.

the process of developing one,[16] or that have put in place strong public policies on AI aimed at making their countries leaders at the continental level.[17]

On a continental level, the African Union is not to be outdone, and has adopted[18] two structuring AI public policy documents, namely an AI white paper[19] and a continental AI roadmap,[20] with a 2033 horizon.

In this context, where Africa, whether at country level or more globally at continental level, has a surge of interest in AI, we also have a strong momentum for an inclusive development of AI at global level. Initiatives such as the Global Partnership on Artificial Intelligence[21] (GPAI), the OECD AI Principles,[22] the G20 AI Principles,[23] the UNESCO Recommendations on AI Ethics,[24] the UN General Assembly Resolution on AI,[25] the Bletchley Declaration[26] of the UK AI Summit (AI Safety Summit), the Seoul Declaration Ministerial Statement[27] et the

[16] https://www.diplomacy.edu/resource/report-stronger-digital-voices-from-africa/ai-africa-national-policies/.

[17] https://www.dentons.com/en/insights/articles/2024/june/13/ai-regulation-and-policy-in-africa.

[18] https://au.int/en/pressreleases/20240617/african-ministers-adopt-landmark-continental-artificial-intelligence-strategy#:~:text=The%20Strategy%20sets%20the%20roadmap,ecosystems%2C%20and%20building%20an%20AI%2D.

[19] https://onedrive.live.com/view.aspx?resid=14DDAD979C3656DF!45406&authkey=!AKJcwcnXeRGANKQ.

[20] https://onedrive.live.com/view.aspx?resid=14DDAD979C3656DF!45405&authkey=!AKJcwcnXeRGANKQ.

[21] https://gpai.ai/.

[22] https://oecd.ai/en/ai-principles.

[23] https://www.mofa.go.jp/policy/economy/g20_summit/osaka19/pdf/documents/en/annex_08.pdf.

[24] https://www.unesco.org/en/artificial-intelligence/recommendation-ethics.

[25] Seizing the opportunities of safe, secure and trustworthy artificial intelligence systems for sustainable development: https://undocs.org/Home/Mobile?FinalSymbol=A%2F78%2FL.49.

[26] https://www.gov.uk/government/publications/ai-safety-summit-2023-the-bletchley-declaration/the-bletchley-declaration-by-countries-attending-the-ai-safety-summit-1-2-november-2023.

[27] https://overseas.mofa.go.kr/viewer/skin/doc.html?fn=20240523095941078.pdf&rs=/viewer/result/202407.

Statement of Intent[28] of the Seoul AI Summit, all promote trusted AI for the benefit of all. Alongside these initiatives, we have two particularly important opportunities for Africa, to turn them into levers for cooperation to facilitate the implementation of various public policies on AI. These are the discussions on the Global Digital Compact,[29] which will culminate in the Future Summit[30] in September 2024, and the work of the UN Secretary-General's High-Level Advisory Body on AI[31] (HLAB), whose final report is expected in August 2024. These last two initiatives are particular opportunities for Africa because they represent the most inclusive, but also because they have a particular interest in helping to bridge the existing gap between the Global South and the Global North, both globally in digital and particularly for AI.

However, if these opportunities are to be exploited to the full, it is important that the leaders of African countries and organisations adopt a sovereign and responsible approach to the development of African AI,[32] to ensure the confidence of the various stakeholders. Indeed, it is essential that the vision is clear and that the resources mobilised already enable the establishment of an African AI ecosystem, so that international cooperation can be grafted onto a dynamic that is already well underway endogenously, with a strong awareness of the ambitions (Arakpogun et al., 2021) that the continent has in this field. On the one hand, this will enable us to break the current trends of AI colonisation, where Africa's place in the global AI economy is de facto defined from the outside, and on the other hand, it will enable us to have Trustworthy AI thanks to mutual confidence between the various players involved.

Sovereign Approach to African AI Leadership

For African countries and organisations to take full advantage of the opportunities offered by AI, it is essential to adopt a sovereign and

[28] https://overseas.mofa.go.kr/viewer/skin/doc.html?fn=20240523101016282.pdf&rs=/viewer/result/202407.

[29] https://www.un.org/techenvoy/global-digital-compact.

[30] https://www.un.org/en/summit-of-the-future.

[31] https://www.un.org/ai-advisory-body.

[32] https://african.business/2024/05/technology-information/why-africas-leaders-need-to-prioritise-ai.

accountable approach that aligns AI development with local values and priorities. African nations must assert their technological sovereignty (Birhane, 2020; Nwankwo & Sonna, 2019) and self-determination by controlling the development,[33] deployment and governance of AI systems within their borders. This is essential to avoid dependence on AI models developed abroad, which can perpetuate digital colonialism and undermine Africa's autonomy. It is therefore essential to strengthen local AI capabilities. AI development in Africa should be anchored in responsible and ethical practices (Shao et al., 2023) to mitigate risks such as prejudice, discrimination and privacy violations, incorporating African philosophies that emphasise collective well-being and human dignity (Nwankwo & Sonna, 2019).

Transparency, accountability and human oversight are essential to maintain public trust (Knowles & Richards, 2021; Olatunji Akinrinola et al., 2024), and explainable AI and human-in-the-loop approaches should be prioritised (Wilchek et al., 2023; Wu et al., 2022). AI development must be inclusive and involve diverse stakeholders, including marginalised communities, civil society, academia and the private sector, to ensure equitable access to AI education and opportunities. Intellectual property frameworks should balance innovation and the public good, and open source models can play an important role. International and intra-African strategic partnerships should accelerate AI capabilities while preserving sovereignty and aligning with local priorities (Kinyua Gikunda, 2023), avoiding exploitative relationships. By prioritising local capabilities, ethical practices, inclusive innovation and strategic partnerships, African nations can fully harness the transformative potential of AI for sustainable development.

If this sovereign approach to AI is to become a reality in Africa, all the players involved need to be aware of this potential and play their part to the full, so that we can have trusted AI for Africa and the world. But who are these players? What is the role of each? How can we guarantee trust between these players?

[33] https://www.fastcompany.co.za/technology/sovereign-ai-an-opportunity-for-uniquely-south-african-powered-artificial-intelligence-6848b668-989a-47c3-bb54-10e1f9a8b306.

African AI Ecosystem Stakeholders

The African AI ecosystem is evolving in a unique way due to the continent's distinct geographical, cultural and political landscape (Wairegi et al., 2021). Stakeholders in this ecosystem include governments, private sector entities, universities, communities and multilateral organisations (Ibeneme et al., 2021). To ensure the equitable development of AI, it is essential to identify the interests, responsibilities and accountability of these stakeholders (Wairegi et al., 2021). Stakeholder consultation is essential to develop a roadmap for AI development in Africa and address power asymmetries (Siminyu et al., 2023).

Key policy dimensions for AI deployment in Africa include gender equity, cultural and linguistic diversity, and labour market developments (Gwagwa et al., 2020). Priorities for AI implementation include data protection, confidentiality and sharing protocols; researcher training and platforms; funding models; evaluation frameworks; forum organisation; and establishing regulations and ethical guidelines (Ibeneme et al., 2021). Government ownership and leadership are essential for sustainable funding and effective scaling of trusted AI-based applications in Africa (Ibeneme et al., 2021).

The stakeholder mapping we propose below is different from that proposed by Wairegi et al. (2021). Our approach takes an ecosystem viewpoint rather than a company viewpoint, with a breakdown of the roles of each player in the ecosystem to guarantee trusted AI in Africa:

- Governments: they play a key role in the African AI ecosystem. In contrast to the global context, where AI development is mainly driven by the private sector, especially big tech, the African AI ecosystem can only reach its full potential if governments are heavily involved. The various roles played by this key player are: (i) strengthening technological infrastructures (computing, storage, Internet access), (ii) implementing a regulatory framework to guarantee Trustworthy AI,[34] (iii) developing public procurement of Responsible AI, (iv) funding R&D and innovation, (v) establishing strategic partnerships as a result of scientific diplomacy[35] and (vi) promoting AI, notably by encouraging the opening up of public data;

[34] Including the implementation of norms and standards.

[35] Including active participation in major international AI initiatives.

- Training and research centres: in the emerging context of AI in Africa, these players also play a central role in ensuring sovereign and trusted AI. The roles assigned to this player are: (i) training AI talent (in all dimensions, not just technical), (ii) developing research and innovation, (iii) supporting the State in public AI policies, (iv) raising R&D and innovation funding, (v) establishing partnerships with research networks at international level and (vi) collaborating with the private sector;
- Organisations that design AI solutions: here we're talking about companies that specialise in developing AI solutions, but also any other type of organisation that implements AI solutions. The various roles assigned to this player are: (i) setting up an internal mechanism to guarantee the implementation of responsible AI, (ii) collaborating with training and research centres, (iii) participating in the animation of the AI ecosystem and (iv) raising funds;
- Grassroots communities: these are equally important in the context of AI development in Africa. Their roles are: (i) ecosystem animation, (ii) AI acculturation and training, and (iii) implementation of structuring projects[36];
- Private sector: not just the AI private sector, but the private sector as a whole. Its roles are: (i) the integration of AI for process improvement and value creation, and (ii) participation in the animation of the ecosystem[37];
- Multilateral organisations: at the African level, these are sub-regional and pan-African organisations; at the global level, these are all organisations working in the global governance of AI. The roles are: (i) promoting responsible AI at continental and international level, (ii) scientific cooperation, (iii) promoting technological inclusion[38] and (iv) setting up a universal regulatory framework for ethical and responsible AI;
- Financial partners: representing investors for the private sector and bilateral cooperation for governments or research centres. Their roles are: (i) financing, (ii) technical support and (iii) networking;

[36] Example of the Masakhane community (https://www.masakhane.io/) on African languages, which is working on a project to create datasets on several local African languages.

[37] For example, agreeing to share company data for hackathons.

[38] For example, facilitating access to computing power or large datasets.

- End-users: these are the citizens and non-profit organisations that use AI solutions. The roles are: (i) acculturation to AI and (ii) responsible use of AI.

A Vibrant Ecosystem for a Trustworthy AI

All the stakeholders identified for this African AI ecosystem have expected roles that enable this ecosystem to be vibrant, dynamic, effective and trusted. Effective stakeholder engagement is key to implementing the ecosystem approach and successfully deploying Trustworthy AI systems (Glomsrud & Bach, 2023; Oates & Dodds, 2017). An ecosystem-based stakeholder management framework can improve organisational performance by strategically managing, monitoring and evaluating stakeholder involvement throughout the stages of a project (Tarode & Shrivastava, 2021). However, in a self-regulating ecosystem such as that of AI in Africa, it is not possible to consider a stakeholder management framework. It is therefore important that each stakeholder ensures its roles fully and that globally the stakeholders in charge of ecosystem animation identify relevant policy frameworks, the creation of inclusive forums, the development of shared visions and the collaborative implementation of engagement actions (Oates & Dodds, 2017). Trust is paramount in these ecosystems, requiring assurance through evidence and knowledge to align stakeholder objectives and manage risk (Glomsrud & Bach, 2023). As emerging industries evolve, stakeholders may undergo role transformations (Lu et al., 2014). This will require the ability to adapt, while being aware of the roles of each player and trusting that they will fully assume them. By implementing effective consultation frameworks between stakeholders, the AI ecosystem in Africa can build trust between players, develop functional relationships and create value globally and individually (Tarode & Shrivastava, 2021).

AI development in Africa evolves in unique ways due to geographical, cultural and political factors, requiring a distinct framework to identify and characterise stakeholders in the African AI ecosystem. This approach aligns with the concept of responsible AI, which emphasises the responsibility of all stakeholders involved in AI development (Lima & Cha, 2020).

Conclusion

The rise of AI in Africa represents both a challenge and a considerable opportunity. Despite the obstacles associated with technology transfer, infrastructure and adaptation to local needs, the growing initiatives of African countries and continental organisations signal a determined commitment to the development of AI. Mauritius' pioneering strategy and the African Union's continental policies underline a collective desire to position themselves as AI leaders on the continent.

However, for Africa to take full advantage of AI's transformative potential, a sovereign and responsible approach is crucial. Integrating local values, managing biases and putting in place appropriate ethical frameworks are essential to ensure AI respects cultural diversity and meets the specific needs of African communities. The importance of endogenous AI development cannot be underestimated, with a clear need for a dynamic ecosystem supported by a variety of players: governments, research centres, companies, communities, the private sector, multilateral organisations and financial partners.

Building a trusted African AI ecosystem relies on the active engagement of these stakeholders. Success will require not only investment in infrastructure and training, but also close collaboration to define robust public policies, promote inclusion and ensure transparency. Global initiatives, such as the Global Digital Compact and the work of the UN Secretary-General's High-Level Advisory Body on AI, offer crucial opportunities to reinforce this momentum, by focusing on the inclusion of the Global South and fostering strategic partnerships.

Ultimately, building trusted AI in Africa will require a delicate balance between technological sovereignty and international cooperation. By adopting an integrated approach that respects local values while exploiting global opportunities, Africa can not only overcome current challenges but also position its AI ecosystem as a model for sustainable and ethical development on a global scale.

References

Ahiara, W. C., Abioye, T., Chiagunye, T., & Olaleye, T. O. (2023). An exploratory data analytics of multivariate observational metrics on generative AI. *MoMLeT+DS*.

Akinrinola, O., Okoye, C. C., Ofodile, O. C., & Ugochukwu, C. E. (2024). Navigating and reviewing ethical dilemmas in AI development: Strategies for transparency, fairness, and accountability. *GSC Advanced Research and Reviews*, 18(3), 050–058.

Akpanudo, S. (2022). *Application of Artificial intelligence systems to improve healthcare delivery in Africa.*

Akter, S., McCarthy, G., Sajib, S., Michael, K., Dwivedi, Y. K., D'Ambra, J. G., & Shen, K. N. (2021). Algorithmic bias in data-driven innovation in the age of AI. *International Journal of Information Management, 60*, 102387. https://doi.org/10.1016/j.ijinfomgt.2021.102387

Ali, A., Yaseen, M. G., Aljanabi, M., Abed, S. A., & Gpt, C. (2023). Transfer learning: A new promising techniques. *Mesopotamian Journal of Big Data.*

Amankwah-Amoah, J., & Lu, Y. (2022). Harnessing AI for business development: A review of drivers and challenges in Africa. *Production Planning & Control.*

Amini, A., Soleimany, A. P., Schwarting, W., Bhatia, S. N., & Rus, D. (2019). Uncovering and mitigating algorithmic bias through learned latent structure. *Proceedings of the 2019 AAAI/ACM Conference on AI, Ethics, and Society.*

Anderljung, M., & Hazell, J. (2023). *Protecting society from AI misuse: When are restrictions on capabilities warranted?* ArXiv, abs/2303.09377.

Anicet KIEMDE, S. M., & Dooguy Kora, A. (2020). The challenges facing the development of AI in Africa. *2020 IEEE International Conference on Advent Trends in Multidisciplinary Research and Innovation (ICATMRI)*, 1–6.

Arakpogun, E. O., Elsahn, Z., Olan, F., & Elsahn, F. (2021). *Artificial intelligence in Africa: Challenges and opportunities.* The Fourth Industrial Revolution: Implementation of Artificial Intelligence for Growing Business Success.

Asiedu, M. N., Dieng, A., Haykel, A., Rostamzadeh, N., Pfohl, S. R., Nagpal, C., Nagawa, M., Oppong, A., Koyejo, S., & Heller, K. (2024). *The case for globalizing fairness: A mixed methods study on colonialism, AI, and health in Africa.* ArXiv, abs/2403.03357.

AUDA-NEPAD. (2024). *AUDA-NEPAD White paper: Regulation and responsible adoption of AI in Africa towards achievement of AU agenda 2063.* African Union Development Agency.

Awan, A. A. (2023). *What is algorithmic bias?* https://www.datacamp.com/blog/what-is-algorithmic-bias. Accessed 6 August 2024.

Azaroual, F. (2024). *L'Intelligence Artificielle en Afrique : défis et opportunités.* Policy briefs 2043, Policy Center for the New South.

Baeza-Yates, R. A. (2016). Data and algorithmic bias in the web. In *Proceedings of the 8th ACM Conference on Web Science* (pp. 1–9).

Balakrishnan, G., Xiong, Y., Xia, W., & Perona, P. (2020). *Towards causal benchmarking of bias in face analysis algorithms*. ArXiv, abs/2007.06570.

Birhane, A. (2020). *Algorithmic colonization of Africa*. SCRIPT-ed.

Bousmalis, K., Silberman, N., Dohan, D., Erhan, D., & Krishnan, D. (2016). Unsupervised pixel-level domain adaptation with generative adversarial networks. *IEEE Conference on Computer Vision and Pattern Recognition (CVPR), 2017*, 95–104.

Caruana, R. (1996). Algorithms and applications for multitask learning. *International Conference on Machine Learning*.

Chisom, O. N., Unachukwu, C. C., & Osawaru, B. (2024). Review of AI in education: Transforming learning environments in Africa. *International Journal of Applied Research in Social Sciences*.

Devries, T., & Taylor, G. W. (2017). *Dataset augmentation in feature space*. ArXiv, abs/1702.05538.

Eke, D. O., Wakunuma, K., & Akintoye, S. (2023). Introducing responsible AI in Africa. In *Responsible AI in Africa: Challenges and opportunities* (pp. 1–11). Springer International Publishing.

Fabi, S., & Hagendorff, T. (2022). *Why we need biased AI—How including cognitive and ethical machine biases can enhance AI systems*. ArXiv, abs/2203.09911.

Farahani, A., Voghoei, S., Rasheed, K. M., & Arabnia, H. R. (2020). *A brief review of domain adaptation*. ArXiv, abs/2010.03978.

Fernandes, E. R., & Graglia, M. A. (2024). Human intelligence and artificial intelligence and the challenges of biases in AI algorithms. *Journal on Innovation and Sustainability RISUS*.

Fletcher, R. R., Nakeshimana, A., & Olubeko, O. (2021). Addressing fairness, bias, and appropriate use of artificial intelligence and machine learning in global health. *Frontiers in Artificial Intelligence, 3*.

Friedman, D., & Dieng, A. B. (2022). *The Vendi score: A diversity evaluation metric for machine learning*. ArXiv, abs/2210.02410.

Fu, R., Huang, Y., & Singh, P.V. (2020). AI and algorithmic bias: Source, detection, mitigation and implications. *InfoSciRN: Machine Learning (Sub-Topic)*.

Ghai, B., & Mueller, K. (2022). D-BIAS: A causality-based human-in-the-loop system for tackling algorithmic bias. *IEEE Transactions on Visualization and Computer Graphics, 29*, 473–482.

Gikunda, K. (2023). *Empowering Africa: An in-depth exploration of the adoption of artificial intelligence across the continent*. ArXiv, abs/2401.09457.

Glomsrud, J. A., & Bach, T. A. (2023). *The ecosystem of trust (EoT): Enabling effective deployment of autonomous systems through collaborative and trusted ecosystems*. ArXiv, abs/2312.00629.

Gondwe, G. (2023). ChatGPT and the global south: How are journalists in sub-Saharan Africa engaging with generative AI? *Online Media and Global Communication, 2*, 228–249.

Gwagwa, A., Kazim, E., Kachidza, P., Hilliard, A., Siminyu, K., Smith, M. J., & Shawe-Taylor, J. (2021). Road map for research on responsible artificial intelligence for development (AI4D) in African countries: The case study of agriculture. *Patterns, 2*.

Gwagwa, A., Kraemer-Mbula, E., Rizk, N., Rutenberg, I., & Beer, J. (2020). *Artificial intelligence (AI) deployments in Africa: Benefits, challenges and policy dimensions*.

Hajian, S., Bonchi, F., & Castillo, C. (2016). Algorithmic bias: From discrimination discovery to fairness-aware data mining. In *Proceedings of the 22nd ACM SIGKDD International Conference on Knowledge Discovery and Data Mining* (pp. 2125–2126).

Ibeneme, S., Okeibunor, J. C., Muneene, D., Husain, I., Bento, P., Gaju, C., Housseynou, B., Chibi, M., Karamagi, H. C., & Makubalo, L. E. (2021). Data revolution, health status transformation and the role of artificial intelligence for health and pandemic preparedness in the African context. *BMC Proceedings, 15*.

Islam, M. (2024). Ethical considerations in AI: Navigating the complexities of bias and accountability. *Journal of Artificial Intelligence General science (JAIGS) ISSN:3006–4023*.

Jaldi, A. (2023). Artificial intelligence revolution in Africa: Economic opportunities and legal challenges. *Policy Center for the New South, Benguerir, 6*.

Johnson, G. M. (2020). Algorithmic bias: On the implicit biases of social technology. *Synthese, 198*, 9941–9961.

Kadam, S., & Vaidya, V. (2018). Review and Analysis of zero, one and few shot learning approaches. *International Conference on Intelligent Systems Design and Applications*.

Katterbauer, K., Syed, H., Cleenewerck, L., Özbay, R. D., & Yilmaz, S. (2024). Impact of generative AI on fintech in Africa. *Yildiz Social Science Review*.

Knowles, B., & Richards, J. T. (2021). The sanction of authority: Promoting public trust in AI. *Proceedings of the 2021 ACM Conference on Fairness, Accountability, and Transparency*.

Kohnert, D. (2022). Machine ethics and African identities: Perspectives of artificial intelligence in Africa. *SSRN Electronic Journal*.

Kumar, A., Mali, Y., & Kumar, A. (2019). Theoretical insights into the role of data augmentation in deep learning model training. *The Pharma Innovation*.

Lima, G., & Cha, M. (2020). *Responsible AI and Its stakeholders*. ArXiv, abs/2004.11434.

Liu, X., Wu, J., & Chen, S. (2022). A context-based meta-reinforcement learning approach to efficient hyperparameter optimization. *Neurocomputing, 478*, 89–103.

Lu, C., Rong, K., You, J., & Shi, Y. (2014). Business ecosystem and stakeholders' role transformation: Evidence from Chinese emerging electric vehicle industry. *Expert Systems with Applications, 41*, 4579–4595.

Manheim, K., & Kaplan, L. (2018). Artificial intelligence: Risks to privacy and democracy. *Yale Journal of Law and Technology, 21*, 106.

Mbunge, E., & Batani, J. (2023). *Application of deep learning and machine learning models to improve healthcare in sub-Saharan Africa: Emerging opportunities, trends and implications.* Telematics and Informatics Reports.

Mbuvha, R., Yaakoubi, Y., Bagiliko, J., Potes, S. H., Nammouchi, A., & Amrouche, S. (2024). Leveraging AI for climate resilience in Africa: Challenges, opportunities, and the need for collaboration. *SSRN Electronic Journal.*

Munoz, S. A., Park, J., Stewart, C. M., Martin, A. M., & Hedengren, J. D. (2023). Deep transfer learning for approximate model predictive control. *Processes.*

Nibigira, N., Havyarimana, V., & Xiao, Z. (2024). Artificial intelligence adoption for cybersecurity in Africa. *Journal of Information Security, 15*, 134–147.

Nwankwo, E., & Sonna, B. (2019). Africa's social contract with AI. *XRDS: Crossroads. The ACM Magazine for Students, 26*, 44–48.

Oates, J., & Dodds, L. A. (2017). An approach for effective stakeholder engagement as an essential component of the ecosystem approach. *ICES Journal of Marine Science: Journal Du Conseil, 74*, 391–397.

Okolo, C. T. (2023). The promise and perils of generative AI: Case studies in an African context. *Proceedings of the 4th African Human Computer Interaction Conference.*

Oluka, A. (2024). Mitigating biases in training data: Technical and legal challenges for sub-Saharan Africa. *International Journal of Applied Research in Business and Management.*

Oriji, O., Shonibare, M. A., Daraojimba, R. E., Abitoye, O., & Daraojimba, C. (2023). Financial technology evolution in Africa: A comprehensive review of legal frameworks and implications for AI-driven financial services. *International Journal of Management & Entrepreneurship Research.*

Osborne, M., & Baldridge, J. (2004). Ensemble-based active learning for parse selection. *North American Chapter of the Association for Computational Linguistics.*

Pantserev, K. A. (2021). Existing practice and risks of malicious use of artificial intelligence in Sub-Saharan Africa. *Asia and Africa Today.*

Pasarkar, A. P., & Dieng, A. B. (2023). *Cousins of the Vendi score: A family of similarity-based diversity metrics for science and machine learning*. ArXiv, abs/2310.12952.

Ravichandran, A., Bhotika, R., & Soatto, S. (2019). Few-shot learning with embedded class models and shot-free meta training. *IEEE/CVF International Conference on Computer Vision (ICCV), 2019*, 331–339.

Rezaeezade, A., & Batina, L. (2022). Regularizers to the rescue: Fighting overfitting in deep learning-based side-channel analysis. *IACR Cryptology ePrint Archive, 2022*, 1737.

Ruder, S., Peters, M. E., Swayamdipta, S., & Wolf, T. (2019). Transfer learning in natural language processing. *North American Chapter of the Association for Computational Linguistics*.

Rutenberg, I., Gwagwa, A., & Omino, M. (2020). Use and impact of artificial intelligence on climate change adaptation in Africa. *African Handbook of Climate Change Adaptation*.

Schoeman, F. R., & Seymour, L. F. (2023). Understanding the low adoption of AI in South African medium-sized organisations. *EPiC Series in Computing*.

Shao, D., Marwa, N., & Matendo, D. (2023). Regulatory strategies for fostering responsible AI innovation in African economies. *First International Conference on the Advancements of Artificial Intelligence in African Context (AAIAC), 2023*, 1–11.

Shin, D., & Shin, E. Y. (2023). Data's impact on algorithmic bias. *Computer, 56*, 90–94.

Siminyu, K., Abbott, J. Z., Túbosún, K., Anuoluwapo, A., Sibanda, B. K., Yeboah, K. A., Adelani, D. I., Mokgesi-Selinga, M., Apina, F. R., Mthembu, A. T., Ramkilowan, A., & Oladimeji, B. (2023). Consultative engagement of stakeholders toward a roadmap for African language technologies. *Patterns, 4*.

Sreerama, J., & Sistla, S. M. (2023). Harnessing the power of transfer learning in deep learning models. *Journal of Knowledge Learning and Science Technology ISSN: 2959–6386 (online)*.

Su, J., Yu, X., Wang, X., Wang, Z., & Chao, G. (2024). Enhanced transfer learning with data augmentation. *Engineering Applications of Artificial Intelligence, 129*, 107602.

Sung, F., Yang, Y., Zhang, L., Xiang, T., Torr, P. H., & Hospedales, T. M. (2017). Learning to compare: Relation network for few-shot learning. *IEEE/CVF Conference on Computer Vision and Pattern Recognition, 2018*, 1199–1208.

Tarode, S., & Shrivastava, S. K. (2021). A framework for stakeholder management ecosystem. *American Journal of Business*.

Tiwari, R. (2023). Explainable AI (XAI) and its applications in building trust and understanding in AI decision making. *International Journal of Scientific Research in Engineering and Management*.

Verma, V. K., & Rai, P. (2017). A simple exponential family framework for zero-shot learning. *ECML/PKDD*.

Wairegi, A., Omino, M., & Rutenberg, I. (2021). AI in Africa: Framing AI through an African Lens. *Communication, technologies et développement*.

Wilchek, M., Hanley, W., Lim, J., Luther, K., & Batarseh, F. A. (2023). Human-in-the-loop for computer vision assurance: A survey. *Engineering Applications of Artificial Intelligence, 123*, 106376.

Williamson, S. M., & Prybutok, V. R. (2024). The era of artificial intelligence deception: Unraveling the complexities of false realities and emerging threats of misinformation. *Inf., 15*, 299.

Wilson, G., & Cook, D. J. (2018). A survey of unsupervised deep domain adaptation. *ACM Transactions on Intelligent Systems and Technology (TIST), 11*, 1–46.

Wong, S. C., Gatt, A., Stamatescu, V., & McDonnell, M. D. (2016). Understanding data augmentation for classification: When to warp? *International Conference on Digital Image Computing: Techniques and Applications (DICTA), 2016*, 1–6.

Wu, J., Huang, Z., Hu, Z., & Lv, C. (2022). Toward human-in-the-loop AI: Enhancing deep reinforcement learning via real-time human guidance for autonomous driving. *Engineering*.

Zhao, S., Yue, X., Zhang, S., Li, B., Zhao, H., Wu, B., Krishna, R., Gonzalez, J., Sangiovanni-Vincentelli, A. L., Seshia, S. A., & Keutzer, K. (2020). A review of single-source deep unsupervised visual domain adaptation. *IEEE Transactions on Neural Networks and Learning Systems, 33*, 473–493.

Zodage, P., Harianawala, H., Shaikh, H., & Kharodia, A. (2024). Explainable AI (XAI): History, basic ideas and methods. *International Journal of Advanced Research in Science, Communication and Technology*.

CHAPTER 4

Trust Me, I Am an Intelligent and Autonomous System: Trustworthy AI in Africa as Distributed Concern

Makuochi Samuel Nkwo and Muhammad Adamu

Introduction

In the 80s, Schank (1987) posed the question: "What is AI, anyway?" Today, this question remains relevant because it seems that we are yet to know with some level of consensus what artificial are. Is it social and moral intelligence, artificial general intelligence, augmented intelligence, or some form of intelligently stupid machines? For Crawford, AI is an "an idea, an infrastructure, an industry, a form of exercising power... a two-word phrase onto which is mapped to a complex set of expectations, ideologies, desires, and fears" (2021, pp. 18–19). For the likes of Schank (1987), Collins (2021), Falk (2021), and Pasquinelli (2023),

M. S. Nkwo (✉)
University of Greenwich, London, UK
e-mail: M.S.Nkwo@greenwich.ac.uk

M. Adamu
University of Nottingham, Nottingham, UK
e-mail: M.adamu@nottingham.ac.uk

D. O. Eke et al. (eds.), *Trustworthy AI*,
https://doi.org/10.1007/978-3-031-75674-0_4

AI is a science project, an art exhibition, technological tool, an instrument of power, or method/technique of technicality. Alvarado (2023, p. 1) believes that AI is an epistemic technology designed and used in contextual inquiries "to manipulate epistemic contents like data…through epistemic operations such as inferences, predictions or analysis". As an instrument of knowledge and a technique of power, AI functions as a method that has the potential to support (and enhance) human epistemic capabilities within a distinctively social and material space.

With diverse interpretation of AI as a thing, Collins (2021, p. 3) noted how the "science of AI is so poor at presenting and testing its claims", as those limitations "arise from methodological and epistemological misconceptions about the capabilities of AI" (Hagendorff & Wezel, 2020, p. 355). If such claims can be adequately substantiated, for which some part of the chapter seeks to pursue, how researchers and practitioners are yet to fully develop a consensus (as regards faith and trust) in the promise of artificial general intelligence. One could argue that charismatic technologies such as AI and Big Data, as demonstrated with the one child per laptop technological project across the global south, operates on the exercise of elegant power where everyday social relations are subdued to present technological systems as humanising apparatus for amplifying human subjectivities.

Artificial Intelligence as a Wildcard

Regardless of such narratives, classic AI as an extensive research programme centres around designing and deploying computer-based agents that exhibit forms of intelligence via rule-based computation or pattern matching at scale. This has led to a series of interdisciplinary dialogue pertaining to ways in which human-friendly AI agents can be designed and adopted based on universal human values and for the common good. Partly due to the AI control and alignment problems that foregrounded the prolonged summers and winters of AI, applied AI researchers have sought to develop computational methods and techniques for simulating the cognitive state of humans as mechanical entities that can be operationally represented and executed with measurable outcomes. Specific to the symbolic AI landscape, researchers have also sought to solve social intelligence as a computation information processing system to be simulated and attained (Toosi et al., 2021). With the framing of AI as an "it" by Pasquinelli (2023, p. 3)—the quest to solve intelligence—with distinctive agency and autonomy—there is a trade-off on how human-like social intelligence can be transformed (or transferred) mechanically. Such intellectual efforts have led to the common understanding that what is often referred to as AI is the abstraction of a range of computational techniques and intelligence argumentation such as machine learning, neural network, and large language models to denote an intellectual aspiration (and not actuality) for the scalability of the human mind and brain. Even with the conflicting accounts as to what AI can (and cannot) do (see Hagendorff & Wezel, 2020), the AI revolution is underway as a modern phenomenon in history (Haenlein & Kaplan, 2019), and the need for closer examination of its trajectory and development is further warranted.

AI as an Intellectual Scientific Project

From cognitive science and computer science, the humanities to critical AI studies, researchers have acknowledged how both technical and social perspectives of AI have embodied the sort of science from the above narrative in its discourse (Brokensha et al., 2023; Buchanan, 2005; Pasquinelli, 2023; Toosi et al., 2021). Consequently, the historical analysis of AI is an attempt to highlight "its genealogy and its historical character: as an intellectual project, a science, an industrial art, a management tool, a promise "....and these histories are meant to present "a clearer picture of what and where AI is, what and where it might be, and what and where it perhaps should not be" (Ali et al., 2023, p. 17). This thus raised the question, going beyond Norbert Wiener and John McCarthy's earlier constructions of AI: How can we as a community of practitioners trust a thing that we don't have a basic understanding of, or are yet articulate how to adopt our modern frames of questioning and answering dialectically to better its histories and futures? What we're getting at is the concept of the AI black box problem; an ethical problem where we're faced with the difficulty of articulating how and why AI systems operate to reach the conclusions it presents.

Relatedly, von Eschenbach (2021, p. 1618) argues that this line of questioning is misguided, arguing instead at length, citing Nickel et al. (2010): "For some, to ask whether we can trust technology is akin to making a categorical mistake because trust can occur only between people or moral agents... To ask if one can trust AI, whether or not it involves black box technology, is the wrong question to ask, according to these views. Instead, we need to ask if we can trust the people who design, implement, and use these technologies". Although we reason with arguments above, our framing of trust as a distributed concern within a complex web of socio-technical systems necessitates posing some fundamental questions as to how trustworthy AI can be better approached and understood across cultures and contexts.

With trust being a core feature of human social relation, we recognised Kiran and Verbeek (2010) and Alvarado's (2023) position that the kind of trust ascribed to intelligent systems during the AI summers are a consequence of the mutation of the absurdities of modernity. Ryan (2020) opines that AI does not have the capacity to be trusted because it is not emotive and cannot be held responsible for their actions. With conflicting account of trust and trustworthy AI, one might reason with Lushetich position that "stupidity is, to a degree, 'baked into' AI" (2022, p. 119), and the long AI winters we've painfully experienced symbolises modernity's quest for new forms of human-artificial stupidity. Even with the continual decidualisation of the society, Falk (2021) has argued that human-machine stupidity could act a *map/script* for reflecting on the complexities of understanding (and representing) the dynamics of human intelligence.[1] Thus, our earlier question: How can we trust a complex web of socio-technical systems that we don't have a fuller understanding of its inner workings? Or are we intelligently stupid enough to trust institutional structure, as in making judgements, when we do have limited concepts to rationalise its assumptions and conclusions? In short, are we to re-trust the instruments of modernity in Africa?

AI in/from Africa

The following section discusses relevant literature that speaks to the complexities around simplistic accounts of trustworthy AI as binaries of risk/reward. To situate trust as a distributed concern, we relied on narratives around AI ethics in Africa, ethical AI application in Health and Agriculture, as well as the discussions around equitable and responsible AI in Africa (see Eke et al., 2023; Ferreira & Tokhi, 2022; Kokuryo et al., 2020) to demonstrate the need for more subtle discursive argumentation about trustworthy AI as an interdisciplinary phenomenon.

[1] See Falk (2021) and Lushetich (2022) for more provocative discussion around the value of human and machine stupidity in AI discussions.

Our discursive argumentation builds on existing work across the continent where researchers have explored the ecological, social, cultural, and political dimension of the development and application of AI. Often, these narratives drew from intersectional perspectives that have sought to counter neo-colonial epistemologies via the centring of African humanism (Brokensha et al., 2023; Eke et al., 2023). Even with the proliferation of AI discourses globally, others have recognised how the "narratives of AI from Africa are missing or are often forgotten" (Eke & Ogoh, 2022, p. 1) but more importantly, within the subfield of African HCI.

For example, Birhane (2020) and Mwema and Birhane (2024) have demonstrated how the conquest patterns embedded in AI digital infrastructure and ecosystem denote an algorithm colonisation of AI. The emphasis on the fourth industrial revolution (4IR) via leapfrogging into sustainable development further solidifies the concerted efforts of Western institutions to control and commodify African entities. While Adamu and Nkwo (2023) wondered that the proliferation of digital technologies (e.g. AI, big data and so on) could signify the re-birth of new forms of digital imperialism under the rubric of the African 4IR other studies argued that AI as an expression of power in the global south is implicated by geopolitical and economic relations, the social imaginaries of whiteness and blackness, the materiality of superiority and inferiority, and the performativity of the dominated and the dominant (Birhane, 2022; Cave & Dihal, 2020; Mwema & Birhane, 2024; Park, 2021), thus, needed to be decolonised (Murphy & Largacha-Martínez, 2022). Even when the framing of AI innovation as a mutation of modernistic values and relations has begun to receive considered scholarly attention, how is it that there is no collective outlook for a good AI-led African society?

From "AI for Good" to "Good AI Society"

Regardless of the fundamental ambiguities and complexities around AI as a wildcard, the notion of "AI for good" and "good AI society", even with its multiple controversies and contractions, has become a forceful research programme and application area across disciplines (Cath et al., 2018; Euchner, 2019; Shi et al., 2020; Wamba et al., 2021). As rightly pointed out by Moore regarding the vagueness of the notion of AI for good: citing Bruno Latour "words are crucial because 'by definition, a technological project is a fiction since at the outset it does not exist, and there is no way it can exist yet because it is in the project phase'...... Vague terms are the wagons of a modern gold rush into the promised riches of a mythic AI frontier" (2019, p. 2). The vagueness of AI for good initiatives denotes technological determinism in action, particularly how anticipatory technologies are rendered as instruments for improving human social conditions. In his words: "AI for good…refers to the projection of the computational discipline onto some definition of public or societal good" (Moore, 2019, p. 2). Green (2019) further demonstrated how modern technological enchantment has rendered invisible the power dynamics of globalisation where often saviourism and solutionist appeals obscure the ethical window-washing underplay in the global south. As a result of this reductionist framing of the social realm, structural social issues are reduced to design problem formulation and technological solution optimisation. And as noted by Green (2019), "Good isn't good enough", perhaps Moore's (2019) inference towards X "for not bad" might provide practical directions on how AI can be designed and adopted for the common public.

As the frontier AI is driven by both the public and private sectors, recent efforts have foregrounded the need for articulating and envisioning what a "good AI society" will look like and how the prosperity of all can be ensured and guaranteed (Cath et al., 2018; Wamba et al., 2021). The requirements for a good AI society have gained a strong interdisciplinary basis as recent developments across the USA, EU, UK and China have demonstrated the limited synergy in the visions of what a good AI society should look like, but more importantly, how those provisional projections could be scaled beyond the normative technological frame of "do no harm" (Wamba et al., 2021). Specific to African HCI, Nkwo and Adamu (2024, p. 4) have considered whether a "concrete visions for a continental African AI society that can be implemented and operationalized to ensure minimal risk and maximal benefit for the common man and the public" is feasible (and attainable) given large Western control of the fundamental infrastructures of AI research and innovation.

Ethics of AI in Africa

Unlike Western and Chinese establishments continual effort to steer AI research and development, AI ethics discourses and applications in Africa are still at the infancy stage. While responsible AI is an approach to design and deployment of AI in an ethical way, AI ethics principles are the code of ethics or frameworks that guide responsible research and development (Adamu & Nkwo, 2023; Dignum, 2022). Some of the AI ethical principles which are needed to build responsible AI systems include transparency & accountability, justice & fairness, beneficence & non-maleficence, security & privacy, freedom & autonomy, sustainability & solidarity. To realise the full potential benefits and mitigate the risks of AI to human well-being and the environment, research has established the need for AI systems to be developed with the human-in-mind approach. However, the adoption of AI technologies into industries such as healthcare, education, commerce, and national security has foregrounded combined multi stakeholder efforts focused to develop and adopt relevant code of ethics and/or guiding principles to inform the entire life cycle of the AI ecosystem. The expansion of the AI ecosystem to include diverse voices aims to chart a socially appropriate approach to the design and implementation of AI interventions for the common good (Floridi, 2019). Due to the potential impact of emerging technologies to human flourishing and environmental sustainability, the landmark EU AI act is a testimony of how the governance and regulation has far-reaching implications on global geo-political and economic relations.[2]

AI Governance in Africa

Although Africa is lagging in the research and development of AI governance mechanisms, there have been fewer regional and national efforts aimed to provide regulatory frameworks and policies for AI on the continental levels. For instance, the African Union (AU) is working to ensure that Africa participates actively in the emerging global AI ethics discussions and is set to launch its regional AI strategy in 2024. Countries such as Mauritius, Egypt, and Nigeria have drafted their national policies and regulations for AI governance in 2018, 2019, and 2022, respectively. For Mauritius, the emphasis was to identify sector-led priority projects that are AI enabled, developing skills and capacities for effective design and adoption, and incentivising research and development as catalyst for upscaled implementation across public services. For Egypt, the focus has been on developing actionable blueprints that could support the realisation of nations sustainable development goals as well as facilitate regional cooperation between Africa and Arab leagues.

[2] https://www.europarl.europa.eu/news/en/press-room/20231206IPR15699/artificial-intelligence-act-deal-on-comprehensive-rules-for-trustworthy-ai.

Even with such projections, a few other countries in Africa such as Uganda, Tunisia, South Africa, Morocco, Rwanda, Kenya, Ethiopia, and Algeria have developed inclusive national regulatory frameworks to govern the adoption of emerging technologies that are central to the 4IR. The Organization for Economic Co-operation and Development (OECD.AI) policy observatory 2022 reveals that the national regulatory frameworks aim to facilitate the design, testing and refinement of governance protocols and policies to maximise the social benefits and minimise the risks of advanced technology in systematically disenfranchised communities. Key actors within the technological landscape have also made significant investment in Africa's AI ecosystem. For instance, Google flagged open their first AI research lab in Accra, Ghana in 2019; and Microsoft followed with the launch of their Africa Development Centre (ADC) with two initial sites in Nairobi, Kenya and Lagos, Nigeria in 2019. These multinational companies have also made significant efforts towards adopting ethical principles that are responsive to new social contexts and emerging markets, thus informing the design and implementation of their AI products and services.

Currently, many AI systems in use globally and in Africa have been found to be potentially susceptible to subtle attacks, bedevilled with bias, privacy, and security issues towards underrepresented groups. Such issues have been identified as leading to mistrust/antitrust in the entire AI landscape (Birhane, 2022). Therefore, we argue that the designers of Africa's AI national regulatory frameworks ought to consider relevant sociocultural, geo-political and environmental specificities that could affect the adoption and use of such AI systems. By approaching ethics and governance as a collective social and political concern, we will not only expand the pool of participation in AI discussions, but also promote and engender confidence in the ecosystem, and amplify the acceptability and sustainability of its practices across various application domains.

Case Studies of Ethical AI from Africa

Across the globe, AI has found application in various domains of human lives including in health, agriculture, commerce, education, finance, defence, etc. Specific to **ethical AI in Health**, Jiang et al. (2017) trace the historical integration of AI in healthcare practices beginning with the early rule-based applications to the evolving machine learning/deep learning techniques utilised to enhance accuracy and efficiency of complex medical processes such as medical diagnosis and imaging, drug discovery and personalised medicine, as well as in prognostics and predictive analytics. In Africa, more specifically, Sallstrom et al. (2019) investigated the ethical concerns connected to the deployment of AI in healthcare across the continent. These include data privacy and security associated with the use of sensitive health data, informed consent, discrimination, and bias among others. Wahl et al. (2018) investigated the application of artificial intelligence (AI) in health care in resource-poor settings, which included diagnosis and treatment, remote monitoring and telemedicine, and outbreak prediction and disease surveillance. The studies above have led to the identification of ethical challenges associated with AI in healthcare (e.g. data ownership and privacy, digital divide, capacity building) and suggested strategies such as community collaboration and partnerships, and responsible and equitable design and utilisation to address such issues. The emphasis of these strategies is to help strengthen AI-enabled healthcare service delivery, optimise resource allocation, and enhance the efficiency of healthcare services in resource-poor countries.

Similarly, the World Health Organization's (WHO) in 2021 offered a robust framework for addressing ethical considerations and establishing governance principles in the context of artificial intelligence (AI) for health care. While prioritising key ethical principles for AI in healthcare (including transparency, accountability, inclusivity, privacy, and fairness), the report suggests that equal access, human-centred approach, data governance and privacy, interoperability and ethics, stakeholder engagement and quality assurance are critical components of an effective AI for healthcare applications. Although AI has the potential to revolutionise healthcare practices not only in Africa but across the globe, it is important to recognise the challenges and opportunities associated with the practical implementation of AI systems in the health sector. For example, Panch et al. (2019) opine that the black-box nature of some of these AI/ML models and the difficulties in integrating AI into the regular clinical workflow make it complicated for community healthcare workers to understand the machine. Moreover, factors such as resistance to change and lack of user-friendly interfaces make it difficult for the healthcare practitioners to develop confidence (as in trust) in the decisions designed using these models, hence impeding the effective implementation of AI in healthcare practices especially in the developing communities (Panch et al., 2019). This calls for the adoption of a distributed approach to building and deploying trustworthy AI systems that are patient-centric, integrative, and cost effective (see Procter et al., 2023).

With specific emphasis on **ethical AI in agriculture**, Songol et al. (2021) examined the current landscape of AI application in agriculture in developing countries with a view to showing emerging themes, opportunities, and challenges in the space. The study described success case studies stories which demonstrates practical insights about the positive impacts of AI on farming practices which include increased productivity, improved crop management, enhanced decision-making, and more sustainable farming practices. Moreover, it discusses the broader challenges with adopting AI in agriculture in developing nations which include limited access to technology, insufficient infrastructure, and the need for capacity building among farmers and stakeholders to effectively integrate AI solutions. To advance the application of AI in agriculture, Songol et al. (2021) highlight the need for the adoption of ethical values (such as data privacy, and equitable access) in the design and deployment of AI technologies in agriculture. But more so, emphasises the role of collaboration among various stakeholders, including governments, researchers, technology developers, and local communities, as well as incentivised policies, financial support, and educational initiatives in maximising the benefits associated with the adopting AI in agriculture.

To advance the application of AI in African agriculture, Gwagwa et al. (2021) aimed to inform research and development of equitable AI for sustainable agriculture. Some of the important questions raised in their study relates to how AI can address data innovation and logistical services, disease diagnosis in animals and crops, and use data analytics to support marginalised communities in tackling issues of economic disruption, social unrest, and, in some cases, political instability. Furthermore, Eli-Chukwu (2019) provided an overview of the diverse applications of AI in agriculture including crop management, weed and pest control, precision agriculture and predictive analytics for crop yield, as well as the use of AI-enabled farming tools for tasks such as planting, harvesting and supply chain management. Although these studies have reflected on the diverse opportunities and challenges connected with the widespread adoption of AI in agriculture (Eli-Chukwu, 2019; Gwagwa et al., 2021; Songol et al., 2021), none have explored the practical implication of trust as an ethical principle of AI and how trustworthiness was built (or could be built) within the entire supply chain landscape of digital agriculture in Africa. From the literature above, it is evident that evolving ethical AI issues are worth looking into since there is currently limited engagement with localised perspectives on how and for whom trustworthy AI is a matter of interest or concern across relevant application areas and communities.

In the remainder of the chapter, we consider how the normative framing of AI in Africa—from ethical, responsible, and trustworthy—can be better understood when their subject matters are conceived as a Latourian "Distributed Concern". Building on Bruno Latour's analytical framing of "matters of facts" as "matters of concerns", we argue that approaching/operationalising Trustworthy AI as a distributed concern entails a continual process of reconciling value(s). Our modern society has preconditioned us to wholeheartedly embrace the idea that we are the naturally intelligent chosen one's even when our inherent stupidity as rational beings can "replace, enslave and delude us, but if it is taken in the right spirit, stupidity can also liberate and inspire us, putting us in touch with aspects of ourselves we usually rationalise away" (Falk, 2021, p. 50).

From Matters of Fact to Matters of Concern

In this section of the chapter, we present the analytical frame that informed our discussion on whether AI as a thing can ever be trustworthy in the African context, but more so, how trust (or the act of becoming trustworthy or being trusted as a result of thinking) can be better approached in discussions around AI in/from Africa. Bruno Latour, the French philosopher of science and technology developed the epistemic concept of "matters of facts" as "matters of concern" as an analytical framework for scaffolding important conversations about technologies, cultures, values, and society (Latour, 2004). The underlying premise of Latour's critique of conventional discourses of science and technology is the need to adopt a realist empirical approach to the study and analysis of the social world—a shift from inquiry (gathering facts) to examination (assembling power-laden dimensions of things) of the order of things in society. This mode of analysis attempts to reassess the terms of scientific and cultural critique by examining how things constituted as given (e.g. facts, opinions, fiction, knowledge, AI, etc.) operate within existing social and political realms (Latour, 2004). For Latour, the shift from matters of fact to matters of concern in contemporary critical discourse presented the need for rethinking the order of things in ways that allow for a more nuanced understanding of the relationship between power, truth, and knowledge.

Although our discursive approach might be novel in the scholarly context of AI in/for Africa, it is not new. The Latourian analytical frame has been adopted across the design literature to demonstrate how digital technologies are an assemblage of matters interacting within the realm of worthiness, and thus their vitalities emerged through the relations that have given rise to new inventions, interactions, and expressions of things (e.g. Lindley et al., 2023; Spencer & Bailey, 2020; Stephan, 2015). Specific to this chapter, we draw strong inspirations from Lindley and colleagues' inquiry into AI discourses to "casts Trust as a notion that is necessarily constructed by complex relationships, disciplinary lenses, and multiple concurrent stakeholders" (2023, p. 1). The narrative constructed by the authors speaks to our earlier questions: How can we trust a complex web of socio-technical systems that we don't have a fuller understanding of how it works?

The value of approaching trust as a matter of scholarly concern has supported mapping interests relational to AI—be it explainability, accountability, reliability, interpretability, and so on. For Lindley and colleagues, "Trust should not be considered as something which is binary (i.e. present, or not) but as a relative concept (i.e. something which exists to a greater or lesser degree)" (2023, p. 6). This is bringing to the fore of AI in/from Africa discussions the need for more subtle engagement with the complexities around what can be characterised as trustworthy, and more importantly how trustworthiness is to be determined and operationalised across context. In short, trust is premised and developed in history, thus the need for a closer examination of its spectrum across cultures and context is warranted.

Trustworthy AI as a Distributed Concern

Trust Is a Wicked Social Construction, so Does the Trust Research Landscape

The subfield of Africa HCI and AI from Africa, for which we're concerned, has foregrounded the need for approaching interactive system research and design beyond the problem-solving paradigm (Oulasvirta & Hornbæk, 2016). To transcend the vicious cycle of problem-solution, we argue that trust is a "wicked" social construct. In urban planning, Rittel and Webber (1974) viewed "wicked problems" as those residual concepts that are extremely difficult to formulate and adequately frame and often led to diverse interpretations and potential (mis)understandings. Even with the conceptual ambiguity and abstraction associated with wicked problems across disciplines (from earlier accounts in social policy planning and design studies more recently) African researchers have identified how such residual social constructions are performative in contemporary discussions (see Kwantes & Kuo, 2021; Niskanen et al., 2021). Across the literature, it is evident that the notion of trust, just as cultures and values, are social constructions emanating from and embedded within social context.

With trust as a wicked construction, in the remainder of the chapter, we sketch a provisional picture of the trustworthy AI landscape as a distributed concern implicated (and impacted) by historical interrelation and intellectual dependencies. The notion of trust has been established as a research and application area across communities of practice (e.g. Kwantes & Kuo, 2021). From cultural studies to organisational studies and political economy, trust has been investigated as a phenomenon, a noun, and a verb. For example, Wright and Ehnert (2010) argue for conceptualising trust as a fluid social construction within cultures where diverse narratives are brought to bear in the processes of its construction and representation. By approaching trust in its verb form(s), one is bringing together both rational and subjective perspectives across layers of influences to articulate a transitory account of trust that is difficult to quantify and measure. Arguably, the social construction of trust could be premise on the interactions and conversations of social actors within a context; and perhaps "understanding trust as an end product or as an aggregation of antecedents dehumanising trust, turning it into an object or commodity" (Wright & Ehnert, 2010, p. 115). Such a constructionist outlook has placed strong emphasis on the narrative of trust-in-the-making across cultures as it is those stories that influence the judgement of actors towards trusting.

Ferrin and Gillespie (2010) further emphasise how the process of trusting varies across cultures. In more individualistic societies, trust is developed through calculative-cognitive-based processes, whereas in collectivist societies, trust is transference-affect based. The authors identify discursive possibilities for approaching normative trust as inherently "universal" within national culture whereas generalised trust is based on perceived ability, integrity, and benevolence of constituting actors. Such divergent views resonate with Thanetsunthorn and Wuthisatian comparative analysis of the construction of national identity that highlighted how countries with "high individualistic and high long-term oriented cultures are the most favourable environment that fosters trust among people in society" (2019, p. 286). Klein et al. (2019) cross-cultural analysis of trust further demonstrate how culture and context impact the trust judgements of actors in relation to others. These studies have foregrounded how the determinant of trust significantly varies across culture and context, but more so the universal consequence of generalised trust on political, economic, and social relations across nations.

Specific to the context of Africa, Idemudia and Olawa (2021) explored the linguistic connotations attributed to trust across different communities in Africa. From Nigeria, to Ghana, and South African languages, the authors identify the plural dimension of trust across cultural narratives—where in some cultures, trust denotes dependence, expectance, faith, and hope, and so on. Ewuoso (2023, pp. 4–6) is of the opinion that trust is constructed within African scholarship as either relational, experience-based, and normative, the core view that trust is about interdependence, interrelationship, and reciprocity: "to make oneself vulnerable and to accept vulnerability…as trust is inseparable from vulnerability". Across sub-Saharan Africa, others have noted how personality and religiosity impact the variation of trust and trustworthiness across communities (Addai et al., 2013; Ezirim et al., 2021). The above studies point to the view that "trust is better seen as part of the ongoing flow of living that should not be artificially halted in order that it can be measured. Actors are never in any state of trust but are in a ceaseless and uneven flow of trusting" (Wright & Ehnert, 2010, pp. 109–110). In short, trust as a social construction is by nature relational and contextual.

Therefore, this current analysis of trustworthy AI builds on established ideals that trust and trustworthiness are wicked social constructions that are implicated (and impacted) by a range of historical and emerging narratives. It is our position that trust—as in trusting—in its verb form denotes a process of reconciling the universal and the specific (author's emphasis). With trust as a process of history and the making-in-history, we identify the values of alternating with the construction of trust as a universal or a specific web of relations that are distributed across domain names and locations.

Trust Is Relative Across Cultures, so Does Trustworthy AI Application Area

One might posit: Is there a general formula for trust, and by extension a specific formula for Trustworthy AI? To provide some formulation of trust across cultures, Thanetsunthorn and Wuthisatian (2019) built on the well-established Geert Hofstede's six cultural dimensions that modelled trust across national culture using the formulation in Fig. 4.1. Other common formulations of trust included Charles Green trust equation:

$$\text{Trustworthiness} = (\text{Credibility} + \text{Reliability} + \text{Intimacy})/\text{Self orientation}.$$

Specific to AI, Freiman (2022) presents a sustained analysis of the "Trustworthy AI" landscape in an effort to highlight how the deliberate attribution of responsibility to social agents that were by design un-liable and unaccountable is misguided. Even with the calls for an overhaul of the frame "trustworthy AI" in place for "reliable AI", conceptual scepticism remains. The mere adoption of the language of ethics doesn't cloud the conceptual ambiguities around the concept of trustworthy AI as a misnomer. As a result of the scepticism that clouds the AI landscape, Braun et al. (2021), and Lewis and Marsh (2022) suggested how formulaic and functionalist approaches to trust might provide relevant prerequisites for building trust in the AI ecosystem. Others have developed the Zero-trust model of AI (ZTA) as a roadmap towards trustworthy AI where literature informed high-level requirements, dimensions/properties, and components for ensuring trust across system level are identified (Tidjon & Khomh, 2022). From the ZTA outlook, trust is not determined by unitary properties or the components of socio-technical systems, but rather partly due to the general reasoning and decisions that occur within complex structures that are impacted by technical, social, and human perspectives.

Furthermore, Alvarado (2022) argues that the type of trust ascribed to/between humans, and machines are both epistemically general and specific; one premise on interaction and the other on reliance (Lewis &

$$Trust_{it} = \alpha + \beta Culture_{it} + u_{it}$$

Fig. 4.1 Benchmark model of trust that build on cultural dimensions theorised by Hofstede (cited in Thanetsunthorn & Wuthisatian, 2019)

Marsh, 2022). From this preview, the kind of trust ascribed to AI as an epistemic technology that operates within an epistemic context is that of an epistemic enhancer or mediator as "using technology, then, implies trusting ourselves to technologies…as deliberately trusting oneself to technology" (Kiran & Verbeek, 2010, p. 409). Ryan (2020) also identifies three paradigms of trust in literature: a rational account, an affective account, and the normative account, arguing that of all three accounts, the kind of trust ascribed to AI is that of reliance on the human agent. Although novel scientific discoveries have foregrounded the relative trust in the "science", the kind of trust demanded by AI systems is neither transferable nor transparent. Emerging technologies require specific "sanctioning" and "appraising" processes, thus a continual formulation of epistemes and practices.

As we've established earlier, trust as a social construction is relational and contextual. The core views about trust in the African scholarship centres around interdependence, interrelationship, and reciprocity. Building on the ethos of relationality and relationship, the benefits of implementing AI in critical sectors of African economies can be realised and sustained through deliberate acts of building trust mechanisms into the ecosystem of AI. Alupo et al. (2022) agree with this view as the need to cultivate "trust" among stakeholders, including governments, AI companies and businesses, and communities at large become amplified. Pérez y Madrid and Wright (2023) hold the position that trustworthiness as it is currently practised within the AI industry (with a focus on ethical considerations, transparency, fairness, and reliability) might not be enough to guarantee the design and adoption of AI in ethical manners. Along with the need for ethical principles (transparency, accountability, reliability, etc.), it is also important to involve relevant stakeholders and beneficiary users/communities in the gradual design and deployment of AI interventions in ways that engender a sense of participation, ownership, and acceptance. The creation of a supportive AI business environment through the enactment of socially appropriate AI regulatory policies and frameworks, education and incentivisation, and public awareness will go a long way in expanding the AI ecosystem to be more inclusive, hence trustworthy AI is a matter of interest or concern to the public.

Trustworthy AI in Is a Matter of Socio-Technical Interest, But More so Concern

As we've attempted to show in the preceding sections, designing and deploying AI that is trustworthy is a matter of socio-technical interest, but more so a global concern. We've argued that there is the need for more concerted efforts aimed at scholarly advocacies, public awareness as well as deliberate actions to construct regulations and guidelines that addresses the practical implications and unintended concerns of AI as a global phenomenon. Below we identify specific concerns we foresee in the development and deployment of AI technologies across the African continent, with specific emphasis on healthcare and agriculture.

Ethical concern: With AI as a socio-technical system of modernity, it is our position that it possesses significant ethical concerns in African healthcare and agriculture. The digital scramble of Africa began with the globalised push for market-led initiatives towards poverty alleviation and economic development. With advances in emerging technologies globally, the ethos of "Green Revolution" has provided the foundation for the "Gene Revolution". For example, it is common knowledge that Editas collect patents of gene-edited organisms in health, which implies that they can technically reconfigure our bodies remotely.[3] The ethical concern with such initiatives across the continent is that algorithms as arbitrary entities with no social personality are conceptually difficult to be held accountable. In short, who should be held accountable and responsible when the machine goes rogue. Some of the concerns we foresee pertain to the reality of Africa becoming a WET LAB (to test biological matters using AI-enabled blueprints), or a SOFT LAB (to experimental with radical ideas before scaling e.g. deep state surveillance).[4]

Educational concerns: As reflexive practitioners, we've witnessed how scholarly endeavours are simplified with the notion of an AI scientist—as this sort of rational man that is objective and abstract, and one that could draw succinct conclusions based on scientific fact and empirical data only. With African universities as modern institutions premised on the culture of the quantification sector—a sector that gives more relevance to

[3] https://www.editasmedicine.com/crispr-gene-editing/.

[4] A practical example is the LAVENDER autonomous weaponry systems developed and deployed by the Israeli Army, see: https://www.972mag.com/lavender-ai-israeli-army-gaza/.

objectification, measurement, and socialisation of education—one might argue that their rhetoric is suited to privilege the forces of global knowledge economies. And with the limited research, innovation and teaching around AI in African universities, there is the pertinent concern that we're embracing naked imperialism via the exploitation of indigenous bodies and bodies of knowledge as the consequence of the forceful co-option to the wagon of the 4IR. There is also the concern that AI as an instrument of modernity will amplify the digital divide that exists in our societies: digital technologies and molecular structures can rework colonial genealogies by reinforcing epistemological, political and economic hegemony (Mwema & Birhane, 2024).

Geopolitical concerns: Academic commentaries have highlighted how the AI landscape will shape emerging global forces and orders (Mwema & Birhane, 2024). If such positions could be further amplified, one needs to identify how global powers and cooperation—from EU, to USA, and China, and Google and Microsoft—are racing to dominate the AI ecosystem. With the colonisation of Africa as a means and ends towards European economic development, it is our position that the algorithm colonisation might have more dire consequences. The concerns to be raised pertained to how African resources, manpower and markets will be further appropriated for capitalist ideals; and often when two elephants fight, it is the grass that suffers.

Furthermore, it is our position that the conception of Africa as a wholesome geographical entity that can be controlled and commanded, just as artificial intelligent systems, might have foregrounded digital colonialism at scale. As noted by Birhane (2020), algorithmic colonisation objectifies subjects as life-less entities to be instrumentalised for capital. Within the global AI pipeline, nature, resources, people, and so on are merely "standing reserves" (in the Heideggerian philosophical sense) to be used within the broader technoscientific landscape. We've seen how Africa is perceived as region of interest to "fuel" the Western EV revolution and the Trans-Saharan gas pipeline to "fill" the energy gap in the WEST, and Africans as objects to be catalogued within data-driven surveillance capitalism; thus, a concern to be raised within the global trustworthy AI narratives.

Technical concerns: The entire AI pipeline is cooperation led; big tech owns the infrastructures supporting AI research and innovation, and as such, could control politics and economics (Mwema & Birhane, 2024). For instance, the utilisation of AI in cyber warfare could erode trust and stir up legal issues of accountability, proportionality, and the possibility for inadvertent consequences. Such issues would have strategic implications to the global and regional power dynamics and peace. The application of AI in e-sabotage (deliberate actions to disrupt, damage, or compromise systems, networks, or services) is evolving and constitutes an ongoing challenge to the cybersecurity industry. Furthermore, AI technologies could be employed as a mass surveillance tool by authoritarian regimes to exert control over public information, monitor citizens, and suppress political opponents thereby violating the human rights of citizens. Also, exploitative data mining practices (including unethical data collection, invasive profiling, identity theft, and discriminatory practices because of bias in algorithms) can cause substantial harm to the well-being of people and the planet.

Conclusion

In this chapter, we presented a forceful case as to how the normative framing of AI in Africa—from ethical, responsible, and trustworthy—can be better understood when their subject matters are conceived as a Latourian "Distributed Concern". Our main contribution to the volume is in the narratives brought to bear as we attempt to account for the complexities around concepts such as trust, AI, trustworthy AI, and so on. With trust and trustworthiness as core features of modern society, one is left with a plethora of conceptions and interpretation. Is trust the right frame for addressing the black box problem? Is trust synonymous with reliability and reliance, relationality and the relative, transparency, and transparent? Is trust a rational or subjective judgement, a transitive or transferable relationship, gain or given?

Researchers and practitioners across the African continent have identified the growing need to investigate the potential opportunities and challenges associated with the design and adoption of AI-mediated technologies in critical sectors of the economy. As our analysis has attempted to show, there is limited engagement with situated perspectives on how and for whom trustworthy AI is a matter of interest or concern. As reflective practitioners, our reporting shouldn't be misunderstood as an attempt to muddle the waters around trustworthy AI design and adoption in Africa; but rather to outline discursive pointers where more than socio-technical challenges and opportunities around AI's trustworthiness can be identified and discussed. In Africa, we're constantly bombarded with the media-led utopia that the 4IR is our chance to leap-frog into sustainable development, the AI revolution is our golden chance to catch up. More recently, researchers have begun to assert that the future of AI is in Africa—perhaps an imagined Africa that is not under the soft power of capitalism and globalisation. Building on Crawford's proclamation that AI is "neither artificial nor intelligent" (2021), it is important to note that the present future of AI in Africa will be merely a recycling of the unfortunate past; the past revolutions were unequally divided, and so will future ones. The tentative formula for Trustworthy AI in Africa can be summed up as, using Audre Lorde's provocative admonishment: "The master's tools will never dismantle the master's house".

Acknowledgements The first author appreciates the University of Greenwich ECA pilot project administrators, while the second author appreciates Research England Beyond Imagination project leadership for their supports in developing this chapter, and Joseph Lindley for insights that have informed the arguments herein (in the title: https://designresearch.works/blog/trust-me-im-an-autonomous-machine).

References

Adamu, M., & Nkwo, M. (2023). AI in Africa. Preliminary notes on design and adoption. *Diid Disegno Industriale Industrial Design, 80*, 44–57. https://doi.org/10.30682/diid8023d

Addai, I., Opoku-Agyeman, C., & Ghartey, H. T. (2013). An exploratory study of religion and trust in Ghana. *Social Indicators Research, 110*, 993–1012.

Ali, S. M., Dick, S., Dillon, S., Jones, M. L., Penn, J., & Staley, R. (2023). Histories of artificial intelligence: A genealogy of power. *BJHS Themes, 8*, 1–18.

Alupo, C. D., Omeiza, D., & Vernon, D. (2022). Realising the potential of AI in Africa: It all turns on trust. In *Towards trustworthy artificial intelligent systems* (pp. 179–192). Springer.

Alvarado, R. (2022). What kind of trust does AI deserve, if any? *AI and Ethics, 3*, 1169–1183.

Alvarado, R. (2023). AI as an epistemic technology. *Science and Engineering Ethics, 29*(5), 1–30.

Birhane, A. (2020). Algorithmic colonisation of Africa. *SCRIPTed, 17*, 389.

Birhane, A. (2022). The unseen Black faces of AI algorithms. *Nature, 610*, 451–452.

Braun, M., Bleher, H., & Hummel, P. (2021). A leap of faith: Is there a formula for "Trustworthy" AI? *Hastings Center Report, 51*(3), 17–22.

Brokensha, S., Kotzé, E., & Senekal, B. A. (2023). *AI in and for Africa: A humanistic perspective*. CRC Press.

Buchanan, B. G. (2005). A (very) brief history of artificial intelligence. *AI Magazine, 26*(4), 53–53.

Cath, C., Wachter, S., Mittelstadt, B., Taddeo, M., & Floridi, L. (2018). Artificial intelligence and the 'good society': The US, EU, and UK approach. *Science and Engineering Ethics, 24*, 505–528.

Cave, S., & Dihal, K. (2020). The whiteness of AI. *Philosophy & Technology, 33*(4), 685–703.

Collins, H. (2021). The science of artificial intelligence and its critics. *Interdisciplinary Science Reviews, 46*(1–2), 53–70.

Crawford, K. (2021). *The atlas of AI: Power, politics, and the planetary costs of artificial intelligence*. Yale University Press.

Dignum, V. (2022). *Responsible artificial intelligence—From principles to practice*. arXiv preprint arXiv:2205.10785

Eke, D., & Ogoh, G. (2022). Forgotten African AI narratives and the future of AI in Africa. *The International Review of Information Ethics, 31*(1).

Eke, D. O., Wakunuma, K., & Akintoye, S. (2023). *Responsible AI in Africa: Challenges and opportunities*. Springer.

Eli-Chukwu, N. C. (2019). Applications of artificial intelligence in agriculture: A review. *Engineering, Technology & Applied Science Research, 9*(4), 4377–4383.

Euchner, J. (2019). Little AI, big AI—good AI, bad AI. *Research-Technology Management, 62*(3), 10–12.

Ewuoso, C. (2023). Black box problem and African views of trust. *Humanities and Social Sciences Communications, 10*(1), 1–11.

Ezirim, G. E., Mbah, P. O., Nwagwu, E. J., Eze, I. C., Nche, G. C., & Chukwuorji, J. C. (2021). Trust and trustworthiness in a sub-Saharan African sample: Contributions of personality and religiosity. *Social Indicators Research, 153*, 1087–1107.

Falk, M. (2021). Artificial stupidity. *Interdisciplinary Science Reviews, 46*(1–2), 36–52.

Ferreira, M. I. A., & Tokhi, M. O. (Eds.). (2022). *Towards trustworthy artificial intelligent systems* (Vol. 102). Springer Nature.

Ferrin, D. L., & Gillespie, N. (2010). Trust differences across national-societal cultures: Much to do, or much ado about nothing. In *Organisational trust: A cultural perspective* (pp. 42–86). Cambridge University Press.

Floridi, L. (2019). Establishing the rules for building trustworthy AI. *Nature Machine Intelligence*. https://doi.org/10.1038/s42256-019-0055-y

Freiman, O. (2022). Making sense of the conceptual nonsense 'trustworthy AI'. *AI and Ethics*, 3, 1351–1360.

Green, B. (2019, December). *"Good" isn't good enough*. In Proceedings of the AI for Social Good workshop at NeurIPS (Vol. 16).

Gwagwa, A., Kazim, E., Kachidza, P., Hilliard, A., Siminyu, K., Smith, M., & Shawe-Taylor, J. (2021). Road map for research on responsible artificial intelligence for development (AI4D) in African countries: The case study of agriculture. *Patterns, 2*(12), 100381.

Haenlein, M., & Kaplan, A. (2019). A brief history of artificial intelligence: On the past, present, and future of artificial intelligence. *California Management Review, 61*(4), 5–14.

Hagendorff, T., & Wezel, K. (2020). 15 challenges for AI: Or what AI (currently) can't do. *AI & Society, 35*, 355–365.

Idemudia, E. S., & Olawa, B. D. (2021). Once bitten, twice shy: Trust and trustworthiness from an African perspective. In *Trust and trustworthiness across cultures: Implications for societies and workplaces* (pp. 33–51). Springer.

Jiang, F., Jiang, Y., Zhi, H., Dong, Y., Li, H., Ma, S., et al. (2017). Artificial intelligence in healthcare: Past, present and future. *Stroke and Vascular Neurology, 2*(4), 230–243.

Kiran, A. H., & Verbeek, P. P. (2010). Trusting ourselves to technology. *Knowledge, Technology & Policy, 23*, 409–427.

Klein, H. A., Lin, M. H., Miller, N. L., Militello, L. G., Lyons, J. B., & Finkeldey, J. G. (2019). Trust across culture and context. *Journal of Cognitive Engineering and Decision Making, 13*(1), 10–29.

Kokuryo, J., Walsh, T., & Maracke, C. (2020). *AI for everyone: Benefitting from and building trust in the technology*. Lulu.com.

Kwantes, C. T., & Kuo, B. C. (2021). *Trust and trustworthiness across cultures*. Springer.

Latour, B. (2004). Why has critique run out of steam? From matters of fact to matters of concern. *Critical Inquiry, 30*(2), 225–248.

Lewis, P. R., & Marsh, S. (2022). What is it like to trust a rock? A functionalist perspective on trust and trustworthiness in artificial intelligence. *Cognitive Systems Research, 72*, 33–49.

Lindley, J., Green, D. P., McGarry, G., Pilling, F., Coulton, P., & Crabtree, A. (2023). Towards a master narrative for trust in autonomous systems: Trust as a distributed concern. *Journal of Responsible Technology, 13*, 100057.

Lushetich, N. (2022). Stupidity: Human and artificial. *Media Theory, 6*(1), 114–126.

Moore, J. (2019). AI for not bad. *Frontiers in Big Data, 2*, 32.

Murphy, J. W., & Largacha-Martínez, C. (2022). Decolonization of AI: A crucial blind spot. *Philosophy & Technology, 35*(4), 102.

Mwema, E., & Birhane, A. (2024). Undersea cables in Africa: The new frontiers of digital colonialism. *First Monday*. https://doi.org/10.5210/fm.v29i4.13637

Nickel, P. J., Franssen, M., & Kroes, P. (2010). Can we make sense of the notion of trustworthy technology? *Knowledge, Technology & Policy, 23*, 429–444.

Niskanen, V. P., Rask, M., & Raisio, H. (2021). Wicked problems in Africa: A systematic literature review. *SAGE Open, 11*(3).

Nkwo, M. & Adamu, M (2024). AI "Ethics Shopping" and "Governance Shrinking" in Africa: A Critical Opinion, 5/02/2024, 10, https://www.research.lancs.ac.uk/portal/en/publications/ai-ethics-shopping-and-governance-shrinking-in-africa(e2e8016f-53f8-4b47-b871-40a2bb031223).html

Oulasvirta, A., & Hornbæk, K. (2016, May). *HCI research as problem-solving*. In Proceedings of the 2016 CHI Conference on Human Factors in Computing Systems (pp. 4956–4967).

Panch, T., Mattie, H., & Celi, L. A. (2019). The "inconvenient truth" about AI in healthcare. *NPJ Digital Medicine, 2*(1), 77.

Park, S. (2021). More than skin deep: A response to "The Whiteness of AI." *Philosophy & Technology, 34*(4), 1961–1966.

Pasquinelli, M. (2023). The *eye of the master: A social history of artificial intelligence*. Verso Books.

Pérez y Madrid, A., & Wright, C. (2023). *Trustworthy AI alone is not enough*. Dykinson Publisher.

Procter, R., Tolmie, P., & Rouncefield, M. (2023). Holding AI to account: Challenges for the delivery of trustworthy AI in healthcare. *ACM Transactions on Computer-Human Interaction, 30*(2), 1–34.

Rittel, H. W., & Webber, M. M. (1974). Wicked problems. *Man-Made Futures, 26*(1), 272–280.

Ryan, M. (2020). In AI we trust: Ethics, artificial intelligence, and reliability. *Science and Engineering Ethics, 26*(5), 2749–2767.

Sallstrom, L., Morris, O., & Mehta, H. (2019*). Artificial intelligence in Africa's healthcare: Ethical considerations* (ORF Issue Brief, 312).

Schank, R. C. (1987). What is AI, anyway? *AI Magazine, 8*(4), 59–59.

Shi, Z. R., Wang, C., & Fang, F. (2020). *Artificial intelligence for social good: A survey*. arXiv preprint arXiv:2001.01818

Songol, M., Awuor, F., & Maake, B. (2021). Adoption of artificial intelligence in agriculture in the developing nations: A review. *Journal of Language, Technology & Entrepreneurship in Africa, 12*(2), 208–229.

Spencer, N., & Bailey, M. (2020). Design for complex situations: Navigating 'matters of concern.' *International Journal of Design, 14*(3), 69–83.

Stephan, P. F. (2015). Designing 'matters of concern' (Latour): A future design challenge. In W. Jonas, S. Zerwas, & K. von Anshelm (Eds.), *Transformation design* (pp. 202–226). De Gruyter.

Thanetsunthorn, N., & Wuthisatian, R. (2019). Understanding trust across cultures: An empirical investigation. *Review of International Business and Strategy, 29*(4), 286–314.

Tidjon, L. N., & Khomh, F. (2022). *Never trust, always verify: A roadmap for Trustworthy AI?* arXiv preprint arXiv:2206.11981

Toosi, A., Bottino, A. G., Saboury, B., Siegel, E., & Rahmim, A. (2021). A brief history of AI: How to prevent another winter (a critical review). *PET Clinics, 16*(4), 449–469.

von Eschenbach, W. J. (2021). Transparency and the black box problem: Why we do not trust AI. *Philosophy & Technology, 34*(4), 1607–1622.

Wahl, B., Cossy-Gantner, A., Germann, S., & Schwalbe, N. R. (2018). Artificial intelligence (AI) and global health: How can AI contribute to health in resource-poor settings? *BMJ Global Health, 3*(4), e000798.

Wamba, S. F., Bawack, R. E., Guthrie, C., Queiroz, M. M., & Carillo, K. D. A. (2021). Are we preparing for a good AI society? A bibliometric review and research agenda. *Technological Forecasting and Social Change, 164*, 120482.

Wright, A., & Ehnert, I. (2010). Making sense of trust across cultural contexts. In *Organisational trust: A cultural perspective* (pp. 107–126). Cambridge University Press.

CHAPTER 5

Afrocentric Trustworthy Framework for Improved Artificial Intelligence Powered Health Management Tool for Africans

Ayodeji Olusegun Ibitoye, Makuochi Samuel Nkwo, Joseph Damilola Akinyemi, and Khadijat Tope Ladoja

Introduction

Background

The rapid advancement of artificial intelligence (AI) has permeated various aspects of global society, presenting both transformative opportunities and ethical challenges. According to Eke et al. (2023b), Africa's diverse socio-cultural landscape, characterised by a multitude of languages and traditions, should inherently position the continent as a fertile ground for the widespread adoption and integration of AI technologies. However, as AI increasingly becomes pervasive, concerns about biases and other

A. O. Ibitoye (✉) · M. S. Nkwo
School of Computing and Mathematical Sciences, University of Greenwich, London, UK
e-mail: a.o.ibitoye@greenwich.ac.uk

M. S. Nkwo
e-mail: m.s.nkwo@greenwich.ac.uk

D. O. Eke et al. (eds.), *Trustworthy AI*,
https://doi.org/10.1007/978-3-031-75674-0_5

ethical considerations have gained prominence. In their exploration of the implications of AI in Africa, Eke et al. (2023a) highlight the pressing need for culturally sensitive approaches. The "one-size-fits-all" approach often seen in AI development can lead to biased outcomes that may inadvertently perpetuate existing disparities.

Africa's linguistic diversity and locally defined innovations provide a unique set of challenges and opportunities for AI applications, particularly in critical sectors such as healthcare. The importance of a nuanced approach is underscored by the fact that health-related challenges in Africa are not only diverse but also deeply intertwined with unique cultural and societal factors (Pell et al., 2011). Against this backdrop, this chapter explores the concept of Afrocentric Trustworthy AI, aiming to address the pressing need for AI technologies that are not only culturally inclusive but also ethically sound. By building upon recent works that emphasise the importance of cultural sensitivity and inclusivity in AI development, this chapter seeks to contribute to the ongoing discourse on creating AI systems that resonate with and benefit the diverse communities across the African continent.

Challenges in AI-Based Healthcare for Africa

One of the critical challenges in AI-based healthcare in Africa lies in drug discovery and pharmacognosis, where the data used to develop drugs often lack representation from Africa (Masimirembwa & Matimba, 2012). The scarcity of African-centric data in drug development not only hinders the efficacy of pharmaceutical interventions but also perpetuates a cycle of underrepresentation and insufficient understanding of the unique genetic and physiological characteristics of African populations. In the context of cancer treatments for example, a notable gap persists in the availability of

J. D. Akinyemi
Department of Computer Science, University of York, Heslington, UK
e-mail: joseph.akinyemi@york.ac.uk

K. T. Ladoja
Department of Computer Science, University of Ibadan, Ibadan, Nigeria
e-mail: kt.bamigbade@ui.edu.ng

medical data from African healthcare facilities. The limited data on prevalent cancer types and variants among African populations pose a significant challenge in tailoring treatments to the specific needs of the citizenry (Ramsay, 2018). Adequate representation in medical datasets is crucial for the development of targeted therapies. The biases in healthcare-based AI tools thus extend beyond algorithmic limitations to systemic issues related to data representation. Addressing these challenges requires concerted efforts to collect and incorporate diverse, region-specific data, ensuring that AI technologies are not only effective but also equitable in meeting the healthcare needs of African populations.

Aim and Objectives

This work is focused on spearheading Afrocentric Trustworthy AI tailored for healthcare. It tackles biases and challenges, crafting an innovative framework that harmonises cultural sensitivity, ethical integrity, and inclusivity for the benefit of diverse healthcare contexts across Africa. The specific objectives it achieves are:

1. To formulate a specialised framework tailored for AI-based healthcare solutions in Africa, prioritising cultural sensitivity and ethical considerations.
2. To investigate and propose solutions to biases and challenges specific to AI-based healthcare solutions in Africa.
3. To advocate for the ethical use of AI in healthcare, emphasising inclusivity, fairness, and transparency in African populations.
4. To encourage collaboration among technologists, policymakers, and local communities to ensure the relevance and effectiveness of the Afrocentric Trustworthy AI framework in addressing healthcare challenges in Africa.

The rest of this chapter discusses the current state and challenges of AI in healthcare in section "AI in Healthcare: Current State and Challenges", the relationship between African cultural values and "trustworthiness" in section "African Cultural Values and Trust", our methodology for building an Afrocentric Trustworthy frame for AI healthcare in section "Afrocentric Trustworthy Framework for AI-Based Healthcare", mechanisms for adopting and scaling AI healthcare technologies in Africa in section "Adoption and Scaling", ethical considerations and regulations in section "Ethical Considerations and Regulation" and conclusion and recommendations in section "Conclusion, Recommendations, and Future Directions".

AI in Healthcare: Current State and Challenges

The contemporary landscape of healthcare-based AI systems reflects a paradigm shift in medical research, diagnosis, and treatment. Advanced machine learning algorithms, powered by extensive datasets and computing capabilities, have demonstrated remarkable capabilities in diverse medical applications. AI-driven diagnostic tools, such as image recognition algorithms for medical imaging (Akinyemi et al., 2023; Oladosu & Ibitoye, 2023), exhibit promising accuracy rates, streamlining the identification of abnormalities and contributing to early disease detection (Esteva et al., 2019). Additionally, natural language processing algorithms are transforming the analysis of clinical texts (Ibitoye et al., 2021), enhancing the speed and precision of information extraction from electronic health records (Miotto et al., 2016). The integration of AI into predictive modelling for patient outcomes and treatment responses is reshaping personalised medicine in Hypertension risk prediction (Ibitoye et al., 2023), and suicide ideation (Oyewale et al., 2024), offering tailored interventions based on individual characteristics and health histories among others.

Despite these advancements, the widespread adoption of AI in healthcare is not uniform across regions, with disparities in access to technology and infrastructure presenting challenges. Developed countries often lead in the integration of AI into healthcare systems, benefiting from well-established technological infrastructures and extensive data resources. In contrast, many developing nations face barriers, including limited access to high-quality data, insufficient computational resources, and inadequate regulatory frameworks (Topol, 2019). Bridging this digital divide is essential to ensure equitable access to the benefits of healthcare-based AI systems. Some challenges in healthcare-based AI systems include:

1. **Data Quality and Availability**: The reliability and representativeness of AI models heavily depend on the quality and diversity of the data used for training. In many healthcare settings, particularly in Africa, there is a scarcity of comprehensive and diverse datasets,

leading to potential biases and limitations in the generalisability of AI models (Njei et al., 2023).

2. **Interoperability and Integration**: The seamless integration of AI systems with existing healthcare infrastructures poses a significant challenge. Diverse data sources, different formats of electronic health records, and varying standards across healthcare providers hinder the interoperability necessary for effective AI implementation (Tarnawski et al., 2021).
3. **Ethical and Regulatory Concerns**: The ethical implications of using AI in healthcare, including issues of patient privacy, consent, and the responsible handling of sensitive medical data, require careful consideration. Developing clear regulatory frameworks to address these concerns is crucial for ensuring trust in AI technologies (Char et al., 2018).
4. **Explainability and Interpretability**: The "black-box" nature of some AI algorithms in healthcare raises challenges in explaining and interpreting their decisions. In critical medical decisions, understanding how AI arrives at conclusions is essential for gaining acceptance from healthcare professionals and building trust in the technology (Rudin, 2019).
5. **Resource Constraints**: Many healthcare facilities, especially in resource-limited settings, face challenges in adopting and maintaining AI technologies. Insufficient computational resources, lack of expertise, and financial constraints hinder the implementation of advanced AI solutions, limiting their accessibility (Litjens et al., 2017).

Addressing these challenges is essential for realising the full potential of healthcare-based AI systems, particularly in the context of developing regions like Africa. As we explore solutions, the aim is to develop strategies that ensure the ethical, equitable, and effective integration of AI technologies into diverse healthcare landscapes.

African Cultural Values and Trust

Africa's rich cultural diversity offers a unique perspective to examine the interplay between cultural values, trust, and healthcare. This section explores the nuances of African cultural values, focusing on trust, community, and respect while evaluating their profound implications for healthcare. As we traverse the continent's diverse cultural landscape, in sub-sections "African Cultural Diversity: A Mosaic of Traditions" to "Trust in Healthcare: Challenges and Opportunities", we also investigate how these values can be applied to modern healthcare and emerging technologies, particularly AI systems.

African Cultural Diversity: A Mosaic of Traditions

Africa's rich cultural diversity stems from complex historical backgrounds marked by migration, trade, and colonial influences, resulting in distinct traditions among its various ethnic groups (Adisa, 2018a). Trans-Saharan trade routes and Bantu-speaking migrations have significantly contributed to cultural diffusion across the continent Manning, P. (2010). The continent's cultural diversity varies widely among its 54 countries, with West Africa's vibrant cultures, East Africa's unique customs, and Southern Africa's rich heritage (Makoni, 2020). These variations are influenced by geography, climate, and historical experiences. Africa's linguistic diversity, with over 2000 languages, reflects its cultural richness, impacting communication, social interactions, and healthcare practices (Makoni, 2020). The holistic perception of health in many African societies includes physical, mental, spiritual, and social well-being views that shape understanding of illness and wellness. Traditional healing practices, rooted in centuries-old wisdom, coexist with modern medicine, promoting collaboration for culturally sensitive healthcare delivery (Nkosi & Abiola, 2017a). Thus, African traditions showcase resilience and adaptability throughout history and understanding this intricate tapestry is crucial for maintaining cultural heritage and providing respectful healthcare services to diverse populations, relying on trust and interconnectedness.

Ubuntu Philosophy: Trust in Interconnectedness

The Ubuntu philosophy, integral to African culture, emphasises individuals' interconnectedness within a community, encapsulated by the saying "I am because we are" (Duru, 2019). Trust is foundational in Ubuntu, as mutual support defines well-being, underscoring the idea that one's identity is tied to the collective, fostering mutual responsibility and shared destiny. Esteeming elders for their wisdom is pivotal in decision-making, as respected elders hold key roles in guiding the community (Nkosi & Abiola, 2017a). Trust in healthcare is influenced by respecting healthcare professionals who appreciate community wisdom and incorporate it into their practices. Building trust involves incorporating elders' perspectives for cultural competence. Also, oral tradition and storytelling transmit knowledge in African cultures, serving as vehicles for community wisdom and shared experiences (Smith, 2015a). Therefore, trust is cultivated through shared narratives that create community connections, fostering a sense of unity and understanding. With many African societies reversing ancestors as guides and protectors, attributing significant influence to their wisdom and guidance (Mbiti, 1990); trust in healthcare practices is established by acknowledging and respecting these beliefs, as they form an integral part of the community's cultural fabric. Hence, understanding the Ubuntu philosophy offers insights for healthcare practitioners aiming for culturally competent care in African communities, strengthening trust bonds and improving health outcomes. In healthcare, storytelling enhances trust by making information culturally relevant and accessible to patients. It serves as a bridge, facilitating mutual understanding and strengthening the bond between healthcare providers and communities. Adopting these cultural nuances presents both opportunities and challenges, as healthcare providers navigate the complexities of integrating cultural beliefs and practices into their care approaches.

Trust in Healthcare: Challenges and Opportunities

Trust is pivotal in healthcare, influencing relationships among providers, patients, communities, and emerging technologies like Artificial Intelligence (AI). In the dynamic healthcare landscape, understanding trust intricacies is vital, presenting both challenges and opportunities. This exploration delves into trust's multifaceted nature, considering historical, cultural, and socio-economic factors shaping its complexities. Navigating these challenges reveals opportunities for building trust within healthcare, striving for more patient-centred, inclusive, and technologically adept practices. No doubt, in the backdrop of historical colonisation and exploitation, the lingering effects continue to shape healthcare trust today (Smith, 2015a). Thus, understanding this historical context is pivotal for healthcare providers, offering insights into the roots of mistrust and guiding efforts to rebuild trust within communities. Bridging the gap in healthcare necessitates cultural competence (Ofori-Atta & Osei, 2016a). Respecting traditional values, integrating cultural rituals, and involving the community in decision-making processes are essential steps in building trust and fostering understanding. Community engagement and participatory healthcare approaches are key to strengthening trust (Ofori-Atta & Osei, 2016a). By actively involving the community in decision-making, seeking their input on policies, and addressing their concerns, healthcare providers can cultivate a sense of ownership and deepen trust within the community. Additionally, examining socio-economic factors is crucial for understanding healthcare trust dynamics (Ofori-Atta & Osei, 2016a). With economic disparities, accessibility challenges, and resource availability significantly influencing trust levels within communities, highlighting the importance of addressing broader socio-economic considerations in healthcare provision remains important. Hence, in navigating the healthcare's complex landscape, recognition of cultural values becomes pivotal, fostering trust, inclusivity, and effectiveness. Having explored trust challenges and opportunities, attention shifts to applying cultural values, especially in traditional practices, and integrating technologies like Artificial Intelligence (AI). Examining the interplay between cultural values, healthcare, and AI reveals pathways to create ethically sound, culturally sensitive, and technologically advanced systems for a globalised and diverse population.

Culturally competent healthcare delivery involves embracing culturally competent approaches, recognising health's holistic nature, incorporating traditional healing practices, and fostering respectful partnerships. Respecting and integrating traditional wisdom enhances trust within healthcare systems, acknowledging cultural significance, and collaborating with traditional healers to create holistic and culturally sensitive healthcare plans. Leveraging storytelling enhances health education, incorporating culturally relevant narratives to bridge communication gaps and make information more relatable to diverse communities. Additionally, acknowledging ancestor reverence, healthcare practices can incorporate cultural rituals, contributing to a more holistic healing experience and enhancing trust. As healthcare embraces AI, infusion of African cultural values becomes crucial, designing AI technologies with cultural sensitivity that respects interconnectedness and holistic health concepts. Ethical considerations in AI applications in healthcare require alignment with African cultural values, addressing data privacy, informed consent, and transparency with cultural sensitivity to build and maintain trust in these technologies.

In the dynamic intersection of healthcare, technology, and diverse cultural values, we stand on the cusp of an era demanding foresight, adaptability, and dedication to inclusivity. Our journey propels us into future directions and the global implications of these integrations, navigating healthcare's evolving landscape, and anticipating trajectories shaped by cultural sensitivity, technological advancements, and global collaboration. Lessons from African cultural values can blueprint culturally sensitive healthcare strategies worldwide, prioritising inclusivity and responsiveness, offering a pathway to a patient-centred, culturally competent, and technologically advanced healthcare future, addressing diverse needs globally.

Afrocentric Trustworthy Framework for AI-Based Healthcare

Trustworthy AI Guidelines and the Need for Afrocentric Framework

The need to foster "trust" among stakeholders (governments, AI companies, and communities) cannot be overemphasised. Along with ensuring data protection and ethical principles (transparency, accountability, fairness, etc.), it is important to involve these stakeholders in developing and deploying AI. This will enable them to contribute to the AI system lifecycle processes, and enhance understanding and acceptance (Alupo et al., 2022). The creation of a structured and supportive AI business environment through the enactment of socially appropriate regulatory policies and frameworks, education and awareness, and iterative enhancement of AI systems based on user feedback is essential in entrenching trust and shaping public perceptions about AI, and what they could be used to achieve (Rossi, 2018). Following the release of the European Commission Ethics Guidelines for Trustworthy AI in 2019 (EU Commission, 2019), Floridi (2019) adapted and identified seven essential requirements to achieving trustworthy AI including (1) human agency and oversight, (2) robustness and safety, (3) privacy and data governance, (4) transparency, (5) diversity, non-discrimination, and fairness, (6) societal and environmental well-being, and (7) accountability. These are critical to promoting fundamental rights and upholding human autonomy while advancing inclusion, accessibility, and sustainability which are values that should drive new AI innovations instead of an afterthought (Floridi, 2019).

Trustworthy AI unlike responsible AI focuses on the technical features of the AI solution which contributes to developing trust and confidence among stakeholders and communities. The shift in focus is necessitated by factors such as resistance to change and lack of user-friendly interfaces (Panch et al., 2019) which makes it difficult for the healthcare workers to "trust" the decisions generated using AI models. It impedes the effective implementation of AI in healthcare practices especially in developing communities. The extent to which the implementation of these ethical guidelines on healthcare technologies could promote "trust" among the community healthcare workers and patients and guide the adoption and utilisation of AI in healthcare practices in Africa remains to be seen.

Moreover, the authors believe that building indigenous AI technologies for healthcare must explore the issues of "trustworthiness" and cultural sensitivity to the ethical values of the people. These are critical because healthcare is a specialised domain and would require predictive models to provide consistent and socially reliable outcomes across the board. To fill these identified gaps, we propose an integrated Afrocentric Trustworthy AI Framework which will guide the development of AI that would win the trust of healthcare stakeholders in Africa.

Prerequisites for an Afrocentric Trustworthy AI Framework for Healthcare

This current research presents an Afrocentric Trustworthy AI Framework for healthcare (Fig. 5.1) that addresses the dearth of Afrocentric values and social complexities in existing trustworthy AI frameworks, especially the EU Trustworthy AI guidelines. This study incorporates relevant African indigenous social values (such as ubuntu, respect—which are relational in nature). Also, it presented People/Human-centeredness, which addresses cultural responsiveness, and sociableness which are crucial to community health sciences/practices Oritsetimeyin et al. (2023).

Below, we identified, contextualised, and tailored seven crucial requirements for an Afrocentric Trustworthy AI framework in healthcare which addresses peculiar complexities associated with healthcare services in the Africa context.

Transparency and Interpretability

The operationalisation of transparency and interpretability in trustworthy AI in African healthcare would include user-centric designs and feedback

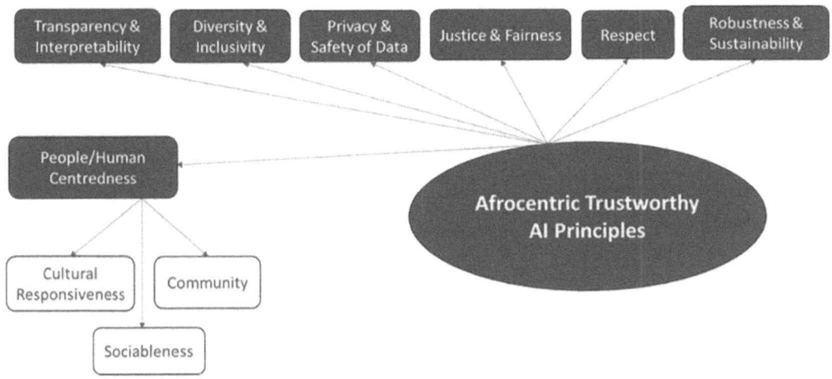

Fig. 5.1 Afrocentric Trustworthy AI framework

mechanisms. These ensure user interfaces are intuitive and available in the local language, and healthcare data and information of patients and related service information (costs) are stored, shared securely (aligning with local and international privacy regulations), and communicated in ways that don't reinforce existing biases. They should be accessible to diverse cultural, language, and literacy levels—via interactive dashboards. Implement feedback mechanisms so users can report health and system issues, provide suggestions, and express concerns in real time. Designers must prioritise the use of explainable AI models that communicate how AI algorithms make decisions, especially in diagnostic and treatment recommendation systems. Our results agree with a recent previous study which shows that prioritising transparency by design and user involvement in building socio-culturally sensitive user interfaces of AI would offer clarity about the functionality, limitations of the AI system to provide feedback should there be erroneous or harmful AI outcomes in the future (Adamu & Nkwo, 2023). We posit that these are fundamental to fostering acceptance and trust in the information presented by AI, ensuring the adoption of ethical practices, and improving healthcare service delivery and patient outcomes.

Diversity and Inclusivity

Diversity and inclusivity entail that AI for healthcare is designed and deployed in ways that are accessible and beneficial to diverse stakeholders regardless of their cultural, linguistic, geographical, or socio-economic status. For instance, inclusivity could be implemented in AI for health to offer accessibility features and interfaces that serve individuals with diverse disabilities including visual, auditory, and motor challenges. This would empower patients to have access and understand their health information, make informed decisions, and actively participate in their care. Involving diverse stakeholders and fostering community engagement in design/development processes would ensure that AI is flexible (allow users to tailor the application to their individual needs), and culturally competent (respects and aligns with values of the people). This can be facilitated through AI capacity building for community healthcare workers and patients with a view to ensuring equitable access to services/facilities and providing user-friendly interfaces and visual aids that are accessible to enhance comprehension and engender trust. These results agree with recent research which suggests that implementing diversity, equity, and inclusion (DEI) in systems would drive effective and authentic advocacy for social change as it will serve as one of the guiding principles for the organisation's business relationship (Gutterman, 2023).

Privacy and Safety of Data

While privacy in healthcare is crucial to safeguard individuals' sensitive health information, safety ensures the health and well-being of healthcare stakeholders. Privacy and safety can be implemented in AI in the African context by anonymising identities of patients in health datasets and providing mechanisms for them to control their health data (access, review, and update their data). Implementing robust security measures (encryption protocols, secure transmission channels, etc.) and tracking measures to monitor access and prevent potential privacy breaches would promote accountability and trust in the AI. Afrocentric AI developers must engage local communities to understand privacy, safety concerns and expectations via education, adopt the principle of data minimisation (collecting only the necessary information for the intended purpose), as well as establish robust informed consent procedures. These approaches will ensure that AI aligns with cultural norms and builds trust in users. These results agree with research which suggests that citizens must have full control over their own data, while data concerning them will not be used to harm or discriminate against them (Floridi, 2019).

Justice and Fairness

Justice and Fairness in Trustworthy AI in healthcare is crucial to ensuring reliable, culturally sensitive, and equitable access to healthcare services across the community and avoiding biased algorithms. This means that adequate bias testing and corrective measures must be done in designing machine learning models (Xivuri & Twinomurinzi, 2023). This implies AI developers must be trained to adapt and engage stakeholders in productive conversations about their research and design intentions. This would assist them in adopting fair processes in the design of AI-based healthcare technologies. Moreover, the AI intervention must provide clear explanations of how it makes its algorithmic decisions and align with local norms and values to make it acceptable and applicable across diverse communities. These can be realised through the adoption of culturally sensitive approaches to data collection which involves social engagement and partnership with community stakeholders who are indigenous to the traditional values of the people. One of the benefits of this technique is that it stimulates community-driven actions and fosters participatory design throughout the AI development lifecycle. Also, fairness can be achieved through the utilisation of healthcare datasets that represent the diverse demographics of the African population (age, gender, socio-economic status, and geographic location), and regular audits of the algorithms to identify and address potential biases. Employing these approaches to mitigate bias and ensure fairness in AI algorithms would promote the development of socially responsive user interfaces for AI-based solutions that are trustworthy, reduce health disparities, and are inclusive and accessible to diverse users.

Respect

Respect emphasises admiration and deference. Considering that "respect" is a cultural value and culture plays an important role in technology adoption and utilisation in many societies (Nkwo, 2019). Implementing respect in AI-based healthcare technology would ensure that it promotes dignity, cultural norms, and preferences of users. Respectful AI system should prioritise privacy and data protection for its users as a way of respecting their autonomy over their health information. This would involve explicit consent seeking and clear communication of the purposes of data collection, storage, and use, and seek explicit consent from users. Incorporating these functionalities into an Afrocentric Trustworthy AI technology for health will ensure that the human rights of the patients are protected, and any form of harm is avoided. For example, an AI system that discriminates against the beliefs and culture of the community and does not acknowledge the traditional values of the potential users would not be considered respectful AI. Rather it will be a turn-off resulting in abandonment. We posit that implementing these features in AI-based healthcare technology will contribute to promoting trust, and respect, fostering a healthcare environment that values and respects the diverse needs of its users.

People/Human-Centeredness
People-centred approaches involve community engagement and require that individuals, patients, and community healthcare workers get involved in the conceptualisation, design, implementation, and deployment of AI. For instance, patient-centred approaches will engender the creation of socially accessible, inclusive, respectful, and customisable interfaces in AI-based telehealth solutions to support individuals with diverse backgrounds, abilities, and levels of digital literacy to access healthcare. This principle also supports the implementation of collaborative features (messaging and feedback mechanism) in the AI-based technologies which help to stimulate shared healthcare decision-making and partnerships among stakeholders (Panch et al., 2019). Afrocentric AI-based monitoring solutions that track public health indicators, and provide early warning and emergency services must be designed to encourage community participation in data collection and health trend monitoring to contribute to the overall health and well-being of the community. It should leverage mobile phones, and social media to develop community-driven health literacy campaigns (in local languages and multimedia formats) that will help people understand how AI could be used in efficient healthcare management. The implementation of people/human-centred principles will not only engender collaboration and effective user experience but will also foster trust, respect, acceptance, and active participation of users in realising their community healthcare goals (Veinot et al., 2013).

Robustness and Sustainability
Robustness is synonymous to resilience and reliability. This should be one of the key considerations for creating resilient and effective AI-based healthcare technologies in Africa as she continues to explore the potentials of AI to achieve the United Nations Sustainable Development Goals.

Robustness can be implemented by prioritising data privacy/security (implementing encryption, secure authentication, and access controls) and adapting to differences in infrastructure availability (such as electricity, and internet connectivity) and varying local conditions (such as climate, environment, and resource availability) during design and deployment. Our guidelines agree with previous studies which posits that since the healthcare domain is complex, AI-based technologies for healthcare must be built to adjust to unforeseen situations without compromising its effectiveness (Amugongo et al., 2023). In addition, sustainability would ensure that relevant environmental and ethically responsible AI-based technologies are adopted to promote shared benefits to all stakeholders in the healthcare system. Due to the unreliable nature of electric supply and internet services across many African nations (Motjoadi & Bokoro, 2023), Afrocentric AI developers might consider energy efficiency and renewability in designing and deploying AI-based healthcare solutions and services. Developers must explore the potentials of using locally sourced materials to create and maintain AI-based healthcare technologies. These would build trust, contribute to improved healthcare and well-being outcomes, promote social acceptance of the AI-based solution, and enhance user experiences.

Adoption and Scaling

In the dynamic healthcare landscape, adopting and scaling Afrocentric trustworthy frameworks is crucial for inclusive and culturally sensitive health solutions. This section explores challenges, opportunities, and strategies for scaling AI health tools in Africa, addressing resistance, promoting adoption, and aligning healthcare with Afrocentric values.

Scaling AI Solutions: Strategies for Health Management Tools

In advancing healthcare with Artificial Intelligence (AI), scaling AI health management tools in Africa is crucial. Below are strategies to be considered for widespread adoption:

i. **Regional Considerations**: Scaling AI tools requires understanding regional variations in healthcare, culture, and technology readiness. Tailoring solutions to each region enhances successful adoption (Makoni, 2020).

ii. **Collaborative Partnerships**: Crucial for success, partnerships between local healthcare, government, and tech developers ensure culturally relevant solutions aligned with local practices (Ofori-Atta & Osei, 2016a).
iii. **Accessibility and Affordability**: Essential for diverse socio-economic contexts, ensuring accessibility through sustainable pricing and user-friendly interfaces is key (Adisa, 2018a).
iv. **Data Privacy and Security**: Addressing data concerns is paramount. Robust protection measures and transparent practices build user trust, facilitating tool adoption (Smith, 2015a).

These strategies for scaling AI in health management tools pave the way for transformative advancements in African healthcare. Transitioning to adoption, and overcoming resistance requires cultural competence, community engagement, education, and sharing success stories. The link between scaling and adoption highlights their interconnected nature, ensuring seamless integration of healthcare technologies. In the subsequent section, we delve into adoption strategies, recognising their crucial role in shaping healthcare's future across Africa.

Overcoming Resistance: Strategies for Adoption

Introducing innovative healthcare technologies faces challenges during adoption, notably resistance to change. This section navigates complexities tied to adopting AI health management tools in Africa, aiming to reveal strategies that acknowledge and address challenges, fostering acceptance of transformative healthcare technologies. Overcoming resistance focuses on cultural competence training, community engagement, education campaigns, and sharing success stories:

i. Cultural Competence Training: To combat unfamiliarity and distrust, cultural competence training for healthcare providers ensures understanding of Afrocentric values in AI health tools, fostering acceptance (Nkosi & Abiola, 2017a).
ii. Community Engagement: Involving local communities in AI solution development is crucial. Soliciting feedback, addressing concerns, and involving community members in decisions empower acceptance and ownership (Ofori-Atta & Osei, 2016a).

iii. Education and Awareness Campaigns: Targeted campaigns dispel myths and misconceptions about AI health tools. Transparent communication about benefits and functionalities builds trust, encouraging adoption (Duru, 2019).
iv. Testimonials and Success Stories: Sharing real-world examples builds confidence and trust. Success stories demonstrate positive impacts, making technology relatable and encouraging adoption (Smith, 2015a)

The interplay between overcoming resistance and scaling AI solutions is evident, forming a symbiotic relationship. Overcoming resistance is an ongoing process, requiring continuous engagement, communication, and responsiveness to evolving community needs. These strategies provide a roadmap for navigating complexities, fostering AI health tool adoption in a culturally respectful manner, building trust, and contributing to improved health outcomes across Africa's diverse landscape.

Challenges to Adoption and Scaling of AI Health Management Tools

The integration of AI in health management promises healthcare transformation, yet faces complexities in adoption and scaling across diverse African landscapes. Challenges include cultural diversity, limited infrastructure, economic disparities, data privacy concerns, workforce readiness, and resistance to change. In navigating the complexities of AI adoption in African healthcare, we encounter a series of interconnected challenges. First, cultural barriers demand tailored approaches that respect and integrate diverse beliefs and traditions. Yet, these efforts are hindered by limited technological infrastructure, necessitating investments to bridge the gap between aspiration and implementation. Also, economic disparities exacerbate the situation, restricting access to AI solutions and widening the gap in healthcare provision. Addressing these concerns leads us to confront the issue of data privacy, a fundamental prerequisite for building trust and ensuring user confidence in AI-driven healthcare. Moreover, healthcare workforce preparedness emerges as a critical link in this chain, requiring targeted training to empower professionals with the skills needed to navigate the digital landscape. Ultimately, overcoming resistance to change becomes imperative, requiring strategic interventions to foster a culture of acceptance and enthusiasm towards AI integration. Thus, each challenge serves as a stepping stone, guiding us towards a future where AI is seamlessly integrated into African healthcare, improving outcomes and transforming lives. Proactive strategies can overcome challenges, paving the way for successful AI integration. Resistance, a response to innovation, requires thoughtful strategies acknowledging cultural, social, and individual nuances. By navigating these, stakeholders can create an environment supporting seamless AI health tool integration, enhancing healthcare outcomes across Africa's diverse landscape.

Strategies for Overcoming Resistance to Change

In the endeavours to navigate resistance to change within African healthcare, a comprehensive approach unfolds: very importantly, cultural competence training and community engagement serve as the bedrock, fostering understanding and acceptance of AI solutions within diverse cultural contexts. Then, education campaigns and testimonials emerge as powerful tools, dispelling misconceptions and highlighting the tangible benefits of AI in healthcare. These efforts are bolstered by incentives and pilot programmes, which not only motivate adoption but also provide real-world evidence of AI's efficacy and potential impact. In tandem, dialogue forums and continuous training ensure ongoing support and address any lingering concerns, nurturing a culture of trust and collaboration. User-friendly interfaces and robust regulatory frameworks then cement this foundation, ensuring accessibility, security, and ethical use of AI technologies. Through this interconnected web of strategies, we pave the way for a future where AI is seamlessly integrated into African healthcare, driving improved outcomes and better health for all. Strategically addressing these challenges can create an environment conducive to successful AI health tool adoption in diverse African landscapes. This not only transforms healthcare delivery but also fosters inclusivity, cultural sensitivity, and overall public health enhancement. Reflecting on these challenges and strategies reveals their profound implications for healthcare's future. The next section emphasises the importance of precise adoption and scaling strategies tailored to cultural, economic, and technological contexts, unravelling the potential for revolutionary healthcare delivery, improved patient outcomes, and sustainable, inclusive health systems.

The Importance of Right Adoption and Scaling

Adopting and scaling AI health tools in diverse healthcare landscapes holds immense potential for the healthcare revolution. By leveraging AI, healthcare can reach even the most remote and underserved regions, democratising access to advanced medical care while streamlining processes, and enhancing diagnostic accuracy. Tailoring AI solutions to local contexts ensures that healthcare interventions align with cultural practices, infrastructure, and specific regional healthcare challenges, empowering healthcare professionals to make informed decisions and deliver personalised care. The accumulation and analysis of vast amounts of healthcare data facilitated by AI enables evidence-based decision-making, leading to targeted public health strategies. Consequently, achieving economies of scale with AI tools enhances their cost-effectiveness over time, fostering sustainability within healthcare systems. Additionally, embracing AI fosters global collaboration, allowing for the exchange of best practices and innovative approaches to healthcare delivery. With AI's focus on preventive measures and early intervention, improved health outcomes are achieved, reducing the burden on healthcare systems. Afrocentric frameworks ensure that AI solutions are culturally sensitive and inclusive, fostering trust and acceptance among diverse communities. The adoption and scaling of these tools usher in an era of accessible, efficient, and culturally sensitive healthcare. By overcoming barriers, tailoring solutions to regional needs, and promoting widespread acceptance, these initiatives transform healthcare systems and improve public health.

Ethical Considerations and Regulation

The ethical considerations and regulatory oversight in developing and deploying AI in African healthcare demand careful attention. Key ethical principles for AI adoption in an African context would include:

1. **Informed Consent and Transparency**: It is important to obtain informed consent for health data and maintain transparency about algorithms and training procedures. These should be clearly explained to citizens in their dialect to ensure proper understanding.

2. **Bias and Fairness**: Bias must be avoided by ensuring a diverse representation of data, training, and validation processes across several regions and cultures within the continent.
3. **Accountability**: Accountability must be ensured by maintaining transparency in process via audits and reports made available to citizens in their local languages and clearly explained
4. **Human Autonomy**: Recognising AI as a supportive tool, decisions impacting healthcare should remain with human providers. AI should augment, not replace, human expertise, and judgement.
5. **Job Displacement**: Responsible AI implementation demands assessing potential job displacement for healthcare workers. Implementing retraining programmes and hybrid AI-human workflows can mitigate workforce challenges.
6. **Culturally Sensitive Design**: Aligning AI solutions with cultural norms, languages, and health practices fosters acceptance and engagement within target communities, ensuring resonance with diverse populations.

A robust regulatory framework is crucial for ethically deploying AI in healthcare. This involves establishing dedicated national or regional bodies to craft and enforce policies, ensuring compliance with ethical AI use. Context-appropriate guidelines, developed through public consultation, align with cultural and ethical values, fostering inclusive regulation and understanding of AI's implications in healthcare. Transparency mandates for AI developers require disclosing algorithm details to build trust and accountability. External audits detect and rectify biases, promoting fairness and preventing discrimination in diverse healthcare settings. Stricter guidelines for health data protection define secure practices for collection, storage and sharing to maintain patient trust. Establishing reporting channels for AI-related adverse events enables prompt monitoring and corrective measures, enhancing regulatory responsiveness. Rigorous efficacy testing before deployment evaluates system performance and safety. Multidisciplinary input ensures comprehensive evaluation of ethical, legal, and societal aspects for informed decision-making, ultimately promoting responsible and trustworthy AI integration in healthcare.

Conclusion, Recommendations, and Future Directions

This chapter advocates for an Afrocentric framework tailored to African healthcare, integrating AI with cultural values, and ethical considerations. It stresses the necessity of AI systems that are culturally sensitive and adaptable to diverse African settings, infrastructure, and health norms. Key elements include incorporating African values into AI principles, fostering collaboration among stakeholders, and prioritising user-centric design to build trust and meet local healthcare needs. Capacity building for healthcare workers in AI literacy is essential, emphasising skills development without replacing expertise. To combat data bias, the Afrocentric framework proposes robust data governance to ensure inclusivity, security, transparency, and prevent discrimination. Pilot testing with localised datasets before full deployment aligns AI solutions with Africa's healthcare landscape. Policymakers are urged to prioritise ethical AI deployment through clear regulations and digital infrastructure investments.

The chapter also highlights the potential of AI to revolutionise African healthcare, focusing on indigenous frameworks as transformative guides. Recommendations emphasise ethical considerations, user-centric design, data governance, and inclusive collaboration among stakeholders. Human-centred design and hybrid models combining AI with local expertise are deemed crucial in addressing healthcare challenges and shortages. Looking forward, intelligent diagnostics and predictive analytics offer hope for improved service access, particularly in underserved areas. It is underscored that AI must align with local knowledge and values through education and collaboration to democratise healthcare while maintaining cultural relevance. In conclusion, the future of AI in African healthcare hinges on indigenous Afrocentric frameworks that harmonise tradition with technology, ensuring ethical, inclusive, and culturally resonant solutions. These frameworks provide a blueprint for transformative healthcare solutions across the continent, empowering communities and embracing cultural diversity.

References

Adamu, M., & Nkwo, M. (2023). AI in Africa. Preliminary Notes on Design and Adoption. Diid Disegno Industriale Industrial Design, (80), 44-57. https://doi.org/10.30682/diid8023d

Adisa, A. (2018a). Technological infrastructure and healthcare in Africa: Challenges and opportunities. *African Journal of Science, Technology, Innovation and Development, 10*(2), 145–154.

Adisa, A. (2018b). Cultural competence training in healthcare: A key strategy for overcoming resistance. *International Journal of Healthcare Management, 11*(3), 213–220.

Akinyemi, J. D., Akinola, A. A., Adekunle, O. O., Adetiloye, T. O., & Dansu, E. J. (2023). Lung and colon cancer detection from CT images using deep learning. *Machine Graphics and Vision, 32*, 85–97.

Alupo, C. D., Omeiza, D., & Vernon, D. (2022). Realising the potential of AI in Africa: It all turns on trust. In *Towards trustworthy artificial intelligent systems* (pp. 179–192). Springer.

Amugongo, L. M., Kriebitz, A., Boch, A., & Lütge, C. (2023). Operationalising AI ethics through the agile software development lifecycle: A case study of AI-enabled mobile health applications. *AI and Ethics*. https://doi.org/10.1007/s43681-023-00331-3

Arun, C. (2019). AI and the Global South: Designing for other worlds forthcoming. In M. D. Dubber, F. Pasquale, & S. Das (Eds.), *The Oxford handbook of ethics of AI*. Oxford University Press. Available at SSRN: https://ssrn.com/abstract=3403010

Char, D. S., et al. (2018). Implementing machine learning in health care—Addressing ethical challenges. *New England Journal of Medicine, 378*(11), 981–983.

Duru, E. J. (2019). Community engagement strategies in healthcare technology adoption: Lessons from successful implementations. *Journal of Community Engagement and Scholarship, 12*(1), 47–63.

Eke, D. O., Chintu, S. S., & Wakunuma, K. (2023a). Towards shaping the future of responsible AI in Africa. In D. O. Eke, K. Wakunuma, & S. Akintoye (Eds.), *Responsible AI in Africa. Social and cultural studies of robots and AI*. Palgrave Macmillan. https://doi.org/10.1007/978-3-031-08215-3_8

Eke, D. O., Wakunuma, K., & Akintoye, S. (2023b). Introducing responsible AI in Africa. In D. O. Eke, K. Wakunuma, & S. Akintoye (Eds.), *Responsible AI in Africa. Social and cultural studies of robots and AI*. Palgrave Macmillan. https://doi.org/10.1007/978-3-031-08215-3_1

European Commission and Directorate-General for Communications Networks, Content and Technology. (2019). *Ethics guidelines for trustworthy AI*. Publications Office. https://data.europa.eu/doi/10.2759/346720

Esteva, A., et al. (2019). A guide to deep learning in healthcare. *Nature Medicine, 25*(1), 24–29.

Floridi, L. (2019). Establishing the rules for building trustworthy AI. *Nature Machine Intelligence.* https://doi.org/10.1038/s42256-019-0055-y

Ibitoye, A. O., Famutimi, R. F., Olanloye, D. O., & Akioyamen, E. (2021). User centric social opinion and clinical behavioural model for depression detection. *International Journal of Intelligent Information Systems, 10*(4), 69–73.

Ibitoye, A. O., Ozuchi, N. J., & Onifade, F. W. (2023). *Hypertension risk prediction model using anthropometric and social behaviour patterns in young adults*. In O. F. W. Onifade, International Conference on Artificial Intelligence Research (ICAIR-23), Virtual, Jakarta Raya, Indonesia, 05th December '23 (pp. 35–42).

Litjens, G., Kooi, T., Bejnordi, B. E., Setio, A. A. A., Ciompi, F., Ghafoorian, M., et al. (2017). A survey on deep learning in medical image analysis. *Medical Image Analysis, 42*, 60–88.

Makoni, S. (2020). Healthcare technology in Africa: Challenges and opportunities. *Journal of Health Informatics in Developing Countries, 14*(2), 1–15.

Makuochi Nkwo. 2019. Designing Cu lturally-appropriate Persuasive Technology to Promote Positive Work Attitudes among Workers in PublicWorkplaces. In 27th Conference on User Modeling, Adaptation and Personalization (UMAP '19), June 9–12, 2019, Larnaca, Cyprus. ACM, NewYork, NY, USA, 9 pages. ACM, New York, NY, USA. 4 pages.

Manning, P. (2010). The African diaspora: A history through culture. Columbia University Press. Chicago

Masimirembwa, C., & Matimba, A. (2012). Pharmacogenomics in Africa: Diversity as an opportunity for personalised health care. In *Genomics applications for the developing world* (pp. 161–182). Springer.

Mbiti, J. S. (1990). African religions & philosophy. Heinemann.

Miotto, R., Li, L., Kidd, B. A., & Dudley, J. T. (2016). Deep patient: An unsupervised representation to predict the future of patients from the electronic health records. *Scientific Reports, 6*(1), 1–10.

Njei, B., Kanmounye, U. S., Mohamed, M. F., Forjindam, A., Ndemazie, N. B., Adenusi, A., et al. (2023). Artificial intelligence for healthcare in Africa: A scientometric analysis. *Health and Technology, 13*(6), 947–955.

Nkosi, T. M., & Abiola, A. (2017a). The role of culture in shaping the perception and adoption of health technologies in Africa. *Journal of Health Informatics in Africa, 3*(2), 22–34.

Nkosi, T. M., & Abiola, A. (2017b). Incentivizing adoption of healthcare technologies: Lessons from global perspectives. *Journal of Incentive Marketing, 1*(1), 56–68.

Ofori-Atta, A., & Osei, A. (2016a). Challenges and opportunities in implementing eHealth strategy in Ghana. *International Journal of Medical Informatics, 94*, 1–7.

Ofori-Atta, A., & Osei, A. (2016b). Overcoming resistance to change in healthcare: Insights from global practices. *Journal of Change Management, 16*(2), 93–109.

Oladosu, O. O., & Ibitoye, A. O. (2023). Brain tumour classification using ResNet50-convolutional block attention module. *Applied Computing and Informatics* (ahead-of-print). https://doi.org/10.1108/ACI-09-2023-0022

Oritsetimeyin, A., Nicola J. B., Anicia P., Jacki O., Oussama M., Amid A., Makuochi S. N., et. al. (2023). *Afrocentric collaborative care: Supporting context specific digital health and care*. In Computer Supported Cooperative Work and Social Computing (CSCW '23 Companion), October 14–18, 2023, Minneapolis, MN, USA (5 pp.). ACM. https://doi.org/10.1145/3584931.3611287

Oyewale, C. T., Akinyemi, J. D., Ibitoye, A. O., & Onifade, O. F. (2024). Predicting suicide ideation from social media text using CNN-BiLSTM. In K. K. Patel, K. Santosh, A. Patel, & A. Ghosh (Eds.), *Soft computing and its engineering applications*. icSoftComp 2023. Communications in Computer and Information Science (vol. 2030). Springer. https://doi.org/10.1007/978-3-031-53731-8_22

Panch, T., Mattie, H., & Celi, L. A. (2019). The "inconvenient truth" about AI in healthcare. *NPJ Digital Medicine, 2*(1), 77.

Pell, C., Straus, L., Andrew, E. V. W., Meñaca, A., & Pool, R. (2011). Social and cultural factors affecting uptake of interventions for malaria in pregnancy in Africa: A systematic review of the qualitative research. *PLoS ONE, 6*(7), e22452. https://doi.org/10.1371/journal.pone.0022452

Ramsay, M. (2018). Precision medicine for Africa: Challenges and opportunities. *Quest, 14*(3), 28–32.

Rossi, F. (2018). Building trust in artificial intelligence. *Journal of International Affairs, 72*(1), 127–134.

Rudin, C. (2019). Stop explaining black box machine learning models for high stakes decisions and use interpretable models instead. *Nature Machine Intelligence, 1*(5), 206–215.

Smith, L. T. (2015a). Technology adoption in healthcare: Lessons from global experiences. *International Journal of Health Policy and Management, 4*(5), 297–299.

Smith, L. T. (2015b). Education campaigns for healthcare technology adoption: Best practices and lessons learned. *Journal of Health Communication, 20*(7), 812–819.

Tarnawski, W., et al. (2021). Benchmarking of 5 AI in health informatics courses. *Studies in Health Technology and Informatics, 281*, 25–31.

Topol, E. J. (2019). High-performance medicine: The convergence of human and artificial intelligence. *Nature Medicine, 25*(1), 44–56.

Veinot, T. C., Campbell, T. R., Kruger, D. J., et al. (2013). A question of trust: User-centered design requirements for an informatics intervention to promote the sexual health of African-American youth. *Journal of the American Medical Informatics Association, 2013*(20), 758–765.

V. Motjoadi, M. G. R. Kilimi and P. N. Bokoro, (2023) "Design and Simulation of Grid-Tied Power Supply System Using HOMER: A Case Study of Lebowakgomo in South Africa," 2022 30th Southern African Universities Power Engineering Conference (SAUPEC), Durban, South Africa, 2022, pp. 1-9, doi: https://doi.org/10.1109/SAUPEC55179.2022.9730770

Xivuri, K., & Twinomurinzi, H. (2023). How AI developers can assure algorithmic fairness. *Discover Artificial Intelligence, 3*, 27. https://doi.org/10.1007/s44163-023-00074-4

CHAPTER 6

Resource Allocation for Trustworthy Artificial Intelligence Projects in African Context

Abiola Joseph Azeez, *Elnathan Tiokou*, *and Edmund Terem Ugar*

Introduction

Can AI be trustworthy? What does it mean to have a trustworthy AI design in Africa? In this chapter, we answer the first question in the affirmative. Our central claim is that, even though trust and trustworthiness

A. J. Azeez (✉)
Canadian Robotics and Artificial Intelligence Ethical Design Laboratory, University of Ottawa, Ottawa, ON, Canada
e-mail: aazeez@uottawa.ca

E. Tiokou
Polytechnique Montréal, Montreal, QC, Canada
e-mail: elnathan.tiokou@polymtl.ca

E. T. Ugar
Department of Philosophy, Centre for Africa-China Studies, University of Johannesburg, Johannesburg, South Africa
e-mail: edmundu@uj.ac.za

D. O. Eke et al. (eds.), *Trustworthy AI*,
https://doi.org/10.1007/978-3-031-75674-0_6

always apply to agents that have the capacity for moral responsibility, trust/trustworthiness can also be extended to AI. However, our use of the term trust in AI differs from the trust we attribute to moral agents—beings capable of responsibility/accountability. We situate the trust in AI within the framework of institutional trust, that is, trust in the institution where the technology is designed.

The need for trustworthy AI design is a serious contention within the literature on AI ethics and government policies and frameworks on AI because of the role AI plays in our current social milieu (Agarwal & Mishra, 2021; Benjamins et al., 2019; Dignum, 2019; Mikalef et al., 2022; Peters et al., 2020; Schiff et al., 2020). The subject of trustworthy AI has received enormous contributions in the last two decades. For example, in 2022, Google Scholar had 11,000 hits on the search on the topic of "trustworthy AI" (Slosser et al., 2023). Many ethical AI guidelines and white papers that have emerged recently have trust as their central topic of discussion (e.g., Gunning et al., 2019; HLEG, 2019; Leslie, 2019; OECD, 2017; United Nations, 2021). While the central or paradigmatic nature of trust is deeply interpersonal, the worry for most discussions on trust is whether we can use trust relationships to describe our relationship with artificial intelligence. The main problem is that, in most instances, rather than a rationally appropriate motive, trust is always considered on the grounds of emotion, intuitions, and the personal history a "trustor" has with a "trustee".

Some theorists proposed the notion of reliability, rather than trust, as that which can be suitably applied to artificial intelligence. These theorists argue that we can rely on AI rather than trust the system (Dur'an & Fromanek, 2018; Nickel et al., 2010; Ryan, 2020). The rationale behind their argument is that we can only trust humans because of their moral capacity for accountability, while technology, on the contrary, can only be relied on given its lack of praise- or blameworthiness. However, the problem with the above view is that technologies such as AI are not merely technical artefacts. AI technologies are socio-technical artefacts that interact differently with humans and are built in ways that fit into the rules of human society (Ugar, 2023a). Furthermore, AI affects our lives differently from other technologies in areas like medicine and healthcare, education, transportation and others (Benk et al., 2022; van de Poel, 2020). As a result, it is crucial that we do not conceptualise the relationship between humans and AI in terms of reliance as applicable to other technical artefacts since AI is more advanced.

In this chapter, we contend that while it is plausible that we cannot trust AI systems because of the moral and emotive implications of trust, relying on AI also does not capture the entirety of the relationship humans share with AI, given their social nature. Thus, we argue that we can trust AI, but from the perspective of institutional trust. While we explain later the meaning of institutional trust, in simple terms, it is the kind of trust that can be applied to non-human subjects within the framework of an institution with natural persons (Misztal, 1996). We adumbrate that for AI to be trustworthy, it must have natural persons who understand the capabilities and limitations of the systems and supervise their functioning. These natural persons ought to monitor overreliance on the system and understand and interpret the systems to approve or override decisions that do not align with the values of human society. Natural persons are entrusted with the role of interfering with the performance of this high-risk AI system, and they form part of the institutional web of trustworthiness.

However, one may ask: what does it then entail to trust an AI system? When we trust an AI, what exactly are we trusting? Are we trusting the technical artefacts, the institution, the rule or the decision makers? We argue that the trust relationship with AI encompasses the artefacts, the institution, the rule makers, and the decision makers as a unit. In line with the above contention, and to address the second question posited at the beginning of this introduction, we underscore that a trustworthy AI design in Africa is one whose institutions are based in Africa, including those providing technical infrastructure for design, algorithm, data storage, data generation, and so on.

African scholars contend that prevailing AI technologies exhibit Western bias that is unsuitable for the African milieu (Azeez & Adeate, 2020; Eke et al., 2023; Wakunuma et al., 2022). In addition, it is argued that because Africans have a historical trajectory that is embedded in colonialism and neo-colonialism, the inadequacy of funding from African governments not only undermines the perception of AI trustworthiness in the African context but also exposes the African population to the manifestation of technological colonialism. In response, this chapter argues that African governmental entities must adopt a proactive strategy by providing an enabling environment for AI development and innovation to thrive. This enabling environment includes the provision of adequate financial resources to fund AI projects within the continent. For example, the estimated global economic value of AI according to PWC is reported to reach $15.7 trillion in 2030. Even though AI is at its early stage, the financial benefits of AI are as follows: $7.0 trillion for China, $3.7 trillion for Northern America, $1.8 trillion for Northern Europe, and $1.2 trillion for Africa. Africa sits at the bottom of the economic gains from AI. Furthermore, in 2022, the US spent $47.7 billion in AI investments, China spent $13.4 billion, and Germany spent almost a billion euros; while in 2021, the European Union Council targeted an annual investment of €20 billion to AI, while Africa spent $2.0 billion in 2021 and $3.0 billion in 2022. Additionally, despite having low investment in AI, some of Africa's AI investments come from Western investors, such as the Google and IBM innovation labs and the Nigerian Kudi AI, which Silicon Valley funds. Given the low financial investment we have highlighted above, we aim to (i) draw on a comparative analysis of global AI advancement projects in Europe, the United States, China, and Africa, our claim is that to develop trustworthy social technologies that resemble the African worldview, the issue of funding deficit must be addressed to advance trustworthy AI research which prioritises setting up trustworthy AI design parameters in the African context and (ii) show how this funding gap obscures and shapes the conversation on design parameters and variables of a trustworthy AI with an African outlook—that is, we show how issues like funding biases can obscure a trustworthy AI design from Africa for Africans.

In other words, an African trustworthy AI, or an AI system that is trustworthy in Africa, is one that is designed in Africa, designed within African institutions, has the African Union as a regulatory body, and African values, norms, and lived experiences shape its policies and frameworks. To put this in simple terms, AI's trustworthy design in Africa must have an African agency at the centre of the design. Our claim is informed by the notion of institutional trust, which we find prize-worthy and which can be applied to the trust relationship we have with AI systems.

Three main reasons shape the novelty and significance of our argument to support the yardstick for a trustworthy design of AI systems in Africa, which is centred around African agencies. First, most of the current institutions responsible for AI designs deployed in Africa are not in Africa, and these systems are not shaped by policies informed by the cultural norms, ethos, worldviews, and ethics emerging from Africa. Second, given African histories of colonialism, neo-colonialism, and techno-colonialism, Africans ought to be wary of designs emerging from elsewhere. Furthermore, current designs of AI have shown evidence of biases and discrimination against Africans, from misrepresentation of black people by facial recognition technology to discrimination in recidivism tools in the US. Lastly, given the previous reasons, on the one hand, and the view that the best version of trust that applies to AI has to be institutional trust, on the other hand, we submit that Africans must rely on their institutions that care for the well-being of Africans, to guide the design of a trustworthy AI.

We divide this paper into three main sections. In the first section, we delve into the philosophical analysis of trust and distinguishing trust from reliability. Additionally, we provide clear reasons why trust is important and why the institutional notion of trust can be applied to AI. The second section shows some of the impediments in Africa that are stumbling blocks to the design of AI in the continent to achieve trustworthiness. One of the problems that we identify is financial constraints. The third section argues that there is no alternative towards trustworthy AI design in Africa. We show what trustworthy AI ought to look like in Africa, encompassing African ontology, along with exuding the relationality and human-centeredness of the African person, and why only Africans can achieve this trustworthy design. Additionally, we make recommendations for AI designers and policymakers on the best approach to designing a trustworthy AI ecosystem in Africa, highlighting a nuanced perspective on channelling financial resources to advance AI projects in Africa, encompassing dormant fund utilisation, corporate social responsibility, partnerships, and community-driven initiatives towards fostering a trustworthy AI framework rooted in the African ethos.

A Philosophical Analysis of the Concept of Trust

What does trust mean? To understand if we can have a trusting relationship with AI, we must expose the meaning of trust. Trust is conceived as the relationship a party has with another party on the account that the former is willing to rely on the latter. The former party, that is one who trusts, is generally known as the trustor, while the party who is trusted is known as the trustee (Jones, 1996). Trust is usually based on the intuitions and histories of past experiences between the trustor and their trustee (Hardin, 2002; Hardwig, 1991). However, prerequisites of trust, like past experiences, are not generalisable to warrant trust or distrust objectively. I can trust Apple to produce their iPhone 16 Pro

Max with exquisite camera features because, based on my past experiences, Apple produces iPhones with the best camera qualities, and Apple has been reliable in this regard in the past. However, my experience with Apple cannot be a yardstick for anyone else to trust Apple since experiences are not the same. Given this, one can then claim that trust is subjective; that is, a trust relationship between a trustor and a trustee is based on the trustor's subjective experience with the trustee. However, it is pertinent to clarify from the onset that the notion of trust that we advance here is not based on subjective estimates, a notion that is ubiquitous in traditional accounts of trust (Bauer, 2019). Our notion of trust is a shared subjectivity. For example, the shared experiences of colonialism, neo-colonialism, capitalism, and techno-colonialism in Africa.

Annette Baier (1986) contends that trust is a concept loaded with normative attitudes. Baier identifies goodwill as an integral component of trust. In Baier's view, a trustor can rely on the trustee because of the trustee's goodwill. When a party expects goodwill from another, and the goodwill becomes non-existent, the trusting party might feel betrayed by the trustee. However, such a dynamic can only exist within the human community because it would be absurd to expect goodwill from non-human entities or for humans to feel betrayed if non-human entities do not meet the demands of goodwill. On this account, Baier believes that trust is an exclusively human attitude (also see Hawley, 2014; Holton, 1994; Jones, 1996). For us not to fall into the trap of ambiguities, it is pertinent that when we use concepts like "trust" in human-AI relationships, we clarify how trust is construed. It is absurd to think that non-human beings can be the object of trust. Why so? Non-human entities cannot be held accountable or responsible for their actions in the absence of goodwill, nor can they commit to upholding certain relationships with humans (Hawley, 2014; Holton, 1994; Ryan, 2020).

As a concept, trust is a mental attitude (Hardin, 2006; Jones, 1996; Sztompka, 1999). When discussing trust, we invoke underlying concepts like reason, emotion, and volitional/behavioural choice. As a result, trust relationships involve a trustor believing in a trustee's agency, feeling safe in their hands, and voluntarily placing their trust in the trustee (Baier, 2013). These three concepts must go concomitantly for a trust relationship to be established. Because of the critical role of agency in a trust relationship, one wonders if non-human entities like AI can be trusted, as expatiated above.

In the AI trustworthy literature, some theorists argue that instead of thinking about AI along the lines of trust, we should rather think about these technologies along the line of reliability (see, for example, Dur'an and Fromanek, 2018; Nickel et al., 2010; Ryan, 2020). Reliability is an alternative to trust or a weak form of trust (Baier, 1986). To put reliability as a weak form of trust into perspective, theorists like Katherine Hawley argue that trust converges with reliability in practical terms because a trust relationship involves a practical reliance on the trustee (Hawley, 2012).

However, the point of divergence between trust and reliance is that reliance is just part of a structural composition of trust on the account that a trustor relying on a trustee does not necessarily require any prior attitude of trust. Furthermore, trust has a moral quality that is not present in reliance (Lagerspetz, 2015). For example, I can rely on my cat to chase out mice from my house. However, my cat does not owe any moral duty to chase out mice from my house, and I cannot hold my cat accountable if it does not chase out mice. In other words, I rely on my cat for practical reasons without any moral obligations attached. While we can rely on animals like dogs and cats or inanimate objects like technology, trust can only be directed to objects to which we can attribute moral responsibility and agency in the trust relationship. Thus, saying a "trustworthy AI" will be missing the point. If we are to introduce the concept of "trustworthiness" to AI, there has to be trust in the AI ecosystem involving humans as agents responsible for praise or blame (Coeckelbergh, 2012). We will return to the above point shortly. Let us briefly engage with the concept of reliance as it applies to AI systems.

The literature on interpersonal trust uses reliance as a weaker version of trust that can be used to describe human-non-human (AI) relationships. For instance, theorists like Dur'an and Formanek (2018) describe human-AI relationships as computational *reliabilism*, while Ryan (2020) believes that such a relationship is based on rational trust, and Nickel and colleagues (2010) argue that it is a thin notion of trust. Even though these concepts are not interchangeable, they have some similarities that warrant that we can use them interchangeably in this chapter. Thus, we group them all into one notion: reliance. We use Ryan's notion of rational trust to expand on them.

According to Ryan (2020), AI cannot be trusted because they do not possess the capacity to be trusted. Ryan alludes that trust requires attribution of some affective and/or normative reasons to act; since AI does not possess any emotive quality or cannot be held responsible for its action, it follows that AI cannot be an object we can attribute trust to (Ryan, 2020, p. 2). Ryan concludes that the only legitimate trust that can be placed in AI should be rational. Ryan exposes rational trust as a situation in which a trustor depends on the trustee regarding certain specific actions, irrespective of whether the trustee is motivated to carry out such actions. As a result, Ryan underscores that the most rational thing to do in human-AI relationships is for the former to rely on the latter rather than trust the latter.

Additionally, Ryan (2020, p. 13) holds that for trustor A to have a trust relationship with trustee B, B must be a moral agent who can recognise the trust A has for them. In this sense, a trustee qualifies to be trusted because they hold moral agency and can be subject to praise or blame. What Ryan introduces here is the requirement of full moral agency for the relationship of trust to take place (2020, p. 10). His rationale for the above is based on the premise that if an entity cannot be held responsible for their actions, it follows that they do not qualify as trustees.

However, we argue that there are exceptions to Ryan's argument. There are cases where one cannot trace the responsibility to a trustee, given that they cannot be responsible. Nonetheless, the institution where the trustee emerges from can be held responsible on behalf of the trustee. For example, I can trust my fourteen-year-old daughter to be responsible and disciplined at school. But if she burns down her school due to indiscipline, I would be held responsible as the parent. Here, my fourteen-year-old teenage daughter is a human being with sound faculties, yet she cannot be directly held accountable for some of her actions. My daughter and her family form the institutional web that collectively takes responsibility for her actions. This is what some theorists term institutional trust. Institutional trust allows us to trust objects, like AI, that are incapable of being held accountable for their actions.

Trust is imperative in human-AI relationships because of what AI represents in our social milieu (Cheng et al., 2021; Clarke, 2019). There are two broad reasons why we need trustworthy AI design and use. First, AI technology is different from other technologies. AI is a socio-technical system that is designed with essentially three building blocks: (I) technical artefacts—they are designed to perform specific technical functions with intentionality (Ugar, 2023a; van de Poel, 2020); (II) agency—the systems exercise some form of agency because they can adapt to their environment, possess semi-autonomy, and can interact with their users (Ugar, 2023a; van de Poel, 2020); (III) rules—AI technologies are designed to follow the rules and social norms of their designers (Ugar, 2023a; van de Poel, 2020). In line with the above view, some thinkers ascribe a weak form of moral agency to AI systems (see Floridi & Sanders, 2004; Ugar, 2023a; van de Poel, 2020).

The second reason for a trustworthy design of AI is because of the role AI plays in various domains like healthcare, justice and criminal system, education, transportation, etc. We have designated various sensitive and intricate roles to AI in the abovementioned domains. In line with the above, the ethics guidelines of the European Union, published in 2019, underscore that trust is an essential and necessary condition for the successful implementation of AI in society (HLEG, 2019). Trustworthiness remains integral to most ethical guidelines and white papers published for AI in society (see Gunning et al., 2019; HLEG, 2019; Leslie, 2019). Furthermore, before we can speak of trustworthy AI in Africa, given how contentious trust is, we must establish how trust should be viewed when it comes to AI. As clearly stated, we place trustworthiness in AI within the scope of institutional trust. We argue that trustworthy AI is not based on trust in AI as a social tool, but a chain that encompasses the institution and agents capable of responsibility from where the technology emerges. Thus, our notion of trustworthy AI is based on institutional trust (for explanations of institutional trust, see entries like Bachmann, 2020; Foley, 2001; Gambetta, 1988; Jones, 2004; Lahno, 2001; Lehrer, 1999; Pettit, 1995).

To understand trust within the context of AI, we must understand the institution that designs the AI. Given that trust is a mental state, they must be an actor to whom the trust is directed towards. This is because of the feasibility of ascribing expectations and responsibility to the trustee (Mollering, 2006). Institutional trust is directed at a system or institutions based on their competencies, honesty, and ability to live up to their commitments. There is an interplay between trust and institution, in the case of AI, for the trust to be effective. For us to trust AIs and the institutions that design them, the institutions must be effective in acting as objects of our trust (Fuglsang & Jagd, 2015, p. 22).

When we trust an institution, it means that we have confidence in the institutional functioning, what it represents, and its performance over time (Mollering, 2006). For an institution to foster trust, it must ensure that the inbuilt rules, routines, and roles that form the basis of an institutional setting are trustworthy. When there is institutional trust, the trustor can see the institutional safeguards measures, decisions, and actions given their level of transparency. When a technology is trusted, it is not the technology itself that is trusted, but the institution where the technology is designed. The extent to which a trustor can rely on a particular AI is influenced or affected by the level of trust the trustor has in the institution where the AI is designed. For instance, when an institution produces a technology that is flawed egregiously, it leads to trustors undermining the institution's trust (Bekker, 2021). To this point, we ask whether Africans can trust AI technology emerging from other climes.

We argue that besides the obvious reasons of colonialism and the aftermaths of colonialism, which have thwarted the trust Africans have in institutions from other climes, especially Euro-America, current designs of AI have undermined the trust relationship between Africa and institutions in the global north due to evidence of biases and discriminations towards Africans and people of colour by their AI designs. For example, facial recognition software designed by these institutions has categorised Africans and people of colour as apes (McCullom, 2017) and has poor recognition of blacks and people of colour (Buolamwini & Gebru, 2018). Additionally, software used for recidivism in the US is biased and discriminatory towards black people, especially African Americans and people of colour (Angwin et al., 2016; Forrest, 2021; Greene, 2023). There were other instances of hand dryers not recognising black people and people of colour during the COVID-19 pandemic (Kennard, 2022). These are clear instances where trust for institutions from other locales by Africans has been undermined. Given the importance of trust in AI and the role that AI plays in our current technologically-driven ecosystem, in the next section, we argue that Africans can circumvent the abovementioned problems of bias and discrimination if they can be agents of their AI designs.

Towards an African Agency in a Trustworthy AI Design

In the previous section, we argued that the best form of trust which captures AI is the notion of institutional trust, that is, trusting the institution which the AI is designed from. Additionally, we pointed out that it is imperative for AI to be designed in Africa to make them trustworthy. Moving forward, we show how Africans can be at the centre of their AI design and the implications this may have in their AI ecosystem.

One of the most important prerequisites for achieving a trustworthy AI design in Africa is funding. Making a case for the imperative of Africans funding their AI projects cannot be isolated from current issues bewildering efforts to create AI systems tailored for the African audience, with emphasis on several critical factors. This section delves into factors necessitating the imperative of crafting trustworthy AI solutions tailored for the African context, encompassing the examination of the three avenues for funding: (A) funding the design locally, (B) sourcing funds elsewhere, and (C) collaboration and partnerships, and the analysis of pros and cons of these avenues. The significance of Africans financing their AI projects could be considered parallel to the efforts of African-born AI Ethics scholars who are engaged in crafting AI solutions tailored to the African context. Some scholars frame the issue of crafting trustworthy AI solutions tailored for the African context from various perspectives such as misalignment between second-wave AI and afro-existential (Azeez & Adeate, 2020), and marginalisation of non-western knowledge systems in the study of AI ethics (Segun, 2021). In more recent times, however, this framing has expanded, encompassing issues of algorithm colonisation of Africa (Birhane, 2020), the importance of local data and knowledge (Abebe et al., 2021), empowering local talent (Ade-Ibijola & Okonkwo, 2023), and technological colonialism (Ugar, 2023b). This chapter acknowledges the issue of funding deficit as a challenge to financing trustworthy AI projects, in line with the notion of institutional trust, tailored to the African audience and demands embracing AI intervention for specific issues on the African continent.

The Onto-Existential Factor

Focusing on the claim of misalignment between second-wave AI and Afro-existential norms, Azeez and Adeate's (2020) analysis could situate the imperative of funding trustworthy AI projects tailored for Africa within an onto-normative context. Making their case, they argued that second-wave AI trends do not reflect the African norms of existence being factored into ordering algorithmic patterns that set up AI systems and programmes, and thus, AI cannot be ingrained within the trustworthiness framework in Africa. The reason for this, they submit, is that Afro-existential practices unsettle with the individualist principle which underlines second-wave AI and therefore, a conversation around the development and application of communal interpretation of AI is important. Justifying this claim, they further argue that Western ethical patterns, which inform the features of second-wave AI, such as statistical patterns, smart algorithms, specialised hardware, and big data sets, emerge from individualist notions. Proposing a way forward, they submitted that codifying communal values of African society into machines and other forms of robotics should narrow down the conversation of global context to Afro-ontological intelligence. Achieving this, we submit, is a step forward in building a robust institution of trust in Africa as well as bringing African values into the conversation on AI designs in the world. For us, Azeez and Adeate make a valid argument, however, leaving out the case of financing trustworthy AI projects by codifying communal values of African society, which we find prize-worthy in building institutional trust, into machines and other forms of robotics.

The Cultural Factor

We acknowledge the foregoing challenge, tracing it to the analysis provided by Segun (2021), in a comparatively expansive work, where this issue of misalignment is framed within the African cultural context. Segun's analysis touches on key issues such as artificial moral agency, patience, personhood, social robotics, and the principle of explicability, focusing on how the African worldview influences how they are understood in the context of AI tailored for African society. Focusing on the critical issue, Segun presents the argument that the Afro-ethical system is a collectivist system and its normative principles, especially the construal of what makes a right or wrong action, rest heavily on a collectivist disposition, demonstrating the view that an AI-tailored for African must imbibe the principles of collectivism. The collectivist society ensures that from birth people are integrated into cohesive in-groups that prioritise harmony, loyalty, and mutual respect, emphasising the defining principle of relationality. The goal is to ensure that AI as an agent has an important place in the decision-making matrix. Like Azeez and Adeate, Segun reckons that an AI tailored for an African audience is far-fetched when the power to create is not with African builders. We engage further with this point shortly.

The Educational Factor

Scholars such as Ade-Ibijola and Okonkwo (2023) have reckoned that the nature of AI education provided for local African talents may not support the tailoring of AI systems for an African audience. This is owing to the idea that much of the AI education curricula is Western-oriented, which is often focused on the guiding notion of individualism—a contrary worldview to the African collectivist and relational worldview. The implication is creating a development gap between the demands of AI solutions for African problems and the nature of education inculcated by Africa's local talents. At best, the local talents will only possess the theoretical skills required but lack the practical skills required for the development, implementation, and use of AI applications, unless they work within a Western-based environment. Making the case, Ade-Ibijola and Okonkwo (2023) argued that any project requires the right expertise to succeed, and AI is no exception. We argue that the right skills can only be given if Africa considers investing in an African AI education curriculum to produce AI engineers who can develop AI systems tailored for the African audience.

The Data Counter-Narrative Factor

Another concern that necessitates financing AI projects by Africans in order to gain robust AI institutions within the continent that can be trustworthy is the adverse implication emerging from non-African stakeholders leading the data-sharing conversation in Africa. The implication is that principles alien to African society are exported, silencing the principles driving the values of relationality and collectivism in African society. Assessing this situation, Abebe et al. (2021) made the case that although the datasets are often extracted from African communities, conversations around the challenges of accessing and sharing African data are too often driven by non-African stakeholders. These perspectives frequently employ deficit narratives, often focusing on the lack of education, training, and technological resources in the continent as the leading causes of friction in the data ecosystem. Therefore, they argued that these narratives obfuscate and distort the full complexity of the African data-sharing landscape. It is worth noting that continuing data access and sharing conversations by non-African stakeholders may frustrate research and policy design to alleviate poverty, inequality, and derivative effects in Africa (ibid.). We argue that tailoring AI projects to an African society requires finance to build a robust data infrastructure, acknowledging that the significance of data in the process of building AI technology has risen to an unparalleled height—data is a critical infrastructure necessary to build AI systems, specifically for the African audience.

The Techno-Colonialism Factor

There is the argument that the West's algorithmic invasion impoverishes the development of local products while also leaving the continent dependent on Western software and infrastructure (Birhane, 2020; Ugar, 2023b). The colonisers' first encounter with Africa in history was characterised by unilateral power and domination over colonised people, as seen in Birhane's (2020) analysis, seizing control of the social, economic, and political spheres by reordering, and reinventing social order in a manner that benefits it. What is worth noting is that traditional colonialism is often spearheaded by political and government forces, and digital colonialism is driven by corporate tech monopolies—both of which are in search of wealth accumulation (ibid.). Sharing the same view, Ugar (2023b) argues that techno-colonialism specifically means the transfer of technology and its values and norms from one locale to another, which has become a serious concern with the advancement of socially disruptive technologies of the Fourth Industrial Revolution (4IR), like artificial intelligence and robots (ibid.). Drawing from Ugar's (2023b) analysis, it is pertinent for Africa to finance their trustworthy AI projects, acknowledging the fact that technologies are not abstractly designed but based on the experiences of human relations in the society where they are designed. This encompasses facts such as technologies that come with the values of their designers and the cultural orientation of the locus from which they are designed (ibid.). We allude that given the histories of technological colonialism and extortion of Africans by foreign tech companies, it is imperative for Africans to build institutions that they can trust to enable them to create their trustworthy AI designs.

The Project-Management Factor

Across the world, AI project owners face three main challenges, but Africa suffers the implications more compared to other regions of the world (Campos-Zabala, 2023). The first challenge has to do with the phenomenon of limited budget, and this refers to low internal funding powers. In responding to this challenge, countries with clear funding strategies and planning consider a phased approach, starting with smaller, less costly AI projects that can provide quick wins (ibid.). Another type of challenge is the issue of limited AI expertise, and this is often tied to the educational reason—the absence of an African-tailored curriculum for African builders, encompassing technical skills, knowledge, certification, soft skills, interdisciplinary skills and so on. In response, non-African countries look for partnerships with universities or consider upskilling current employees (ibid.). The third main challenge is perhaps the most difficult to address: high data costs. This is a bigger problem in the African context due to the lack of a robust and structured data ecosystem (Ade-Ibijola & Okonkwo, 2023). Responding to this issue, most countries leverage open-source data, negotiate partnerships for data sharing, or invest in generating their data (ibid.). Peculiar to the African context is the absence of a trust framework that can coordinate approaches to gathering data AI for projects in African society. We argue for heavy financial investments into the African social technology space, enabling a healthy procedure of gathering and handling locally sourced data within the African context for AI projects.

Examining Available Avenues for Funding Africa's Trustworthy AI Projects: Pros and Cons

In the African setting, the successful path to trustworthy AI is closely related to the availability and distribution of financial resources. Despite the growing interest in AI in Africa, a critical concern arises when examining the funding landscape for trustworthy AI development, particularly the glaring disparities between developed countries and Africa. We contend that designing trustworthy AI in Africa requires human agency and oversight, technical robustness and safety, privacy and data governance, transparency, etc., which come at a cost, however critical for driving innovation, fostering the growth of AI technologies, and building trustworthy AI institutions and ecosystems in Africa (Díaz-Rodríguez et al., 2023). However, the continent lags in this area, with limited funding available for AI-related projects.

Funding is the lifeblood of any AI initiative, and securing it requires careful planning and strategy (Campos-Zabala, 2023). As of today, no document can be referenced that contains Africa's strategy for sourcing funds, locally and internationally, in executing AI projects tailored for the

African audience. When embarking on an AI journey, the interconnection between funding, implementing AI initiatives, and measuring their impact is vital (ibid.). In this area today, there is a huge gap between African funders and the rest of the world. Global AI advancement projects in Europe, the United States, and China cannot be compared with Africa in terms of funding and how designers are responding to their people's experiences with AI solutions. Focusing on this as a fact amplifies the call for building trustworthy AI institutions to develop trustworthy social technologies that resemble the African worldview while acknowledging that the issue of funding deficit must be addressed to advance trustworthy AI research, which prioritises setting up trustworthy AI design parameters in the African context.

According to Gerrard et al. (2019) of the World Economic Forum (WEF), the estimated global economic value of AI is $15.7 trillion in 2030. Even though AI is at its early stage, the financial benefits of AI are as follows: $7.0 trillion for China, $3.7 trillion for Northern America, $1.8 trillion for Northern Europe, and $1.2 trillion for Africa. Africa sits at the bottom of the economic gains from AI. Furthermore, in 2022, the US spent $47.7 billion in AI investments, China spent $13.4 billion, and Germany spent almost a billion euros; while in 2021, the European Union Council targeted an annual investment of €20 billion to AI, while Africa spent $2.0 billion in 2021 and $3.0 billion in 2022. Additionally, despite having low investment in AI, some of Africa's AI investments come from Western investors, such as the Google and IBM innovation labs and the Nigerian Kudi AI, which Silicon Valley funds. Given the low financial investment we have highlighted above, we aim to show how this funding gap obscures and shapes the conversation on design parameters and variables of a trustworthy AI with an African outlook.

Funding the Design Locally

This funding option is sometimes described as internal funding, and usually, it is used to describe the funding that comes from within. It may include reinvestment of profits, operating budgets, or internal fundraising efforts (Campos-Zabala, 2023). In most cases, it is preferred for some reasons, such as possessing control for using funds, greater flexibility, and reduced risk in terms of not depending on their parties (ibid.). Considering some worth noting pros, local funding AI design for African audiences creates local empowerment, surrendering control and both resource and man management to the indigenous users of AI products. Another key advantage is the attainment of cultural relevance. This speaks to the fact that the people can do as they see fit to a project, in most cases, reflective of cultural norms, since the project activities are funded internally. One other advantage that is often mentioned is sustainable development. There is the argument that any monies used are expected to result in a commensurate return to where the monies are taken. Internal funding is released with the idea that it drives development in society. While internal funding has numerous benefits, there are downsides to it. For example, one of the downsides is the problem of limited resources. Most organisations or countries in Africa lack resources to execute their scale of projects, and in most cases, the lack of resources is often measured in terms of funding. Another way that internal funding is measured is to acknowledge the expertise gap. Inadequate internal funding means that the right expertise, which is most of the time expensive, cannot be hired. The risk of isolation is another disadvantage of relying on internal funding. Most AI project initiatives pool together internal and external funding from different sources to expand their access and reach. In cases where there is total reliance on internal refunding, expansion is difficult, leading to risk isolation and denying exposure to global perspectives and best practices.

Sourcing Funds Elsewhere

As the previous funding option, this funding option is sometimes described as external funding, encompassing funding sources which may include government grants and incentives, venture capital and private equity, corporate partnerships and collaborations, crowdfunding, and alternative financing methods (Campos-Zabala, 2023). In essence, funders send the message, "If you want the money, then build trustworthy AI!" (Gardner et al., 2022). As requirements, a compelling business case and a clear demonstration of potential return on investment must be included in the proposal. What is worth thinking about is whether African AI project owners approach potential funders with a business case. Nevertheless, there are some advantages to this funding option. For example, there is access to capital, sometimes referred to as venture capital or private equity (ibid.). Firms provide both funding and expertise. However, they require, in exchange, an equity stake in your business and usually, they ask for a term sheet—a document that outlines the key terms of an investment agreement. It includes information such as the amount of investment, the valuation of the company, and the terms of repayment. Another advantage is that external funding allows for large-scale projects with the potential for greater impact and innovation. On the other hand, the disadvantages are numerous. There is a case of dependency on external funding, which may make the project susceptible to changes in global economic conditions, geopolitical factors, or the agenda of the funding organisations. Also worth considering is the problem of cultural misalignment, where projects funded from abroad might face challenges in terms of cultural practices, potentially leading to implementation issues. In addition, there is the issue of stringent conditions whereby external funders may impose conditions and expectations that could conflict with the project's original goals, potentially compromising its integrity. Additionally, there might exist stringent control from external funders on what kinds of technologies out to be produced. This problem is similar to what is conceptualised as funding bias in evidence-based medicine (Ugar, 2023c). This form of control may pertain to what kinds of design, policies, and frameworks ought to govern the AI ecosystem in Africa, a similar problem faced in the development of technologies like vaccines and medications in evidence-based medicine (Ugar, 2023c).

Collaboration and Partnerships

Another viable funding source involves collaboration and partnership. It is a usual practice in this type of funding that partners or collaborators provide financial support and potentially access to resources, market opportunities, and expertise (Campos-Zabala, 2023). Identifying companies with an interest in AI and negotiating mutually beneficial terms are critical steps in this process (ibid.). Considering some advantages of this funding option, one is the synergy of resources. Collaboration brings together diverse skills, resources, and perspectives, enhancing the overall strength of the project. Another advantage is risk sharing; it involves partners sharing financial and operational risks, making the project more resilient to challenges. Worth considering is the advantage of global–local balance in the sense that partnership allows for a balance between local knowledge and global expertise, ensuring a more comprehensive and effective project. There are several disadvantages, and one is coordination challenges. It is a matter of fact that managing collaboration can be complex, especially when dealing with diverse partners with varying priorities and working styles. Another disadvantage is that decision-making may be slower due to the need for consensus among partners, potentially impacting the project timeline. Lastly, the challenge of intellectual property concerns, in which issues related to the ownership and control of intellectual property can arise in collaborative projects, requiring careful negotiation.

Recommendations

As hypothesised, this chapter has demonstrated that trustworthy AI is not based on trusting the technologies but on the institution where the technology emanates. We further argued that Africa can only achieve a trustworthy AI ecosystem when they become agents of their designs; that is, designing their AI technologies within their institutions and crafting policies from their socio-ethical and cultural practices to shape the designs and use of AI. Nonetheless, we are not oblivious to some challenges that may arise in achieving a trustworthy design of AI in Africa. The major problem which we addressed is the issue of funding deficit, which is the bane of trustworthy AI projects tailored for the African audience. Based on the discussions and findings, we provide some novel and actionable recommendations.

a. Hybrid Funding Approach: We recognise that project interests may be diverse, and it is crucial to be flexible to take advantage of available funding options. Therefore, we propose a funding policy that keeps all three funding options open for easy access.
b. Innovative Programmes: Launch a Tech Collaborators Fellowship programme that pairs African AI enthusiasts with global mentors, in terms of connecting local innovators with international funding opportunities and creating an avenue for local designers to showcase their commitment to upskill for knowledge transfer, to both help African designer develop local expertise and foster cross-cultural collaboration, injecting fresh perspectives into the tech experience of their people.

c. Financial Security for Innovative Safeguarding: This involves creating a smart funding charter that transparently records and verifies project goals to help external funds adhere to agreed-upon terms, safeguarding against mission drift. This will encompass project alignment with local needs and a financial safety net, providing stability even if a funding source experiences changes.
d. Collaborative Governance Framework: This goal is to develop an AI platform that can facilitate real-time decision-making in collaborations that is adaptable to the evolving needs of the project to minimise delays. This governance will encompass defining roles and responsibilities in a visually engaging format—a co-creation compact movement and providing constant communication support for collaborators, thereby mitigating communication gaps, and maintaining engagement throughout the project.
e. Forming Local AI Pressure Group: The problem of funding deficit in Africa's conversation of trustworthy AI projects has a political undertone. There must be an advocacy group that can pressure the government into channelling resources into more fruitful endeavours in support of widening and developing the tech ecosystem in Africa.

Conclusion

This chapter highlighted the importance of designing trustworthy artificial intelligence (AI) systems grounded in the African context. It argues that most current AI designs deployed in Africa are not shaped by policies informed by the cultural norms, ethos, worldviews, and ethics emerging from Africa. The chapter identified financial constraints as one of the impediments to the design of AI in Africa to achieve trustworthiness. It recommended a hybrid funding approach, innovative programmes, financial security for innovative safeguarding, a collaborative governance framework, and forming a local AI pressure group to address the funding deficit. The chapter also emphasised the need for African governments to provide an enabling environment for AI development and innovation to thrive. Overall, the chapter argued that Africans ought to be wary of designs emerging from elsewhere, given African histories of colonialism, neo-colonialism, and techno-colonialism. The chapter recommended that Africans build institutions that care for the well-being of Africans to guide the design of trustworthy AI.

References

Abebe, R., Aruleba, K., Birhane, A., Kingsley, S., Obaido, G., Remy, S. L., Sadagopan, S. (2021, March). *Narratives and counternarratives on data sharing in Africa.* In Proceedings of the 2021 ACM conference on fairness, accountability, and transparency (pp. 329–341).

Ade-Ibijola, A., & Okonkwo, C. (2023). Artificial intelligence in Africa: Emerging challenges. In *Responsible AI in Africa: Challenges and opportunities* (pp. 101–117). Springer.

Agarwal, S., & Mishra, S. (2021). *Responsible AI*. Springer.

Angwin, J., Larson, J., Mattu, S., & Kirchner, L. (2016). *Machine bias*. ProPublica. https://www.propublica.org/article/machine-bias-risk-assessments-in-criminal-sentencing. Accessed: 29 September 2023

Azeez, A., & Adeate, T. (2020). Second-wave AI and Afro-existential norms. *Filosofia Theoretica: Journal of African Philosophy, Culture and Religions, 9*(3), 49–64.

Bachmann, R. (2020). Trust and institutions. In D. C. Poff & A. C. Michalos (Eds.), *Encyclopedia of business and professional ethics* (pp. 1–6). Springer. https://doi.org/10.1007/978-3-319-23514-1

Baier, A. (1986). Trust and antitrust. *Ethics, 96*(2), 231–260.

Baier, A. (2013). What is trust? In D. Archard et al. (Eds.), *Reading Onora O'Neill*. Routledge.

Bauer, P. C. (2019). Conceptualizing trust and trustworthiness. *Journal of Trust Research*, 9(1), 1–17. https://doi.org/10.1080/17513072.2019.1573460

Bekker, S. (2021). *Fundamental rights in digital welfare states: The case of SyRI in the Netherlands.* Netherlands Year Book of International Law 2019: Yearbooks in International Law: History, Function, and Future.

Benk, M., Tolmeijer, S., von Wangenheim, F., & Ferrario, A. (2022). The value of measuring trust in AI-a socio-technical system perspective. arXiv preprint arXiv:2204.13480

Benjamins, R., Barbado, A., & Sierra, D. (2019). *Responsible AI by design in practice.* arXiv preprint arXiv:1909.12838

Birhane, A. (2020). Algorithmic colonization of Africa. *SCRIPTed, 17*, 389.

Buolamwini, J., & Gebru, T. (2018). Gender shades: Intersectional accuracy disparities in commercial gender classification. *Proceedings of Machine Learning Research, 81*, 1–15.

Campos-Zabala, F. J. (2023). Scaling AI. *Grow your business with AI: A first principles approach for scaling artificial intelligence in the enterprise* (pp. 479–507). Apress.

Cheng, L., Varshney, K. R., & Liu, H. (2021). Socially responsible ai algorithms: Issues, purposes, and challenges. *Journal of Artificial Intelligence Research, 71*, 1137–1181.

Clarke, R. (2019). Principles and business processes for responsible AI. *Computer Law & Security Review, 35*(4), 410–422.

Coeckelbergh, M. (2012). Can we trust robots? *Ethics and Information Technology, 14*, 53–60.

Díaz-Rodríguez, N., Del Ser, J., Coeckelbergh, M., de Prado, M. L., Herrera-Viedma, E., & Herrera, F. (2023). Connecting the dots in trustworthy Artificial Intelligence: From AI principles, ethics, and key requirements to responsible AI systems and regulation. *Information Fusion, 99*, 101896.

Dignum, V. (2019). *Responsible artificial intelligence: How to develop and use AI in a responsible way* (Vol. 1). Springer.

Du'ran, J. M., & Formanek, N. (2018). Grounds for trust: Essential epistemic opacity and computational reliabilism. *Minds and Machines, 28*, 645–666.

Eke, D. O., Chintu, S. S., & Wakunuma, K. (2023). Towards shaping the future of responsible AI in Africa. In *Responsible AI in Africa. Social and cultural studies of robots and AI* (pp. 169–193). Palgrave Macmillan. https://doi.org/10.1007/978-3-031-08215-3_8

Floridi, L., & Sanders, J. W. (2004). On the morality of artificial agents. *Minds and Machines, 14*(3), 349–379.

Foley, R. (2001). *Intellectual trust in oneself and others*. Cambridge University Press.

Forrest, K. (2021). *When machines can be judge, jury, and executioner: Justice in the age of artificial intelligence*. World Scientific Publishing Co., Pte. Ltd.

Fuglsang, L., & Jagd, S. (2015). Making sense of institutional trust in organisation: Bridging institutional context and trust. *Organisation, 23*(1), 23–39.

Gambetta, D. (1988). *Trust: Making and breaking cooperative relations*. Blackwell.

Gardner, A., Smith, A. L., Steventon, A., Coughlan, E., & Oldfield, M. (2022). Ethical funding for trustworthy AI: Proposals to address the responsibilities of funders to ensure that projects adhere to trustworthy AI practice. *AI and Ethics, 2*, 277–291.

Gerrard, J., Webster, K., McNaughton, S., & Kukutai, T. (2019). *By 2030, AI will contribute $15 trillion to the global economy*. World Economic Forum. https://www.weforum.org/agenda/2019/08/by-2030-ai-will-contribute-15-trillion-to-the-global-economy/. Accessed: 30 November 2023.

Greene, C. (2023). AI and the social science: Why all variables are not created equal. *Res Publica, 29*, 303–319. https://doi.org/10.1007/s11158-022-09544-5

Gunning, D., Stefik, M., Choi, J., Miller, T., Stumpf, S., & Yang, G.-Z. (2019). XAI—Explainable artificial intelligence. *Science Robotics, 4*(37).

Hardin, R. (2002). Trust and Trustworthiness. New York: *Russell Sage Foundation.*

Hardin, R. (2006). *Trust*. Polity Press.

Hardwig, J. (1991). The role of trust in knowledge. *The Journal of Philosophy, 88*(12), 693–708.

Hawley, K. (2012). *Trust: A very short introduction*. Oxford University Press.

Hawley, K. (2014). *How to be trustworthy*. Oxford University Press.

HLEG. (2019). *Ethics guidelines for Trustworthy AI*. European Commission. https://ec.europa.eu/futurium/en/ai-alliance-consultation.1.html

Holton, R. (1994). Deciding to trust, coming to believe. *Australasian Journal of Philosophy, 72*(1), 63–76.

Jones, K. (1996). Trust as an affective attitude. *Ethics, 107*(1), 4–25.

Jones, K. (2004). Trust and terror. In P. DesAutels & M.U. Walker (Eds.), Moral Psychology: *Feminist Ethics and Social theory* (pp. 3–18). Rowman & Littlefield.

Kennard, J. G. (2022). 'Trusting-to' and 'trusting-as': A qualitative account of trustworthiness. *Philosophical Studies*, 179(8), 2509–2539.

Lagerspetz, O. (2015). *Trust, ethics and human reason*. Bloomsbury Academic.

Lahno, B. (2001). Institutional trust: A less demanding form of trust? *Revista Latinoamericana de Estudios Avanzados, 15*, 19–58.

Lehrer, K. (1999). Self-trust: A study of reason, knowledge and autonomy. *Philosophical and Phenomenological Research, 59*(4), 1045–1055.

Leslie, D. (2019). *Understanding artificial intelligence ethics and safety*. Alan Turing Institute. http://arxiv.org/abs/1906.05684

McCullom, R. (2017). *Facial recognition technology is both biased and understudied* [Online]. https://undark.org/2017/05/17/facial-recognition-technology-biased-understudied/?msclkid=b913148dd10911ec932962fbfdac1591

Mikalef, P., Conboy, K., Lundström, J. E., & Popovič, A. (2022). Thinking responsibly about responsible AI and 'the dark side'of AI. *European Journal of Information Systems, 31*(3), 257–268.

Misztal, B. A. (1996). *Trust in modern societies: The search for the bases of social order*. Blackwell.

Mollering, G. (2006). *Trust: Reasons, routine, reflexivity*. Emerald Group Publishing.

Nickel, P. J., Franssen, M., & Kroes, P. (2010). Can we make sense of the notion of trustworthy technology? *Knowledge, Technology & Policy, 23*(3), 429–444. https://doi.org/10.1007/s12130-010-9124-6

OECD. (2017). *OECD guidelines on measuring trust*. OECD Publishing. https://doi.org/10.1787/9789264278219-en

Peters, D., Vold, K., Robinson, D., & Calvo, R. A. (2020). Responsible AI—Two frameworks for ethical design practice. *IEEE Transactions on Technology and Society, 1*(1), 34–47.

Pettit, P. (1995). The cunning of trust. *Philosophy & Public Affairs, 24*(3), 202–225.

Ryan, M. (2020). In AI we trust: Ethics, artificial intelligence, and reliability. *Science and Engineering, 26*, 2749–2767.

Schiff, D., Rakova, B., Ayesh, A., Fanti, A., & Lennon, M. (2020). *Principles to practices for responsible AI: Closing the gap*. arXiv preprint arXiv:2006.04707

Segun, S. T. (2021). Critically engaging the ethics of AI for a global audience. *Ethics and Information Technology, 23*(2), 99–105.

Slosser, J. L., Aasa, B., & Olsen, H. P. (2023). Trustworthy AI: A cooperative approach. *Technology and Regulations*, 58–68. https://doi.org/10.26116/techreg.2023.006

Sztompka, P. (1999). *Trust: A sociological theory*. Cambridge University Press.

Ugar, E. T. (2023a). Rethinking remote work, automated technologies, meaningful work and the future of work: Making a case for relationality. *Philosophy and Technology, 36*(32). https://doi.org/10.1007/s13347-023-00634-7

Ugar, E. T. (2023b). The fourth industrial revolution, techno-colonialism, and the Sub-Saharan Africa response. *Filosofia Theoretica: Journal of African Philosophy, Culture and Religions, 12*(1), 33–48.

Ugar, E. T. (2023c). Evidence-based medicine and patient-centred care: A patient's best interest analysis. *Revista Opinao Filosofica, 14*, 1–18. https://doi.org/10.36592/opiniaofilosofica.v14.1072

United Nations. (2021). *Recommendation on the ethics of artificial intelligence.*

van De Poel, I. (2020). Embedding values in artificial intelligence (AI) systems. *Minds and Machines, 30*, 385–409.

Wakunuma, K., Ogoh, G., Eke, D. O., & Akintoye, S. (2022, May). *Responsible AI, SDGS, and AI governance in Africa*. In 2022 IST-Africa Conference (IST-Africa) (pp. 1–13). IEEE. https://doi.org/10.23919/IST-Africa56635.2022.9845598

CHAPTER 7

Context-Aware Africa-Led Designing of Responsible Artificial Intelligence Technologies

Michael Zimba, Maha Jouini, and Angella K. Ndaka

Artificial intelligence (AI) is a general purpose technology (GPT), which is currently enjoying increasing use in strategic decision-making and military affairs. The AI revolution brings significant changes into the current and future socio-economic national and international systems, with AI applications expected to tilt the global balance of power in favour of actors who strategically invest and use this emerging technology. AI-assisted automation is also changing prevailing socio-economic production models on the global scale, and sooner or later, these technologies are expected to

M. Zimba (✉)
Malawi University of Science and Technology, Mikolongwe, Malawi
e-mail: mzimba@must.ac.mw

M. Jouini
Witwatersrand University, Johannesburg, South Africa

A. K. Ndaka
University of Otago, Dunedin, New Zealand

D. O. Eke et al. (eds.), *Trustworthy AI*,
https://doi.org/10.1007/978-3-031-75674-0_7

exert systemic impacts on the current global order. However, the distribution of AI technologies and skills is not uniform, with the global north dominating the space. Even within the global south, Africa lags way behind other continents. TIME100AI, a list of world's 100 top AI influencers released in September, 2023, confirmed this dominance by the global north. While this has been the trend with all the three preceding industrial revolutions, Africa needs to change this narrative and champion context-aware Africa-led designing of responsible AI technologies. In this chapter, we argue for the need for Africa to rise and lead the development of its own AI technologies that are reflective of the rich Africa's socio-cultural societies. We begin by demonstrating the extent to which Africa lags behind other continents, by analysing the landscape of AI technologies and skills. Secondly, we highlight the cost of inaction should Africa continue to wait on other continents for the development of AI technologies. We then go ahead to make recommendations on what African governments, universities and other institutions can do to increase local capacity in terms of AI skill sets, feeder datasets, foundational infrastructures and potential local AI market. Throughout our discussion, we advocate for responsible ethical AI-by-design whose co-creation is not left only to AI technologists and engineers, but includes a diversity of stakeholders such as AI ethics experts, sociologists and civil society leaders. We believe that you can only develop a more representative and fair AI technology through involvement of an inclusive diverse team of co-creators.

Introduction

Artificial intelligence (AI) has taken the world by storm. It has truly emerged as a "general purpose technology" (GPT). AI is currently enjoying increasing use in strategic decision-making and military affairs. The AI revolution brings significant changes into the current and future socio-economic national and international systems, with AI applications expected to tilt the global balance of power in favour of actors who strategically invest and use this emerging technology. However, the distribution of AI technologies and skills is not uniform, with global north dominating the space (Endo et al., 2021; Graham, 2015). Even within the global south, Africa lags way behind other continents. This typical narrative of Africa's approach to many technological revolutions has to be seriously discussed and challenged.

In this chapter, we argue for the need for Africa to rise and lead the development of its own AI technologies that are reflective of Africa's socio-cultural societies. In Section "Analysis of the AI Technologies and Skills Landscape for Africa" we demonstrate the extent to which Africa lags behind other continents, by analysing the landscape of AI technologies and skills. Section "Power, Politics and Knowledge Hegemony" highlights the dominance of the global north, the intricate intimacy of AI and our ways of life, our cultures and beliefs, the power, politics and knowledge hegemony. Section "Current Policy and Regulatory Landscape" unveils the policy and regulatory efforts taking place on the Continent. We cluster the locus nations for our discussion into Anglophone and Francophone and we sample some countries from these two clusters and look closely at their AI governance initiatives. In Section "Regulatory Landscape in Anglophone Africa", we highlight the cost of inaction should Africa continue to wait on other continents for the development of AI technologies. We conclude the chapter in Chapter 6 by making recommendations on what African governments, universities and other institutions can do to increase local capacity in terms of AI skill sets, feeder datasets, foundational infrastructures and potential local AI market. Throughout our discussion, we advocate for responsible ethical AI-by-design whose co-creation is not left only to AI technologists and engineers, but includes a diversity of stakeholders such as AI ethics experts, sociologists and civil society leaders. We believe that you can only develop a more representative and fair AI technology through involvement of an inclusive diverse team of co-creators.

Analysis of the AI Technologies and Skills Landscape for Africa

In most parts of the world, Africa is not well understood, a kind of *terra incognita*. While many misconstrue the continent as a country, many see it only from the prism of its problems: slavery, poverty, droughts, wars, underdevelopment, diseases and human rights violations. It is not clear to such people that Africa is a continent filled with a diverse collection of countries, peoples, beliefs and cultures. It is not a place often associated with technological innovations.

This gloomy picture of Africa is not entirely incorrect. Africa is indeed underdeveloped. Many regions within the continent grapple with sporadic electricity, limited and inconsistent internet access and poor infrastructure. Furthermore, there are no or incomplete datasets due to a lack of comprehensive data collection mechanisms. Even when data is available, its accuracy and standardisation can be questionable, with institutions and agencies collecting data in varied formats, making consolidation and analysis a daunting task. Infrastructural limitations further exacerbate the situation. Limited and inconsistent internet access, especially in rural locales, hinders real-time data collection and the use of cloud-based AI processing. Moreover, the sporadic electricity supply in certain areas disrupts consistent AI operations.

The lack of hyperscalers offering public cloud services in Africa is also a challenge to the continent as far as AI development and uptake is concerned. With the exception of South Africa, in which Amazon, Microsoft and Oracle provide public cloud services with Google joining the list lately, the lack of public cloud services in Africa mean that enterprises need to invest in their own AI infrastructure on premises along with a complimentary workforce, which makes AI deployments even more complex and challenging. The continent also faces a significant skill gap in digitalisation. While there's a burgeoning interest in AI, there's a palpable shortage of professionals' adept in AI. Financial constraints pose another hurdle. On the other hand, the initial setup for AI, encompassing both hardware and software, can be prohibitively expensive, and securing adequate investment remains challenging.

Despite the myriad of challenges that, not surprisingly, make Africa lag behind on AI development and uptake, the continent is beginning to bridge the gap with several initiatives. Many African countries are recognising the potential of AI in improving data collection, analysis and decision-making. International organisations and partnerships are also helping in this regard. AI adoption in Africa is currently limited to a few countries like South Africa, Nigeria, Ethiopia, Kenya, Zimbabwe, Togo, Libya, Rwanda, Morocco, Egypt and Ghana. Many African nations are putting in place the essential elements for technology adoption, including infrastructure, data ecosystems, STEM education and governance systems.

Nevertheless, AI is being developed and used in specific cultural, economic, political and social contexts across Africa. The development and use of AI is not at the same pace among African countries, and we note most advanced countries in terms of AI use and AI Market size are English-speaking countries such as: Kenya, Nigeria, South Africa, Egypt, Ghana and Uganda. These countries benefit from strong innovation hubs supported with many accelerators and incubators in the region, such as Nailab, or iHUB in Kenya, SPARK and 440NG in Nigeria, or TechStars in South Africa. These countries also rely on government initiatives, such as the ecosystem village with multiple innovation spaces, e.g. Innovation Village Kampala in Uganda. In Ghana, the African Artificial Intelligence Research Centre (CAIR) was established in 2018. This Centre aims to train AI experts and develop innovative projects in different fields such as health, agriculture and energy. In South Africa, the African Institute of Mathematical Sciences offers a master's degree in AI sponsored by Facebook and Google.

Developmental partners of Africa are also aiding development, uptake and governance of AI. At the global AI summit, the UK government and other partners announced a $100 million programme on responsible AI, starting with Africa. Nearly half of this will come from the UK to invest in technology partnerships, while the International Development Research Centre (IDRC) in Canada is contributing more than $8 million. Other partners include the Bill and Melinda Gates Foundation and USAID. IDRC has already committed nearly $50 million in more than 30 countries to support AI research and innovation, with a focus on areas such as feminist AI, AI for global health and AI for COVID response.

Power, Politics and Knowledge Hegemony

While it is generally accepted that AI technologies have significant social implications, this is often viewed as an externality especially at design stages, until it is time to deploy and evaluate those innovations. Technology is both physical (artefacts/hardware) and non-physical (virtual/software), it is an intellectual result of people, things, interests and other abstractions and occurrences (Agnew, 2013; Jordan, 2014). The socio-cultural, corporate and political relations that underlie AI design, while they form implicit basis of technical decision-making, are often obscured by explicit attention given to technological innovations (Hasselbalch, 2021, 2022; Šabanović, 2010). Hasselbalch, (2021) argues that technology conception is done through imaginations by experts and powerful actors, who transform these imaginaries to actual artefacts. This transformation involves a symphonic relationship of interests, politics and power that shapes the realities of technology design and deployment. She further presents AI sociotechnical imaginaries as fertile spaces that are waiting to be colonised, and hence "open for active occupation of interests"

(p. 17). These power voids often get occupied by powerful tech actors, who in turn shape how power is distributed—including how institutions are assembled, how technology funding policies are framed, how business models are positioned and how different interests are positioned within the technology design and adoption (Ndaka, 2023). Depending on which group is more privileged in these ecosystems, certain knowledge, contexts, realities and expertise are being marginalised (Eke & Ogoh, 2022; Eke et al., 2023; Rosendahl et al., 2015), and their perspectives are continuously being fenced out.

Studies have shown that, more often, the socio-material context and dynamics of use and potential users come into focus once AI and robotic technologies have been developed and are ready to be evaluated (Ndaka, 2023; Šabanović, 2010). The association of AI with advanced technology is so complex and invisible that its functioning can only be understood by experts (Diefenbach et al., 2022), further promotes the distancing of social and technological decision-making in AI and emerging technologies from broader society (Griffin et al., 2023; Šabanović, 2010). Faced therefore with the complexity of advanced sociotechnical systems, everyday people—the potential users of technologies—hand over their agencies and leave decisions about the directions for the current and future development of AI to technical experts and powerful technology actors (Griffin et al., 2023). Most of the time, such developments move ahead without contextual and inclusive discussions of the consequences of technological innovation for relevant user groups, contexts and society as a whole. The potential users of AI technologies come to occupy a secondary role in the process of designing AI and robotic technologies; they are present in the field as objects of study, rather than active subjects and participants in the construction of the future uses of AI and robots (Hoffman, 1990). It is assumed that the AI technologies are neutral and therefore, not harmful to the users (Hasselbalch, 2021; Latour, 2011). In this techno-optimistic perspective on the place of AI in society, technological innovation pushes society to a better, though vaguely described, future (Šabanović, 2010).

Contrary to the dominant narrative and practices in AI, the relationship between AI and society is neither autonomous nor linear. AI-based systems design is influenced from its very inception by the socio-cultural assumptions of designers, as well as political and corporate interests of technology owners and other powerful technology actors (Hasselbalch, 2021, 2022; Šabanović, 2010). Thus, the applicability, reproducibility and sustainability of AI outcomes as well as the other implications are heavily dependent on socio-cultural and socio-material contexts in which AI is funded, developed and deployed, respectively (Ndaka, 2023; Ruttkamp-bloem, 2023). Some studies have shown that the impact of "faulty" AI (incompatible and/or biased), even when it has been removed from circulation or corrected, leaves imprints that cannot be obliterated (Ehsan et al., 2022). Evaluation of the social interactions and socio-material dynamics that shape AI are therefore important in that they regulate the production relations as well as define how ideals and notions of the social relations are inclusively enacted at design and reproduced in AI (Ndaka, 2023; Šabanović, 2010). Since social choices, whether explicit or implicit, form an integral part of daily decision-making practices in AI development, the same choices are the drivers of how design is conceptualised, how investment is done, including how significance of AI results are measured (Šabanović, 2010).

The examples above share a techno-centric, linear view of history, in which both technological growth and social progress are inevitable, the former driving the latter. This reflects what STS scholars call technology determinism which drives permissionless innovation—which rarely allows for the perspectives of the users to emerge (Dotson, 2015). In such framing, technological development can be predicted and controlled, while societal dynamics are less easily determined, but expected to follow the technological imperative. There is little recognition that AI and emerging technologies might have differentiated effects on different parts of society including socio-cultural contexts (Ruttkamp-bloem, 2023). While studies also show that the ethics that govern technology will be dominantly shaped by societal values (Robinson, 2020), these aspects are also getting little or no recognition in the current AI debates in Africa (Eke et al., 2023). The technologically optimistic view of the future of AI in society assumes an upper-middle-class, and white male Caucasian subject, similar to AI and robotics researchers themselves, as its main consumer (Šabanović, 2010). But more importantly they are meant to foreground unlimited capitalistic growth of technology (Mclennan, 2015). In an environment where technology growth in Africa has been a preserve of foreign technology companies and discourses (Endo et al., 2021; Graham, 2015), this potentially closes out rich perspectives from African indigenous communities, as well other diverse groups.

Furthermore, other potential complexities relating to legal liability may arise, raising questions like who is responsible when systems get it wrong—the technology owners, software developers, the subject matter experts, or the Internet service providers? (Susskind & Susskind, 2017). The possibility for technological progress to have controversial or socially disruptive effects, such as in the bombings of Nagasaki and Hiroshima or the Bhopal disaster, also evades the purview of these reductionist depictions of our AI and robotic futures (Šabanović, 2010). This is especially because of the layers of barriers created by power asymmetries which not only reduce users to objects of technology, but also transform tech designers to ethical chameleons who have to adapt to different, and sometimes conflicting interests (Liu et al., 2022). Worse is when conceptualisation of technology from regions like Africa is controlled by large corporates who provide funding. In such cases, choices about who is included in conceiving tech for Africa are problematically made by people in power to address a desired outcome. Thus, the politics of mattering as discussed by Burch and Legun (2021), who questioned who matters to be included and how far can they be included in conceiving technology that impacts them directly. Exercise of power by those who wield it creates a barrier to existing perspectives to emerge in technology (Hadorn et al., 2008; Rosendahl et al., 2015), but also induces complacency to the local actors in the way they imagine technology (Ndaka, 2023), and allow for local perspectives to emerge.

Current Policy and Regulatory Landscape

On the regulatory front, the absence of robust data protection laws in many African countries raises concerns about data privacy and ensuring the ethical use of AI. Cultural and societal factors play a role too. There's often scepticism or a lack of understanding about AI, leading to hesitancy in the adoption of AI-driven methods. Additionally, AI models trained on non-local data might miss the unique socio-cultural nuances intrinsic to African regions.

Murat Drumus considers that: "*The problem is not the AI itself but the biased data with which AI models are driven. Many see data preparation and data labelling as deadly trouble and want to start as soon as possible with training or model optimization*" (Durmus, 2021).

On the policy front, several countries, including Ethiopia, Ghana, Morocco, Rwanda, South Africa, Tunisia and Uganda, are taking steps to formulate AI policies. Ghana and Uganda have participated in the Ethical Policy Frameworks for Artificial Intelligence in the Global South project, conducted in 2019 by UN Global Pulse and the German Federal Ministry for Economic Cooperation and Development. This project aimed at developing local policy frameworks for AI, and Ghana continues to collaborate with UN Global Pulse to map its AI ecosystem and craft a blueprint for its national AI strategy. Rwanda has also developed a national AI policy centred on the ethical and responsible use of AI for social and economic progress.

Mauritius unveiled its AI strategy in 2018, emphasising the transformative potential of AI and emerging technologies in addressing the nation's socio-economic challenges. It envisaged AI as a crucial driver for revitalising traditional economic sectors and forging a new path for national development in the coming decade and beyond. The strategic areas highlighted encompassed manufacturing, healthcare, fintech, agriculture, and the management of smart ports and maritime traffic.

Since May 2022, the African Union High-Level Panel on Emerging Technologies (APET) has been working on the AU's AI strategy, (AUDA-NEPAD, 2024). In addition, South Africa, Benin, Egypt, Ghana, Nigeria, Senegal, Tunisia, Côte d'Ivoire, Ghana, Morocco, Nigeria and Senegal have all made significant progress in developing their own AI strategies or frameworks. While encouraging, these national strategies also complicate the implementation of a comprehensive AU strategy.

Francophone African countries are slightly lagging behind the Anglophone counterparts, in terms of AI governance. However, we notice the recent establishment of the appropriate climate for AI uses in several Francophone countries. Senegal, Rwanda, Mauritius and Benin have officially launched their AI policy, national roadmaps and Data regulations. We now sample a few strategies from the two clusters of African countries.

Regulatory Landscape in Anglophone Africa

Anglophones countries have seen government initiatives and policies framework on AI. Egypt, for example, launched its national AI strategy in 2021, with the aim of benefiting from AI in achieving the country's sustainable development goals. The Strategy will spur Egypt's regional cooperation with the African and Arab countries and place Egypt as an engaged international player in AI. Egypt AI national strategy considers Arabic language processing a "vital" sector, "allowing not only a more user-friendly way of interacting with other AI and advanced systems but also a powerful tool for extracting contextual information".

Egypt has identified four major challenges in the AI strategy, starting with Brain Drain of AI talent. Trained workforce is leaving the country to work in other economies post training. The second challenge is the slow adoption of and resistance to AI by the private sector, the main contributor to GDP. The private sector in Egypt contributes up to 60% of national GDP, having an employment share of ~74% (European Bank for Reconstruction and Development EBRD). The third challenge is the large capital investments required for many AI projects and the slow, uncertain return of investment (ROI) associated with them. These deter many investors. The fourth challenge is the relative monopolisation of AI research by so-called AI superpowers which includes few countries, as well as large technology companies. The monopoly makes it difficult for a country like Egypt to put its stamp on the map of international AI research. These challenges are not necessarily unique to Egypt.

Regarding Regulation, the national council for AI launched the Egyptian charter for responsible AI. The charter is divided in two parts. Firstly, the Charter highlights general guidelines overarching rules applicable to all members of the ecosystem in order to:

- Use AI for well-being of citizens (SDG Goals)
- Ensuring transparency and explainability so that any end-user using an AI system has the fundamental right to know when he or she is interacting with an AI system and not a human being, and call the AI ecosystem to promote capacity building and public awareness programmes about AI.
- Ensuring accountability principle so that all stages of the lifecycle of the AI system are subject to the relevant laws of the Arab Republic of Egypt, including laws of consumer protection, personal data protection and anti-cybercrimes.

Secondly, the Charter highlights the implementation guidelines, which are technical considerations, mainly applicable to any entity developing, deploying, or managing AI systems. Such guidelines include ensuring that:

- AI projects should be preceded by a pilot or proof of concept (PoC) to ensure the technical viability of the solution.
- Government entities, private companies, academic and research organisations and any other entities developing AI systems should work with a representative sample of the beneficiaries of their AI systems.
- Developers of AI systems are encouraged to examine and address the cultural impact of AI systems.
- All members of the AI ecosystem should facilitate access by the scientific community to their data for research purposes, provided that such access does not come at the expense of privacy.
- Foreign companies looking to roll out their AI products in Egypt must adhere to the Egyptian Charter for Responsible AI.

The second country we sample from the Anglophone cluster is Kenya. Kenya developed a six action plan to spur using AI to uphold Kenya's economy, using AI to filter out deserving candidates for allotting, using AI in Health, Finance, Agriculture and Food Security.

Similarly, Kenya has proposed a Robotics and Artificial Intelligence Society Bill, whose primary objective is to formally establish the Kenya Robotics and Artificial Intelligence Society as a professional body, mandated to regulate, promote and facilitate the activities of robotics and AI practitioners within the country. The Bill provides for a framework for AI ethical use in the Kenyan AI ecosystem as well as urging AI stakeholders to establish and enforce standards and best practices for robotics and AI. The Bill calls for the development and use of robotics and AI in Kenya guided by following principles:

- The public good: Robotics and AI shall be developed and used for the benefit of the people.
- Human safety and security: Robotics and AI shall be developed and used in a manner that is safe and secure for humans.
- Privacy and data protection: The privacy and data protection of individuals shall be respected in the development and use of robotics and AI.
- Accountability: Those who develop and use robotics and AI shall be accountable for their actions.

- Diversity and inclusion: The development and use of robotics and AI shall be inclusive of all Kenyans

In fact, Kenya's tech sector is opposed to a new bill aimed at regulating artificial intelligence in the country, arguing that it would stifle innovation and put off investors (Siele, 2023). The Bill has not yet passed for approval by the Kenyan Parliament.

In South Africa, despite a growing AI ecosystem which includes startups, think tanks and academic institutions, there is not yet a comprehensive legislation that governs the use of AI and machine learning in the country. Personal information, on the other hand, is governed by the South African Protection of Personal Information Act (POPIA). However, South Africa was part of the Southern African countries which authored the Windhoek Statement on Artificial Intelligence in Southern Africa in September 2022. Broadly, the Statement recommends advancing of standard-setting initiatives, fostering of cooperation and exchanges of expertise involving all AI stakeholders, as well as to strengthening cooperation between Southern African countries and UNESCO, as foreseen through the SADC-UNESCO Joint Programme of Action 2022–2025, including through the establishment of a Southern African coordination mechanism for the Implementation of the UNESCO Recommendation on the Ethics of AI. In addition, the Windhoek Statement calls for:

- AI and Responsible Data Governance: Establish frameworks for Data Governance and Promote transparency of AI algorithms and mitigate the digital divide by fostering open and competitive markets and so on.
- Capacity Building and awareness building: Launch programmes to promote public awareness and literacy, strengthen the capacities of governments, civil society and the private sector to understand and make sense of AI technologies and applications.
- Investment and Infrastructure: Expand investments towards infrastructure development, to address issues such as access to electricity, connectivity, spectrum, data centres, cybersecurity (CSIRTs) and cloud. Support the establishment of an AI incubation centre and empower mutual understanding of the AI-related investment needs among technology experts and policymakers who determine the funding of these initiatives.

- Education, Research, Development and Innovation: Promote the decolonisation of the design and application of AI technologies, including by decolonising education at all levels, developing Africa-centric AI curricula and involving communities to co-design inclusive and ethical AI applications, taking into account heritage and indigenous knowledge systems, as well as Increasing investment in ethical AI-related research, development and innovation.

The statement also highlighted the role of AI in Environment and Disaster Risk Reduction and called for using AI as leverage to enhance gender equality and empower Female entrepreneurship.

Landscape Regulatory in Francophone Africa

In Francophone countries of Africa, we take a closer look at Senegal's AI Governance. Recently, Senegal has experienced rapid adoption of information and communication technologies, a successful digital transformation, with factors that have accelerated the emergence of Artificial Intelligence. The Senegalese Government has lined up initiatives to support its tech-industry, including defining a roadmap. The roadmap aims at shaping the future of Senegal's digital landscape and making a meaningful impact on society through AI responsible use. The roadmap has four aspirations, namely.

- Make AI, a locomotive of the global digital economy, the catalyst for the PSE for the benefit of youth employment, economic performance, public transformation, sovereignty digital technology and the attractiveness of Senegal.
- Direct AI in Senegal as a priority towards improving the living conditions of the population and the achievement of the SDGs.
- Make AI an opportunity for Senegal to be the driving force behind a technological partnership on a regional or sub-regional stage.
- Ensure that AI in Senegal is responsible, ethical, trustworthy and respectful of sovereign prerogatives.

We also consider the case of Rwanda. The National Artificial Intelligence Policy for the Republic of Rwanda, calls for using AI towards its socio-economic development and attainment of SDGs, with a clear vision of enabling Rwanda to become a global centre for AI research and innovations well as achieving the following national Rwandese objectives of:

- Positioning Rwanda as Africa's AI Lab and Responsible AI Champion
- Building 21st Century Skills and AI Literacy
- Creating an Open, Secure, Trusted Data Ecosystem as an Enabler of the AI Revolution
- Driving Public Sector Transformation to Fuel AI Adoption
- Accelerating Responsible AI Adoption in the Private Sector

In terms of regulations, the Government of Rwanda is working on strengthening the capacity of regulatory authorities to understand and regulate AI aligned with emerging global standards and best practices such as fairness and bias mitigation, trust and transparency, accountability, social benefit and privacy and security.

Generally, among the Francophone countries, Senegal, Rwanda and Tunisia lead the way. They are in the phase of training and enhancing the legal processes in digital transformation and AI ethical governance. Legislations and laws are yet to be updated especially to respond to the rise of foundation and generative models. Generative AI brings new intricate data protection policies.

Given the complexity of generative AI issues and its medium and long-term impacts, it is necessary to create a sovereign entity (a centre of competence) dedicated to research and training on the ethical issues of AI systems related to their scientific, technical, societal and environmental issues (CCNE, 2023).

Implication of AI Inaction

If Africa does not take deliberate measures to invest in the development of its own technologies, it risks falling prey to digital colonisation. Digital colonialism, which refers to the use of digital technologies for the purpose of politically, economically and socially dominating another nation or territory, has detrimental consequences on the socio-economic development of the colonised nations. "Classical" European colonialism was based on the annexation of territories, the establishment of infrastructures, the exploitation of resources, indigenous knowledge and almost free labour. This organised the world by an unequal international division of labour (Kwet, 2019).

Digital colonialism is rooted in the domination of what the digital world encompasses: software, hardware and connection networks, mainly by the global north. Today it is inseparable from the traditional tools of capitalism and authoritarian governance, labour exploitation, intelligence services and the hegemony of the ruling classes.

In 2016, the French Philosopher, Éric Sadin, described the dominance of the global north as "*colonisation of a new kind, which is not experienced as violence suffered, but as an aspiration ardently desired by those who intend to submit to it*" According to Eric, the spirit of Silicon Valley would be a world colonisation enterprise. The digitalisation of the world will establish an industry of life thanks to the support of actions by algorithms. The capacity for initiative and creativity is denied, reduced to exalting orders emanating from programmes administered by external providers.

Artificial intelligence is now created as a kind of «surmoi» endowed with the intuition of truth and called to guide in all circumstances of our lives towards the greatest comfort and supposed efficiency as observed by Eric Sadin.

> It is not the human race that is in danger, but the human figure endowed with the faculty of judgement and that of acting freely and consciously. (Sadin, 2016)

As a result of this new colonialism, Africa may face a technological dependency especially with the rise of Generative AI and other foundational models. The dependency can harm the African future by choking Africa's socio-economic development. Big Data and other international companies benefit from African industries and control it. The immediate effect we note is the increase in brain drain and decrease in Africa-led niche AI initiatives.

Indeed, the lack of appropriate technologies is threatening African digital sovereignty as observed by Pierre Belanger (2019).

> Digital sovereignty is control of our present and destiny as manifested and guided by the use of technology and computer networks. Pierre Belanger

AI systems function by being trained on a set of data relevant to the topic they are tackling. However, companies often struggle to "feed" their AI algorithms with the right quality or volume of data necessary, either because they don't have access to it or because that quantity doesn't yet exist. This imbalance can lead to discrepant or even discriminatory results when operating your AI system. This issue, otherwise known as the bias problem, can be prevented if you make sure to use representative and high-quality data. In addition, it would be best to start your AI journey with simpler algorithms that you can easily comprehend, control for bias and modify accordingly. Africa cannot afford to be inactive in this aspect. She needs to generate data, representative of her diverse context and build capacity to develop effective and efficient algorithms. She needs to develop or domesticate AI governance policies and standards.

Utilising public and global AI tools offers numerous advantages but also comes with its own set of challenges. One notable benefit is the accessibility of these tools. Open-source frameworks like TensorFlow and PyTorch provide a cost-effective entry point for developers, enabling a broader community to leverage the power of AI.

Community support is another significant advantage. With a large user base, public AI tools benefit from collaborative efforts, resulting in constant updates, improvements and a wealth of shared knowledge. Developers can tap into online forums and resources, making problem-solving more efficient.

However, there are drawbacks to relying solely on public AI tools. Security and privacy concerns are paramount. Since these tools are open to the public, there's an inherent risk of unauthorised access and data breaches. It becomes crucial to implement additional security measures when handling sensitive information. Moreover, customisation can be a limitation. Public AI tools might not align perfectly with specific business needs. Companies with unique requirements may find it challenging to adapt pre-existing models to suit their distinctive use cases.

In summary, the advantages of public AI tools lie in their accessibility, affordability and the strength of their user communities. On the flip side, the potential security risks and limitations in customisation may prompt organisations to carefully weigh the benefits against their specific requirements. Striking a balance between public and private AI tools often proves to be an effective strategy, ensuring a mix of innovation, accessibility and security in AI development.

Recommendations to African Institutions and Individuals

In light of the preceding discussion, we recommend that every African country should define its AI agenda. There should be substantial investment in national AI infrastructure to support, coordinate and drive the agenda. Countries should identify national universities and institutes to facilitate skills and policy development in order to institutionalise the national AI ecosystem. There should also be deliberate efforts to drive AI literacy and awareness among the populace. Attention should be paid to demographic communities that are usually under-represented in technology development.

African institutions of higher learning should be strengthened in AI, particular computer science, IT, ICT and other departments which offer AI training. It is vital that these departments keep track of rapid research advances in AI. They also need to recruit and retain top notch expertise in AI.

On the policy and regulatory front, African countries need to pace up in putting the necessary frameworks. Currently, the corpus of text relating to the digital sector, in several countries in Africa, does not take into account the ethical principles established by international organisations, notably those of UNESCO and the resolution 473 of the African Commission on Human and Peoples' Rights (ACHPR). As a result, we recommend the establishment of normative frameworks consistent with the societal values of African people and the principles on AI of the OECD, UNESCO AI guidelines and Windhoek Proclamation on AI ethics among others. We call for cooperation between governments, the private sector and civil society organisations. Countries should also promote the advancement of AI by creating collaborative platforms, such as councils and working groups. We encourage businesses and traders based in Africa or in Diaspora, to invest in AI research and Tech-industry and working to change classic investment models such as purchasing land and construction, explaining the importance of investing in technology and the future of the digital economy in Africa especially with the progress of African Free trade Zone and its impact on facilitating business in Africa. We wish to see an increase in the number of national AI strategies and policies. We advocate for the advancing of African Value Systems and Principles in AI Ethics such as the Windhoek Statement on Artificial Intelligence in Southern Africa. We call upon African policy makers to enhance their efforts to build a secure and inclusive infrastructure to support the local development of an inclusive AI.

References

Agnew, J. A. (2013). Arguing with regions. *Regional Studies, 47*(1), 6–17. https://doi.org/10.1080/00343404.2012.676738

AUDA-NEPA. (2024). *AUDA-NEPAD white paper: Regulation and responsible adoption of AI in Africa towards achievement of AU agenda 2063.* https://www.nepad.org/blog/taking-continental-leap-towards-technologically-empowered-africa-auda-nepad-ai-dialogue

Burch, K. A., & Legun, K. (2021). *Overcoming barriers to including agricultural workers in the co-design of new AgTech: lessons from a COVID-19-present world.* https://doi.org/10.1111/cuag.12277

CCNE. (2023). *Systèmes d'intelligence artificielle générative : enjeux d'éthique.* Avis 7 du CNPEN. 30 juin 2023. https://www.ccne-ethique.fr/sites/default/files/2023-07/CNPEN-Avis7-%20SIAgen-enjeux%20d%27e%CC%81thique-2023-07-04-web.pdf

Diefenbach, S., Christoforakos, L., Ullrich, D., & Butz, A. (2022). Invisible but understandable: In search of the sweet spot between technology invisibility and transparency in smart spaces and beyond. *Multimodal Technologies and Interaction, 6*(10). https://doi.org/10.3390/mti6100095

Dotson, T. (2015). Technological determinism and permissionless innovation as technocratic governing mentalities: psychocultural barriers to the democratization of technology. *Engaging Science, Technology, and Society, 1,* 98–120. https://doi.org/10.17351/ests2015.009

Ehsan, U., Singh, R., Metcalf, J., & Riedl, M. (2022). The algorithmic imprint. In ACM International Conference Proceeding Series (pp. 1305–1317). https://doi.org/10.1145/3531146.3533186

Eke, D., & Ogoh, G. (2022) Forgotten African AI narratives and the future of AI in Africa. *The International Review of Information Ethics, 31*(1). https://doi.org/10.29173/irie482

Eke, D., Chintu C. S., & Wakunuma, K (2023). Introducing responsible AI in Africa. In: *Responsible AI in Africa: Challenges and opportunities* (pp. 1–11). Springer International Publishing Cham.

Endo, M., Onoma, A. K., & Neocosmos, M. (2021). African politics of survival: Extraversion and informality in the contemporary world. M. Endo, A. K. Onoma, & M. Neocosmos (Eds.). [Book]. LANGAA RPCIG.

Graham, M. (2015). Contradictory connectivity: Spatial imaginaries and technomediated positionalities in Kenya's outsourcing sector. *Environment and Planning A, 47*(4), 867–883. https://doi.org/10.1068/a140275p

Griffin, T. A., Patrick, B., & Jos, G. (2023). The ethical agency of AI developers. *AI and Ethics*, 0123456789. https://doi.org/10.1007/s43681-022-00256-3

Hadorn, G. H., Pohl, C., Hoffmann-Riem, H., Biber-Klemm, S., Wiesmann, U., Grossenbacher-Mansuy, W., Zemp, E., & Joye, D. (2008). Handbook of transdisciplinary research. In *Handbook of transdisciplinary research*. Springer Netherlands. https://doi.org/10.1007/978-1-4020-6699-3

Hasselbalch, G. (2021). Data ethics of power. In *Data ethics of power*. https://doi.org/10.4337/9781802203110

Hasselbalch, G. (2022). Data pollution & power: White paper for a global sustainable development agenda on AI.

Hoffman, L. W. (1990). Constructing realities: An art of lenses. *Family Process, 29*, 1–12. https://doi.org/10.1111/j.1545-5300.1990.00001.x

Jordan, T. (2014). Deliberative methods for complex issues: A typology of functions that may need scaffolding. *Group Facilitation: A Research and Applications Journal, 13*(13), 50–71.

Kwet, M. (2019). *Digital colonialism: US empire and the new imperialism in the Global South*. https://doi.org/10.1177/0306396818823172

La Silicolonisation du monde l'irrésistible expansion du libéralisme numerique. (2016). Eric Sadin. L'ECHAPPE publication.

Latour, B. (2011). Drawing things together. In *The map reader: Theories of mapping practice and cartographic representation* (pp. 65–72). Wiley. https://doi.org/10.1002/9780470979587.ch9

Liu, Z., Zhang, H., Wei, L., & Ge, X. (2022, March). Moral Chameleons: The positive association between materialism and self-interest-triggered moral flexibility. *Journal of Research in Personality, 100*, 104268. https://doi.org/10.1016/j.jrp.2022.104268

Mclennan, S. J. (2015). Information technology for development techno-optimism or information imperialism: Paradoxes in online networking, social media and development techno-optimism or information imperialism: Paradoxes in online networking, social media and development. https://doi.org/10.1080/02681102.2015.1044490

Ndaka, A. K. (2023). *Sustainable AI techno-futures? Exploring socio-technical imaginaries of Agtech in Aotearoa New Zealand* (Dissertation). University of Otago.

Pierre Belanger, La souverainete numerique. (2019). *les diners de l'Institut Diderot , Diderot Institute publication*. https://www.institutdiderot.fr/wp-content/uploads/2019/12/Diner-La-Souverainete%CC%81-nume%CC%81rique-Page.pdf.

Robinson, S. C. (2020, October). Trust, transparency, and openness: How inclusion of cultural values shapes Nordic national public policy strategies for artificial intelligence (AI). *Technology in Society, 63*. https://doi.org/10.1016/j.techsoc.2020.101421

Rosendahl, J., Zanella, M. A., Rist, S., & Weigelt, J. (2015). Scientists' situated knowledge: Strong objectivity in transdisciplinarity. *Futures, 65*, 17–27. https://doi.org/10.1016/j.futures.2014.10.011

Ruttkamp-bloem, E. (2023). Epistemic just and dynamic AI ethics in Africa. *Springer International Publishing*. https://doi.org/10.1007/978-3-031-08215-3

Šabanović, S. (2010). Robots in society, society in robots. *International Journal of Social Robotics*. https://doi.org/10.1007/s12369-010-0066-7

Siele. (2023). Kenya's tech industry is fighting AI regulation plans. *Semafor Magazine*. https://www.semafor.com/newsletter/12/05/2023/kenya-ai-regulation-tech

Susskind, R., & Susskind, D. (2017). The future of the professions: How technology will transform the work of human experts. *Journal of Nursing Regulation*. https://doi.org/10.1016/s2155-8256(17)30099-6

The AI Thought Book. 2021. Inspirational thoughts & quotes on artificial intelligence. Murat Durmus , Hardcover Publication.

CHAPTER 8

Exploring Trustworthy AI in Nigeria: A Focus on Safety in Road Traffic

Memunat A. Ibrahim, Elizabeth Williams, and Kehinde Aruleba

Introduction

While Africa's realities and perspectives are grossly under-represented in artificial intelligence (AI) research, regulation, and ethics discourse (Eke et al., 2023; Jobin et al., 2019), AI systems like chatbots and autonomous drones are increasingly being adopted in many African countries to solve local problems (Borokini et al., 2023; Roberts, 2022). This is potentially problematic: African AI ethics experts have expressed concerns about the under-representation of African voices and contexts in trustworthy AI

M. A. Ibrahim (✉)
Australian National University, Canberra, ACT, Australia
e-mail: memunat.ibrahim@anu.edu.au

E. Williams
Australian National University, Canberra, ACT, Australia
e-mail: elizabeth.williams@anu.edu.au

K. Aruleba
University of Leicester, Leicester, UK
e-mail: ka388@leicester.ac.uk

D. O. Eke et al. (eds.), *Trustworthy AI*,
https://doi.org/10.1007/978-3-031-75674-0_8

research and regulation (Rathenau Instituut, 2021). AI systems' performances rely on their training dataset's familiarity with their use cases. Hence, they tend to perform erroneously, discriminately, or harmfully when used in situations (NTSB, 2019) or populations that are under-represented in their training data (Buolamwini & Gebru, 2018; Koenecke et al., 2020). According to Abebe et al. (2021), a reason for their discriminatory or unsafe performances in such scenarios is the asymmetry in the voices shaping AI development and regulation. These make the safety and trustworthiness of AI in Africa questionable.

Trustworthy AI systems are systems in which the values, goals, and welfare of their users, stakeholders, and the societies in which they are deployed are integrated into their design (European Commission AI HLEG, 2019; Nevala, 2020). To guide AI systems' trustworthy development and use in different contexts, many agencies have published various trustworthy or ethical AI principles, including: *Recommendation on the ethics of artificial intelligence* (UNESCO, 2021) and *Ethics guidelines for trustworthy AI* (European Commission AI HLEG, 2019). For instance, the European Union's (EU) trustworthy AI guideline targets the development and use of AI systems in the EU, regardless of where they originate. Hence, it reinforces ***European values or ethics*** (European Commission AI HLEG, 2019). These efforts towards ensuring that AI systems are trustworthy is crucial in facilitating their large-scale adoption and ensuring they benefit society and individuals upon adoption. Although African values, goals, or welfare are currently under-represented in global trustworthy AI discourse, many African countries are working towards publishing trustworthy or ethical AI principles (GNA, 2022; Tijani, 2023; UN Global Pulse, 2019).

The trustworthiness of an AI system can only be adequately defined, understood, and evaluated when that system is considered with respect to environmental and social contexts that are representative of where it will be used. However, most trustworthy AI principles originate from Western contexts, and most AI systems are designed and trained for such contexts. In addition, most African cultures, ethics, and contexts differ significantly from Western contexts, yet many of these systems are deployed for use in Africa. It is, therefore, imperative that African perspectives are represented in trustworthy AI discourse.

To further this discussion, we will focus on safety as an example of key trustworthy AI requirements. AI safety has no standard definition, but is nevertheless a critical requirement for any AI system's use (House,

2023) and trust (Leslie, 2019). This is because AI systems have demonstrated their ability to be erroneous, exposing people to discrimination and dangers when carelessly used in unanticipated or under-represented real-world scenarios (NTSB, 2019; Staff, 2020). Ensuring AI safety in their deployed environments requires critically and holistically considering their safety implications in their potential use cases and deployed (social) environments and integrating these into their development and lifecycle. But how do we ensure AI safety in Africa?

In this chapter, we explore this question by adopting a sociotechnical lens to AI safety in Africa. This is because safety issues are sociotechnical and are relevant beyond AI technologies. We believe AI safety research can benefit from existing safety research and conversations in safety-critical sociotechnical systems like road transportation systems, which maintain well-established and tested safety cultures and mechanisms (Zachmann, 2014), and have continuously integrated new technologies. This chapter presents an African perspective on AI safety through a case study of the Nigerian road transport system, exploring the question: "What lessons can be learned about safety in the Nigerian road transport system to help ensure AI safety in Nigeria?"

We begin exploring this question by defining AI safety and safety approaches as documented in literature. Afterwards, we contextualise our discussion of the potential safety implications of AI systems in Nigerian social systems by presenting how some existing safety issues in the Nigerian road transport system can be traced to the design, introduction, and regulation of automobiles—widely adopted technological artefacts—in Nigeria, and then exploring AI safety in the context of AI-driven vehicles or autonomous vehicles (AV) in Nigeria. We conclude this chapter by highlighting lessons and recommendations that may aid AI systems' safety in Nigeria and similar countries.

We take Nigerian road traffic as the research focus because it is a high-risk multi-agent environment where conversations around safety are critical and ongoing. Nigeria is a dominant vehicle import market in Africa, where vehicles with AI-enabled features are increasingly being introduced (National Bureau of Statistics, 2021), thereby offering a useful case study for: (a) exemplifying how the large-scale adoption of technologies in sociotechnical systems can impact society, (b) demonstrating the importance of Africa's representation in AI safety and trustworthiness discourses, and (c) ensuring AI safe adoption in Nigeria and Africa by learning from past and current issues.

Background

AI Safety and Safety Element Definitions

Generally, safety is defined as *freedom or security from danger, risk, loss, harm or when an agent or object is not likely to be harmed or cause harm* (Leveson, 2011; Merriam Webster, 2023). There are various descriptions of AI safety (Jobin et al., 2019), some of which we highlight here. The IEEE's Ethically Aligned Design (EAD) defined AI safety as *"the probability that a system will either perform its functions correctly or will discontinue its functions in a well-defined safe manner"* (Laplante, 2017). They essentially described safety as the prevention of errors from AI systems. In contrast, systems engineers noted that a system can perform its functions correctly or reliably and still be unsafe, and vice versa; and accidents can occur from the interaction of its various reliable and faultless components (Leveson, 2011; Sommerville, 2011). That is, system safety goes beyond reliability; it is a system-level property that emerges from the interactions of the system's parts. With AI systems, safety transcends technological failures and impacts; it includes *"social impacts on individual wellbeing and public welfare"* (Leslie, 2019), and preventing harmful outcomes from AI systems by ensuring they behave as intended when used (European Commission AI HLEG, 2019).

Risk-Based Approach to AI Safety

Leslie (2019) described ensuring AI safety in real-world environments—which are usually filled with uncertainties—as "a difficult and unremitting task" involving AI risk management. This view conforms with the predominant approach to AI safety in existing trustworthy AI guidelines (European Commission, 2021; Tabassi, 2023; UNESCO, 2021). A risk-based safety approach requires identifying and managing the potential risks and harms of AI systems to people, their communities, and the environment, and adopting safety mechanisms that reflect the scale of the identified risks for the AI system in various contexts and use cases (European Commission AI HLEG, 2019). The EU's AI Act adopts this approach; therein, AI systems were first categorised into levels based on their potential risks (minimal to unacceptable) and were then regulated based on their risk level. AI used in automobiles, medical devices, and law enforcement were categorised as high-risk AI systems—high-risk AI are used in high-risk or life-and-death scenarios where mistakes can result in deaths (NTSB, 2019)—and they recommended that humans are kept in the loop of their decision-making (European Commission, 2021; UNESCO, 2021).

Towards AI risk management, various AI risks have been identified. These include functional failures, erroneous or adversarial performances, malicious use of AI, cyberattacks, privacy breaches, national security, human rights violations, fatalities, and mass surveillance (European Commission, 2021; House, 2023; UNESCO, 2021). In addition, the potential harms of AI systems identified so far relate to physical, economic, social, political, cultural, or mental harms to humans, which can diminish people's trust in AI (European Commission AI HLEG, 2019; Leslie, 2019; Tabassi, 2023; UNESCO, 2021). Overall, AI safety and risk management mechanisms must reflect the safety factors in the diverse real-world environments where AI systems might operate, including their environments, the people and their values, and other technologies involved.

A Snapshot of Safety and Its Elements
From the highlighted descriptions above, we define AI safety as the security of humans and the environment from harms and risks stemming from the development and use of AI. We also present some recurring elements of AI safety. These elements relate to safety but are not safety. They are:

i. Risks—the probability of hazards resulting in harm (Sommerville, 2011).
ii. Hazards—conditions that can cause harm, such as failures (Leveson, 2011).
iii. Harm—loss or damages experienced by one or more individuals (Sommerville, 2011).
iv. Risk assessment—determines the possibility of harm and informs perceived safety (Sommerville, 2011).

The Need for African Realities and Values in Shaping AI Safety

While existing trustworthy AI guidelines like the EU's are good starting points, the values represented so far do not represent global human cultures or realities. The under-representation of African perspectives and African AI safety requirements in global trustworthy AI means that currently, there are no comprehensive guides to help stakeholders identify and manage AI risks and safety issues peculiar to Africa, and protect Africans' safety, values, and welfare; potentially exposing Africans to avoidable harm from AI systems. This is evidenced by findings relevant to AI-enabled AV. In 2017, Mercedes noted that South African road conditions introduce unique challenges for AV intelligence (Luchian, 2017). As such, there is a need to explore the safety of AI systems like Tesla's partial self-driving vehicles currently being manufactured overseas and sold to Africa (Okonkwo, 2023).

Exploring AI safety in African contexts presents an opportunity: adequately considering African realities and experiences in AI design and AI safety will diversify the research contexts informing the design and use of such technologies and may help identify new challenges of AI integration in society. This can facilitate the design of AI systems that are safer and more robust. In the following section, we explore Nigerian road traffic as an example of sociotechnical systems that are increasingly integrating AI-driven technologies. We highlight some of its safety practices and challenges towards identifying safety considerations for AI in Nigerian road traffic.

Exploring Safety in Nigerian Road Traffic

The Nigerian road transport system is a sociotechnical system that fulfils a societal function: safe mobility. Sociotechnical systems integrate humans, societal structures, infrastructure, networks, user practices, regulation, knowledge, technologies, and symbolic meanings to fulfil their function (Geels, 2005). This section discusses the societal aspect of the topic. It presents a brief history of automobiles in Nigeria and highlights existing safety challenges, factors, and mechanisms in road traffic based on a critical review of road safety literature, reports, and data from the Nigerian Federal Road Safety Corps (FRSC) and the National Bureau of Statistics (NBS).

Automobility Adoption in Nigeria—Why and How?

In the early 1900s, Nigeria's increasing population size, urbanisation, and progress in agriculture and manufacturing created challenges in its road transportation, such as poor traffic management, inefficient transport services, and inadequate infrastructure (Commerce & Wilken, 1964;

Ogunbodede, 2008; Pavoris, 2021). Automobiles, including lorries and motor cars from Britain, were introduced into the Nigerian road transport system to address these challenges. Afterwards, road networks were developed to facilitate the automobiles' smooth integration into society, connect railway stations with the major urban centres, and enhance the movement of extracted resources and the British colonial officers in Nigeria (Ogunbodede, 2008).

These developments enabled the large-scale adoption of vehicles in Nigeria, making road transportation Nigeria's primary mode of transportation (Asunloye, 2019). The transitions also introduced and amplified safety challenges and hazards like vehicle overloading, road degradation, road insecurities, and accidents. These were managed by establishing policies, regulations, and an automotive industry (Ede & Chamberlain, 2013), as well as road agencies such as the FRSC—created in the late 1980s to monitor and ensure road safety across Nigeria (FRSC, 2007)—and jobs like traffic police. Despite these efforts, Nigeria still records road safety challenges like a high road crash rate, indicating a gap between its current road safety mechanisms and its safety needs.

Safety Impacts of Automobility in Nigeria: Road Accidents and Hazards

Road Accident Causes

One of the major impacts and challenges of automobile adoption on Nigerian road traffic is its high accident rate. In 2022, the FRSC recorded 13,656 road crash cases and 45,836 road casualties (National Bureau of Statistics, 2023). To identify the causes of Nigerian road accidents, we analysed the 2022 Nigerian road transport data (National Bureau of Statistics, 2023). Therein, the FRSC identified accident causative factors (or road hazards) and categorised them into environmental (the road), mechanical (the vehicles), and human (road users) factors, and others (FRSC, 2022). As shown in Table 8.1, human factors constituted 14,273 (79.21%) of the 18,019 road crash causes recorded in 2022—disproportionately the highest cause of road crashes. Most human causative factors were speed violations, sign light violations, and dangerous driving, accounting for 51.99%, 7.61% and 5.93% of road crashes causes respectively (National Bureau of Statistics, 2023).

However, looking at road accident causes in isolation of their contexts is simplistic; it inherently omits how the interactions between the different

Table 8.1 Frequency distribution of road crash causative factors

Causative factors' category	*Frequency*	*Proportion*
Human	14,273	0.79211
Mechanical	1936	0.10744
Environment	85	0.00472
Others	1725	0.09573
Total	18,019	1

causative factors systemically contribute to road crashes. Taking a systems perspective, we drew on news articles to gather more context about road accident causes. This showed that while accidents caused by reckless driving are due to human factors, reckless driving is sometimes due to environmental factors like bad roads. On bad roads, drivers are forced to drive slowly or maneuver recklessly to avoid damaging their vehicles because of the deplorable state of the roads. Criminals may also lay ambush on motorists on such roads, exposing motorists to heightened insecurities and damages (Ajide, 2020; Boniface, 2021). In such situations, drivers may drive aggressively and break some traffic laws to avoid ambush and protect their lives and property (Naku, 2022). This demonstrates that: (a) road accidents are both hazards (can result in harm like death) and harm (an outcome of another hazard like reckless driving), and (b) road accident factors are systemic, as accidents are generally caused by a combination of these causative factors. Addressing road safety issues, therefore, requires systems approaches.

Other Road Hazards
Drawing on road safety manuals, news articles, and literature on Nigerian road users' safety experiences, we identified additional relevant road hazards that affect Nigeria's road safety that are not reported in the NBS' road transport data.

Insecurity
Road insecurity refers to road users' exposure to dangers and crimes such as kidnapping, theft, and ambush from criminals (Ugwuoke et al., 2023). It is a major challenge on Nigeria's highways and has negatively impacted the transport sector and the nation's economy (Boniface, 2021). In the case of kidnapping, mass transit passengers are most vulnerable to being robbed or kidnapped by criminals who pretend to be commercial drivers

(Sahara Reporters, 2023). These criminals may attack the passengers and cause adverse physical, financial, or mental harm to them. Similarly, drivers may be attacked by road criminals, especially on isolated or bad roads, to rob, carjack, or potentially murder them (Boniface, 2021).

Non-compliance with Traffic Laws

Unskilled or reckless driving, which translates to traffic law non-compliance, is prevalent on Nigerian roads, especially from commercial drivers, motorcyclists, and tricyclists (Ayoyinka, 2023; Uzondu et al., 2022). While traffic laws exist to guide road users' safe interactions on roads, commercial drivers, motorcyclists, and tricyclists tend to disregard traffic laws and speed limits (Uzondu et al., 2022); thus, most accidents happen with commercial vehicles (National Bureau of Statistics, 2023).

Traffic Congestion and Pollution

The large-scale adoption of vehicles on Nigerian roads negatively impacts the environment and public health. Nigeria currently imports about 98% of its vehicles, most of which are used and old vehicles from Europe and the USA (National Bureau of Statistics, 2021). Used or old vehicles are hazardous as many of them are degraded, faulty, or discarded vehicles with expired parts from developed countries, and are prone to breaking down. Such imports are a form of e-waste dumping in Nigeria and Africa as a whole (UNEP, 2020a). These vehicles' usage heightens traffic congestion, accident rates, and they emit 90% more carbon than new ones (Segun, 2019; UNEP, 2020b). Smoke and gas emissions from vehicles significantly contribute to air pollution in Nigeria, which impacts the climate and the residents' health.

Existing Road Safety Mechanisms

Various safety mechanisms have been introduced to address the safety challenges that emerged from automobility adoption in Nigeria. Existing road safety mechanisms are designed around the three main categories of current road accident causes—humans, vehicles, and the environment. These mechanisms vary; they can be formal, technological, or cultural. The formal safety mechanisms in Nigeria are usually based on global standards and the safety mechanisms in the countries where the vehicles are from (FRSC, 2012). They are then adapted to fit the specificities of Nigerian road traffic. This section discusses some existing road safety mechanisms in Nigeria that are relevant to AI safety discourse.

Road Laws and Regulation

Laws and regulations are official safety mechanisms that ensure road users sense their environments, communicate with others, behave in accordance with the set standards, and manage commuters' shared expectations on roads. These regulations may be focused on technology and infrastructure engineering, or road users and their interactions (Admin, 2019; FRSC, 2012).

Vehicle design standards are examples of technology-focused regulations. They specify the mandated features in vehicles and dictate the standards for vehicle parts for them to be considered safe by design and roadworthy (iRAP, 2022). Since most of the vehicles used in Nigeria are imported and used, this means that the standards of these vehicles are primarily not defined in Nigeria. For instance, AI-enabled driver assistant features have been mandated in vehicles in the EU and USA since 2022—the two major suppliers of vehicles used in Nigeria (European Commission, 2019; NHTSA, 2016). This means that from 2022, cars imported from these regions to Nigeria may have AI-driven driving automation (Okonkwo, 2023), whether they are standardised and regulated in Nigeria or not.

Traffic laws are human-focused safety mechanisms that guide road users' behaviours and interactions towards ensuring their collective safety. Traffic laws' validity depends on the geographical levels they cover. They may be (1) global-level, e.g. the UN Geneva Convention on Road Traffic; (2) national-level, e.g. the Nigeria highway code; or (3) regional-level or state-level laws. National and regional traffic laws and road signages are usually designed to address the local road traffic and safety issues they regulate while considering their road users' communication styles and abiding by international and national standards (FRSC, 2012). Figure 8.1 depicts a state-level road sign that uses visual and textual instructions and local terms like "danfo"—which means commercial bus—to communicate what vehicles are allowed on a Lagos bridge to diverse road users with varying communication needs.

Education, Management, and Enforcement

To promote road law compliance and enhance road safety, the government draws on various mechanisms to educate road users, manage road

Fig. 8.1 A road sign specifying the vehicles banned on Lagos Lekki-Ikoyi Link Bridge

safety, and enforce road laws. They include: regulatory road signages; traffic control; vehicle safety checklist and checks; traffic policing and monitoring; traffic violation punishments; vehicle registration—which also enforces vehicle insurance; regular vehicle roadworthiness test; drivers' licensing; drivers' education on traffic laws, norms, vehicle safety checks; and public education (DRTS, 2018; FRSC, 2007, 2022). Non-compliance with traffic laws is consequential. It can result in fines, jail time, or licence revocation for those culpable. To enhance road law compliance, data and AI-driven road technologies such as smart traffic control lights, CCTV cameras, and automatic number plate recognition are increasingly being adopted for traffic management and law enforcement (Bolanle, 2023; Burt, 2022; Nwafor, 2023).

Road Users' Situational Awareness and Communication

Road users' awareness of road traffic risks is essential for road safety as it enables them to detect impending danger and adjust their behaviours towards preventing harm. Appropriate and timely communication enhances road users' awareness of impending risks and is also important for maintaining road safety. Road traffic communications involve various channels, including road signs and markings (FRSC, 2022) as well as other aural, visual, oral, or written communication means; and road users from different countries, regions, or cultures prefer differing road traffic communication media (Nordfjærn et al., 2014). For instance, Nigerian road users are usually sensitive on roads and may alert one another of impending dangers by honking (Olasunkanmi et al., 2014) or headlight flashing.

Localised Safety Efforts by International Ride-Hailing Platforms

The introduction of ride-hailing platforms in Nigeria has provided passengers with options for commercial transit that enhance their safety and minimize their exposure to hazards like kidnapping (Olawole, 2022). These platforms increasingly roll out safety features that address safety issues encountered by their users—drivers and passengers—in Nigeria (Kansal, 2018). These include enabling passengers to:

(a) live share their location with close contacts for safety.
(b) assess the driver's skills prior to the trips based on their ratings.
(c) review drivers' performances or report drivers' misbehaviours after their rides and hold the drivers responsible for misconduct through the company.
(d) contact the companies for assistance and complaints both during and after a trip (Michael, 2023)

A Holistic View of Road Safety in Nigeria

The adoption of automobiles as a technological solution in the Nigerian road transport system introduced and amplified safety challenges that are still being managed by road transport stakeholders using various mechanisms, some of which are increasingly integrating AI-driven technologies to improve road safety. However, lessons from automobile adoption demonstrate that road safety goes beyond road collisions or accident avoidance, and it cuts across both road users' experiences and the road transport system. Road safety involves securing their lives, properties, environments, the climate, and public health from crimes and damages.

Therefore, developing AI systems that operate safely in their social environments similarly requires taking a sociocultural perspective on safety and considering social factors in AI design. In the case of Nigerian road transport, this will involve considering Nigerian road accident factors, the road environments, the road and societal cultures, and road users' behaviours and communication styles, and exploring AI design approaches and solutions that are sensitive to these. In this regard, the following section presents some sociotechnical and environmental factors for ensuring AI safety on Nigerian roads.

Considerations for AI Safety in Nigerian Road Traffic

In the last section, we presented safety considerations for Nigerian road transport systems as they currently are. In this section, we draw on that knowledge to highlight some likely safety considerations that might emerge on Nigerian roads as AV and other AI-driven transport technologies become more prevalent in Nigerian road traffic.

Nigeria's Environmental Factors

Despite NBS's (2023) report that poor weather contributes the least—approximately 0%—to Nigerian road crashes, studies have shown that Nigeria's poor weather conditions, like rain or harmattan—a dry season in West Africa—increase road accident frequency (Amidu & Oni, 2012). Coupled with evidence that poor weather negatively affects driving automation performance (Vargas et al., 2021), this suggests that environmental factors must be considered when thinking about the safe widespread adoption of AV in Nigeria. Currently, Nigerian climate or road scenarios are under-represented in AI training data, likely exacerbating AV's potential for harm when integrated into Nigerian road traffic to enhance road safety.

Situational Applications of Traffic Laws

In 2022, a driverless vehicle did not give way to a fire truck driving to an emergency in California, USA (Marshall, 2022). It is widely known that ambulances and fire engine trucks are legally allowed to disregard traffic lights and have the right of way when driving to an emergency, and the driverless vehicle's unawareness and disregard of this resulted in more damages from the fire incident. This example demonstrates the need to train AI systems to not only be aware of traffic laws, but also consider how they apply in real-world situations. For instance, in Nigeria, highly congested traffic may be controlled by both a traffic light and a human traffic warden. In such cases, commuters are expected to obey the traffic warden if the traffic warden's directive contradicts the traffic light. Considering these societal nuances in formal and tacit laws, which exemplify the complexity of real-world scenarios, is critical to ensuring that AI systems operate in a safe and socially acceptable manner.

Slow Down and Avoid Collisions—For Whose Safety?

Another challenge we anticipate in AV is their lack of "common sense"—the ability to make good judgments, especially in unsafe road situations. Road traffic environments are not always safe. As highlighted previously, there are existing issues of insecurities and other hazards on some roads, and commuters may draw on their "common sense" and use a risk-based approach to make safety judgements. In theory, driving automation trained to always obey traffic laws or slow down to avoid collisions when approaching pedestrians are prioritising pedestrians' safety. In practice, these "safe" actions may result in additional harm to motorists, given that drivers sometimes escape dangerous highway scenarios where insecurity is prevalent by speeding or not slowing down (Naku, 2022). Deploying AV on roads without realistic and systemic consideration of the safety of those within and around the vehicles in such unsafe situations may result in harmful actions by the vehicles. Therefore, it is vital that AI engineers in automotive companies approach road safety systemically and consider road safety issues from various road stakeholders' perspectives, especially from multidisciplinary and multicultural perspectives.

Locally Unintelligent AI Sensing and Behaviours

AVs are typically trained in highly mapped and structured road traffic—and even there, they have been involved in some accidents that demonstrate their insufficient intelligence for the environments in which they work (Siddiqui et al., 2022). Urban Nigerian traffic scenarios that differ from these highly controlled road settings by density and composition are scarcely represented in AI training for real-world scenarios. This is dangerous for AV adoption in Nigeria, as their intelligent and safe operation in Nigerian contexts depends on their ability to rightly sense and interpret Nigerian road objects and communication cues from other road actors. This, in turn, hinges on the degree to which the Nigerian road traffic and road users' interactions are represented and considered in their AI design and training. Training AVs in local contexts prior to widespread introduction is therefore critical for ensuring public safety, and by extension, AV reliance and trustworthiness.

Emergent Road Safety Behaviours

In 2016, TechPlus deployed a remotely controlled self-driving car in Lagos. Some road users reacted with disbelief, while others intentionally walked in front of it to test if it could detect them and react appropriately (Techplusng, 2016)—a reaction that will typically not be observed with a human-driven vehicle but emerges from road users' interactions with a perceived AV. This indicates that in addition to understanding the current systems and how people interact, AI safety considerations also need to anticipate how the introduction of AI-driven agents into road traffic might unveil new, potentially unsafe behaviours from road users, transform current road norms, and how the AI-driven agents might behave in these situations.

AI/Software Safety Checks and Maintenance

In the introduction of AI systems to replace humans in performing some driving or road management functions, we also need to consider how this might affect existing safety mechanisms like vehicle roadworthiness tests, regular safety checks, car servicing, and repairs. Replacing the human driver with AI agents pushes additional safety responsibilities on those involved in carrying out mandatory vehicle safety checks and repairs in Nigeria, because in doing so, they are effectively testing and influencing both the car hardware and its AI driver. Given that driving automation may act independently in road traffic, which will have safety consequences, it is imperative that: (a) Nigeria's vehicle safety protocol assesses vehicles' AI components and their performances in varying realistic Nigerian road traffic, (b) car manufacturers consider how vehicle safety checks need to adapt to new AI components and communicate what this needs to look like in Nigeria, and (c) regulators and car manufacturers consider how Nigerian automobile owners, users, and repairers might easily upskill and access the required resources for maintaining, fixing, or checking the safety of these AI features and their future software update releases—an emerging issue for Tesla users in Nigeria (Olubi, 2023).

Broader Societal Impacts of AI Systemic Adoption

E-waste, Pollution, Public Health, and the Climate

The significant environmental impacts and dangers of Large Language Models (LLMs) (Bender et al., 2021) demonstrates why AI safety and trustworthiness considerations in Nigeria must also consider AI systems' footprints on their environments and the continent, as well as the potential health hazards of these. African countries are already disproportionately the most vulnerable to climate change impacts, even though Africa's contribution to global carbon emission is currently relatively insignificant—about 4% (AJLabs, 2023).

A quarter of global road accidents happen in Africa despite only utilising 2% of the global vehicle fleets (UN, 2023), demonstrating the disproportionate impact of automobility on Africa. Most of the vehicles in Africa are old used vehicles, which have been flagged as dangerous and a major source of emissions and pollution (UNEP, 2020a). Considering Africa's fast-rising population, the large-scale adoption of AV and other AI systems in Nigeria and across Africa may exponentially intensify the continent's carbon footprints and vulnerability to emissions and climate change impacts if not adequately managed, amplifying the continent's existing safety challenges. This indicates that designing AI systems that are environmentally sustainable is also crucial for AV and their AI safety impacts in Nigeria and other African countries.

Therefore, we urge relevant government and non-government stakeholders and regulators to proactively address the potential manifestations of e-waste dumping in AI and data-driven systems, as well as the longer-term environmental impacts of AI products like AV, especially in Nigeria and other African countries. Also, AI and automobile engineers should prioritise designing their products to be safe and sustainable throughout their lifecycle, especially in their end-of-life years, and develop sustainable plans for their safe decommissioning at their end-of-life stage.

AI Responsibility and Accountability
Human-in-the-loop (where humans intervene in every AI decision cycle) as a recommended risk mitigation strategy for high-risk AI systems like AV (European Commission, 2021) raises concerns about the responsibility and accountability for consequential AI errors. Human-in-the-loop enables humans to draw on their domain knowledge, emotional intelligence, and situational awareness to enhance or correct AI performances. However, implementing human oversight in AV without proper governance can be unsafe for human drivers, as Nigerian traffic laws are yet to recognise AI agents as autonomous or accountable road actors and may hold the drivers responsible for the faults and inefficiencies of automation and their manufacturers. Therefore, it is important for AI stakeholders and regulators to critically explore what responsibility and accountability look like with AI as humans' collaborators or assistants in Nigeria and develop effective policies and mechanisms to manage their potential risks and impacts.

Lessons and Recommendations for AI Safety in Nigeria and Africa

Lessons from road transport have shown that safety is emergent, contextual, and collective. As observed with accidents, road safety emerges from road users' interactions, and ensuring road safety requires the cooperation of the road users as well as systemic efforts that transcend road traffic, as other road stakeholders—automobile manufacturers, lawmakers, and road safety agencies—play their part in promoting road safety through regulations, standardisation, traffic management, and designing and testing road technologies for safety.

Despite these, Nigeria records a high accident rate, indicating the ineffectiveness of these mechanisms. Most of Nigeria's formal road safety mechanisms originated from countries with varying social values and road systems than Nigeria, and likely do not represent Nigeria's indigenous values and cultures. Since laws and standards reflect societal values and desires (European Commission, 2021; Friedman & Hendry, 2019), this raises the questions: What would road safety mechanisms and their enactments look like if vehicles and their standards originated in Nigeria or other African countries? How would African values have shaped road safety design and regulations? And now, going beyond AI in road transport, how can AI regulations in Nigeria and Africa be rooted in Nigeria's and Africa's values and needs?

AI safety—a key trustworthy AI requirement—predominantly involves a risk-based approach, which inherently requires accounting for an AI system's diverse operational contexts and stakeholders in the adopted safety mechanisms. As our exploration of the Nigerian road transport system has illustrated, proper considerations of AI safety and trustworthiness require holistically considering both technical and social perspectives on safety and risk management, where the social perspective helps to consider and adequately design for the various operational contexts or environments of an AI system. Such perspectives must draw on contextual research and system-level approaches (Ibrahim et al., 2022; Pasandideh et al., 2022). In that vein, it is essential to define and foreground: (1) whose safety is being assured—the impacted stakeholders being considered, (2) the scope of analysis—e.g. individual versus collective, (3) the context or environment of use, (4) the AI system being deployed and its potential impacts, and (5) the stakeholders' values and welfare given the various AI use cases.

Recommendations for AI Safety in Nigeria and Africa

Drawing on the existing safety issues, mechanisms, and patterns observed in road transport, we make the following recommendations to support the development of safe and trustworthy AI systems for Nigeria and potentially other African countries:

Prioritise Africa's Safety in AI Systems

African countries are mostly consumers, rather than active producers, of foreign high technologies—and as the road system demonstrates, they pay a disproportionate price for this in the form of high accident rates. This indicates a need to prioritise African safety in technologies—including AI—developed globally: to design for Africa by default. As AI models are being integrated into various technologies, some destined to operate in safety-critical road contexts with potentially lethal consequences, we urge regulators, researchers, and engineers in Africa and beyond to proactively ensure the safety of these models and avoid them from causing disproportionate harm in Africa or to Africans. This work may benefit stakeholders beyond Africa: prioritising the safety of Nigerians and other Africans in AI systems developed or used there increases their robustness, sustainability, and trustworthiness.

AI Safety Can Benefit from Indigenous Values, Morals, and Approaches
Nigeria's and other African countries' current Data Protection Regulation and emission standards are based on the Europe's (Isa, 2023; UNEP, 2016), which indicates that AI regulation and trustworthiness requirements efforts from African governments might draw on the EU Act and trustworthy requirements. With AI safety, there is an opportunity for regulators to lean towards Nigerian and African indigenous safety traditions, morals, and values like communal care, interests, and duty (Ikuenobe, 2015) for establishing AI safety and trustworthiness requirements that are value-sensitive, resonate with the public, empower them, and effectively promote safety cultures in AI development and use.

Local Empowerment and Research to Guide AI Adoption and Regulations
Representing African voices and values in global trustworthy AI discourse through the development of trustworthy AI principles, requirements, and regulations that protect Africa's interests needs to be powered by research and development originating in Africa. Local research and efforts that consider African realities, challenges, values, and ethics in identifying AI safety requirements and procedures for Africa. African governments can facilitate this through empowering policies and investments that foster thriving environments for local AI research, interdisciplinary and intracontinental collaborations, education, and public debates that publicly drive critical discourses about AI ethics and AI impacts on the continent. Offering opportunities that enable AI research and developments that are sensitive to Africa's sociocultural environments and needs, fostering the development of ethical or trustworthy AI that Africans can identify with; and equipping academic researchers, policymakers, and other relevant experts with the skills and resources to critically examine the safety and trustworthiness of AI systems, promptly inform or propose AI safety standards or requirements, and protect the welfare and values of Africans.

Diversity and Localisation Are Key for Global AI Trustworthiness
The design of global AI safety and trustworthiness standards is a complicated endeavour that can benefit from localisation. As seen with the diversification and localisation of international road safety standards and mechanisms in Nigeria's road transport, developing AI safety requirements and standards that reflect the diversity of its potential contexts and cultures is an enormous task that requires inputs from global communities. AI researchers and regulators can borrow this communal approach to navigate how to design AI systems, their standards, and safety mechanisms in ways that are inclusive, empowering, and adaptable to diverse environments and communities—especially those who are most vulnerable to AI's negative impacts. This should involve inviting various (potentially) impacted communities to the conversation to understand their values, welfare, and effective approaches for protecting them, and ensuring that their contributions are well represented in global AI principles. We also urge the global AI ethics communities to continuously reflect on and critique their assumptions of what safety and trustworthiness are, their viewpoints—e.g. individual versus communal view, and their limitations, and create spaces for engaging and learning from diverse communities and their cultures.

Recommendations for AI Safety Globally
AI Safety Requires Systemic Approaches
Road safety—an emergent property of a sociotechnical system—requires systemic approaches that consider road users' overall experiences, interactions, cultures, environments, and their impacts on infrastructures, the climate and ecosystem, and public health. Similarly, designing for safety in AI systems requires considering their potential unsafe situations or interactions upon deployment, and designing to mitigate against such possibilities. That is, systemically considering AI systems' diverse environments, cultures, stakeholders and their values, and designing for them accordingly. With the awareness that the introduction of automation into an environment can manifest unanticipated actions from people and change some of the existing processes or cultures, AI systems should be proactively designed to encourage safe and desirable actions and prevent or discourage unsafe and undesirable actions from their users and those in their environments (Davis, 2020; Penzenstadler et al., 2018).

Public Awareness and Accountability
Human-in-the-loop as a critical risk management strategy for high-risk AI systems like AV comes with accountability caveats. To avoid holding the "human" in the loop responsible for AI mistakes and their consequences, we urge regulators to proactively explore AI systems' risk management, governance, and accountability in society. This may be facilitated by creating public awareness on AI systems' capabilities, limitations, and possibilities to misbehave or make mistakes, as well as creating comprehensive AI risk management frameworks that hold companies accountable for deploying unsafe AI products for public use. Developing such AI systems' risk management framework and regulations should be informed by diverse AI stakeholders such as government agencies, industries, activists, AI experts, the public, and others. Lastly, existing laws and risk management frameworks in the various contexts or sectors in which AI systems are being adopted should also be assessed and amended to sufficiently integrate AI risks.

Conclusion

Safety is contextual, subjective, cultural, and situational; it is systemic and sociotechnical. The lack of adequate representation of trustworthy AI principles and safety requirements from African nations presents a blind spot in AI developers' and regulators' abilities to ensure Africans' welfare and safety in AI systems development and use. This potentially excludes Africans from the benefits of AI while disproportionately exposing them to harm. Hence, there is a need for more African values-informed trustworthy AI guidelines and definitions that systematically consider the diverse African histories, cultures, ethics or morals, realities, as well as existing and future challenges. These should ideally be co-designed by diverse stakeholders—from the public to the government. Ensuring AI safety and trustworthiness in Africa requires a communal approach, as well as commitments from the local and global AI stakeholders to (1) Prioritise Africa's and Africans' safety in AI systems; (2) Treat safety and trustworthiness of such systems as systemic properties shaped by the current and future sociocultural environments in which they are deployed; (3) Empower African researchers and regulators—both locally and globally—to systematically create robust research and regulations that are for Africa and by Africans; (4) Respect African values, approaches, agency, experiences, and contributions to global AI discourse; and finally (5) Create avenues for public awareness, debates, and communal contributions to AI safety in Africa. AI systems cannot be truly trustworthy for global use if Africa and Africans' safety are not considered and integrated in their design and use, and considering Africans' safety requires including African perspectives, values, experiences, and environments.

References

Abebe, R., Aruleba, K., Birhane, A., Kingsley, S., Obaido, G., Remy, S. L., & Sadagopan, S. (2021). Narratives and counternarratives on data sharing in Africa. In *Proceedings of the 2021 ACM Conference on Fairness, Accountability, and Transparency* (pp. 329–341). https://doi.org/10.1145/3442188.3445897

Admin, L. N. (2019, July 18). *Nigerian standards and specifications for road vehicle engineering—Standards*. https://standards.lawnigeria.com/2019/07/18/nigerian-standards-for-road-vehicle-engineering/

Ajide, F. M. (2020). Criminal activities and road accidents in Nigerian transport industry. *Transportation in Developing Economies, 6*(1), 6. https://doi.org/10.1007/s40890-020-0094-4

AJLabs. (2023, August 4). *How much does Africa contribute to global carbon emissions?* Al Jazeera. https://www.aljazeera.com/news/2023/9/4/how-much-does-africa-contribute-to-global-carbon-emissions

Amidu O., A., & Oni, S. (2012). Seasonal climatic variations and road accidents in Lagos, Nigeria.

Asunloye, A. (2019, October 31). *Why Nigeria should develop other transport modes*. Businessday NG. https://businessday.ng/transport/article/why-nigeria-should-develop-other-transport-modes/

Ayoyinka, J. (2023, September 8). *Rising road crashes during ember months due to reckless driving*. The Guardian Nigeria News—Nigeria and World News. https://editor.guardian.ng/news/rising-road-crashes-during-ember-months-due-to-reckless-driving/

Bender, E. M., Gebru, T., McMillan-Major, A., & Shmitchell, S. (2021). On the dangers of stochastic parrots: Can language models be too big? In *Proceedings of the 2021 ACM Conference on Fairness, Accountability, and Transparency* (pp. 610–623). https://doi.org/10.1145/3442188.3445922

Bolanle, O. (2023, July 28). *Lagos, technology and traffic management*. ThisDay Live. https://www.thisdaylive.com/index.php/2023/07/28/lagos-technology-and-traffic-management

Boniface, E. (2021, December 15). Nigeria's highways of risks and insecurity. *Thisday*. https://www.thisdaylive.com/index.php/2021/12/15/nigerias-highways-of-risks-and-insecurity

Borokini, F., Wakunuma, K., & Akintoye, S. (2023). The use of gendered chatbots in Nigeria: Critical perspectives. In D. O. Eke, K. Wakunuma, & S. Akintoye (Eds.), *Responsible AI in Africa: Challenges and opportunities* (pp. 119–139). Springer International Publishing. https://doi.org/10.1007/978-3-031-08215-3_6

Buolamwini, J., & Gebru, T. (2018). Gender shades: Intersectional accuracy disparities in commercial gender classification. In *Conference on Fairness, Accountability and Transparency* (pp. 77–91).

Burt, C. (2022, May 11). *VerifyMe Nigeria launches license plate verification API to enable car insurance services | biometric update*. https://www.biometricupdate.com/202205/verifyme-nigeria-launches-license-plate-verification-api-to-enable-car-insurance-services

Commerce, U. S. B. of I., & Wilken, A. A. (1964). *Market for U.S. products in Nigeria*. U.S. Government Printing Office.

Davis, J. L. (2020). *How artefacts afford: The power and politics of everyday things*. MIT Press.

DRTS. (2018, November 28). *The official DRTS website: Vehicle inspection schedule in Nigeria*. http://drts.gov.ng/the-official-drts-website-vehicle-inspection-schedule-in-nigeria/

Ede, E. C., & Chamberlain, O. (2013). History of automobile past and present challenges facing automobile production in Nigeria. *IOSR Journal of Research & Method in Education (IOSRJRME), 2*(4), 11–16. https://doi.org/10.9790/7388-0241116

Eke, D. O., Wakunuma, K., & Akintoye, S. (2023). *Responsible AI in Africa: Challenges and opportunities*. Springer Nature.

European Commission. (2019, November 27). *Vehicle safety and automated/connected vehicles—European Commission*. https://ec.europa.eu/growth/sectors/automotive-industry/safety-automotive-sector_en

European Commission. (2021, April 24). *The Act | EU Artificial Intelligence Act*. https://artificialintelligenceact.eu/the-act/

European Commission AI HLEG. (2019, April 8). *Ethics guidelines for trustworthy AI | Shaping Europe's digital future*. European Commission. https://digital-strategy.ec.europa.eu/en/library/ethics-guidelines-trustworthy-ai

Friedman, B., & Hendry, D. G. (2019). *Value sensitive design: Shaping technology with moral imagination*. Mit Press.

FRSC. (2007). *About us—FRSC official website* [FRSC official website]. Federal Road Safety Corps. https://frsc.gov.ng/about-us/

FRSC. (2012). *Nationalroad traffic regulations, 2012*. https://frsc.gov.ng/NATROADTRAFFICREGS2012.pdf

FRSC. (2022). *2022 compendium for assistant route commanders*. FRSC. https://frsc.gov.ng/wp-content/uploads/2022/12/ARC-COMPENDIUM-2022.pdf

Geels, F. W. (2005). The dynamics of transitions in socio-technical systems: A multi-level analysis of the transition pathway from horse-drawn carriages to automobiles (1860–1930). *Technology Analysis & Strategic Management, 17*(4), 445–476. https://doi.org/10.1080/09537320500357319

GNA. (2022, May 6). *Project for artificial intelligence begins at KNUST | News Ghana*. https://Newsghana.Com.Gh. https://newsghana.com.gh/project-for-artificial-intelligence-begins-at-knust/

House, T. W. (2023, October 30). *Executive order on the safe, secure, and trustworthy development and use of artificial intelligence*. The White House. https://www.whitehouse.gov/briefing-room/presidential-actions/2023/10/30/executive-order-on-the-safe-secure-and-trustworthy-development-and-use-of-artificial-intelligence/

Ibrahim, M. A., Assaad, Z., & Williams, E. (2022). Trust and communication in human-machine teaming. *Frontiers in Physics*, *10*. https://doi.org/10.3389/fphy.2022.942896

Ikuenobe, P. (2015). Relational autonomy, personhood, and African traditions. *Philosophy East and West, 65*, 1005–1029. https://doi.org/10.1353/pew.2015.0101

iRAP. (2022, April 18). *Motor vehicle standards*. Road Safety Toolkit. https://toolkit.irap.org/safer-vehicle-treatments/motor-vehicle-standards/

Isa, P. A. (2023, July 3). The journey towards the Nigeria Data Protection Act 2023. *Tribune Online*. https://tribuneonlineng.com/the-journey-towards-the-nigeria-data-protection-act-2023/

Jobin, A., Ienca, M., & Vayena, E. (2019). The global landscape of AI ethics guidelines. *Nature Machine Intelligence*, *1*(9), Article 9. https://doi.org/10.1038/s42256-019-0088-2

Kansal, S. (2018, October 17). *New safety toolkit arrives in Nigeria*. Uber Newsroom. https://www.uber.com/en-NG/newsroom/new-safety-toolkit-arrives-nigeria/

Koenecke, A., Nam, A., Lake, E., Nudell, J., Quartey, M., Mengesha, Z., Toups, C., Rickford, J. R., Jurafsky, D., & Goel, S. (2020). Racial disparities in automated speech recognition. *Proceedings of the National Academy of Sciences, 117*(14), 7684–7689. https://doi.org/10.1073/pnas.1915768117

Laplante, P. A. (Ed.). (2017). *Dictionary of computer science, engineering and technology*. CRC Press. https://doi.org/10.1201/9781315214740

Leslie, D. (2019). Understanding artificial intelligence ethics and safety: A guide for the responsible design and implementation of AI systems in the public sector. *Zenodo*. https://doi.org/10.5281/ZENODO.3240529

Leveson, N. (2011). *Engineering a safer world: Systems thinking applied to safety*. MIT Press.

Luchian, E. (2017, December 15). Going autonomous in South Africa—The self-driving Mercedes-Benz S-Class has reached Cape Town. *Mercedes-Blog*. https://mercedesblog.com/going-autonomous-in-south-africa-the-self-driving-mercedes-benz-s-class-has-reached-cape-town/

Marshall, A. (2022, May 27). An autonomous car blocked a fire truck responding to an emergency. *Wired*. https://www.wired.com/story/cruise-fire-truck-block-san-francisco-autonomous-vehicles/

Merriam Webster. (2023, November 1). *Definition of SAFE*. https://www.merriam-webster.com/dictionary/safe

Michael, C. (2023, July 17). *Uber's in-app emergency support to address safety in Nigeria*. Businessday NG. https://businessday.ng/technology/article/ubers-in-app-emergency-support-to-address-safety-in-nigeria/

Naku, D. (2022, July 17). Rivers driver evades kidnappers, escapes with passengers. *Punch Newspapers*. https://punchng.com/rivers-driver-evades-kidnappers-escapes-with-passengers/

National Bureau of Statistics. (2021). *Foreign Trade Statistics—Q3 2021.pdf* (Q3 2021). National Bureau of Statistics. https://nigerianstat.gov.ng/elibrary/read/1241099

National Bureau of Statistics. (2023, October). *Road Transport Data Q4 2022*. National Bureau of Statistics. https://nigerianstat.gov.ng/elibrary/read/1241392

Nevala, K. (2020, November 28). Ethical AI isn't the same as trustworthy AI, and that matters. *VentureBeat*. https://venturebeat.com/2020/11/28/ethical-ai-isnt-the-same-as-trustworthy-ai-and-that-matters/

NHTSA. (2016, March 17). *U.S. DOT and IIHS announce historic commitment of 20 automakers to make automatic emergency braking standard on new vehicles | NHTSA* [Text]. https://www.nhtsa.gov/press-releases/us-dot-and-iihs-announce-historic-commitment-20-automakers-make-automatic-emergency

Nordfjærn, T., Şimşekoğlu, Ö., & Rundmo, T. (2014). Culture related to road traffic safety: A comparison of eight countries using two conceptualizations of culture. *Accident Analysis & Prevention, 62*, 319–328. https://doi.org/10.1016/j.aap.2013.10.018

NTSB. (2019). *Collision between vehicle controlled by developmental automated driving system and Pedestrian, Tempe, Arizona, March 18, 2018* (Highway Accident Report NTSB/HAR-19/03 NTSB/HAR-19/03; National Transportation Safety Board, p. 78).

Nwafor. (2023, October 18). Travel advisory: Sanwo-Olu unveils Lagos traffic radio life camera update service. *Vanguard News*. https://www.vanguardngr.com/2023/10/travel-advisory-sanwo-olu-unveils-lagos-traffic-radio-life-camera-update-service/

Ogunbodede, E. F. (2008). Urban road transportation in Nigeria from 1960 to 2006: Problems, prospects and challenges. *Ethiopian Journal of Environmental Studies and Management, 1*(1), 7.

Okonkwo, O. (2023, February 4). 7 things to know about owning and driving a Tesla in Nigeria. *Nairametrics*. https://nairametrics.com/2023/02/04/7-things-to-know-about-owning-and-driving-a-tesla-in-nigeria/

Olasunkanmi, A., Dotun, I., & Ikenna, A. (2014, October 13). Horn-Free-Day: Mixed feelings as Lagos moves to tackle noise pollution. *Vanguard News*. https://www.vanguardngr.com/2014/10/horn-free-day-mixed-feelings-lagos-moves-tackle-noise-pollution/

Olawole, M. O. (2022). *Ride-hailing services in Nigeria: Adoption, insights and implications* (pp. 121–147).

Olubi, E. (2023, December 17). *I have come to the conclusion that the biggest challenge with driving a tesla in a country that's not officially supported are the software issues that will inevitably come up. My car is currently stuck in a boot loop thanks to a botched firmware update to 2023.44.1* [Tweet]. Twitter. https://twitter.com/0x/status/1736321648255504879

Pasandideh, S., Pereira, P., & Gomes, L. (2022). Cyber-physical-social systems: Taxonomy, challenges, and opportunities. *IEEE Access, 10*, 42404–42419. https://doi.org/10.1109/ACCESS.2022.3167441

Pavoris. (2021, January 3). *File: First car that arrived Nigeria.jpg—Wikimedia Commons*. Wikimedia Commons. https://commons.wikimedia.org/wiki/File:First_car_that_arrived_Nigeria.jpg

Penzenstadler, B., Duboc, L., Venters, C. C., Betz, S., Seyff, N., Wnuk, K., Chitchyan, R., Easterbrook, S. M., & Becker, C. (2018). Software engineering for sustainability: Find the leverage points! *IEEE Software, 35*(4), 22–33. https://doi.org/10.1109/MS.2018.110154908

Rathenau Instituut. (2021, July 26). *Trustworthiness of AI is mainly a socio-technical concept*. Rathenau Instituut. https://www.rathenau.nl/en/living-together-digital-world/trustworthiness-ai-mainly-socio-technical-concept-not-technical-check

Roberts, L. (2022, April 18). *BOOM or BUZZ: Drones on the rise in Africa*. Forbes Africa. https://www.forbesafrica.com/technology/2022/04/18/boom-or-buzz-drones-on-the-rise-in-africa/

Sahara Reporters. (2023, October 8). *How we were abducted, robbed of life savings by 'one-chance' criminals in Nigeria's capital city, victims narrate ordeals | Sahara Reporters*. Sahara Reporters. https://saharareporters.com/2023/10/08/how-we-were-abducted-robbed-life-savings-one-chance-criminals-nigerias-capital-city

Segun. (2019, December 26). Lagos adopts technology for vehicle inspection services. *The Nigerian Xpress*. https://www.thexpressng.com/lagos-adopts-technology-for-vehicle-inspection-services/

Siddiqui, F., Lerman, R., & Merrill, J. B. (2022, June 15). Teslas running Autopilot involved in 273 crashes reported since last year. *Washington Post*. https://www.washingtonpost.com/technology/2022/06/15/tesla-autopilot-crashes/

Sommerville, I. (2011). *Software engineering* (9th ed). Pearson.

Staff, T. M. (2020, December 15). *Algorithms behaving badly: 2020 edition—The markup*. https://themarkup.org/2020-in-review/2020/12/15/algorithms-bias-racism-surveillance

Tabassi, E. (2023). *Artificial Intelligence Risk Management Framework (AI RMF 1.0)* (error: 100-1; p. error: 100-1). National Institute of Standards and Technology (U.S.). https://doi.org/10.6028/NIST.AI.100-1

Techplusng. (Director). (2016, July 5). *Tech Plus driverless car*. https://www.youtube.com/watch?v=9clHIu9J1H4

Tijani. (2023, August 29). *Co-creating a national artificial intelligence strategy for Nigeria | LinkedIn*. LinkedIn. https://www.linkedin.com/pulse/co-creating-national-artificial-intelligence-strategy-tijani/

Ugwuoke, C. O., Ajah, B. O., Akor, L., Ameh, S. O., Lanshima, C. A., Ngwu, E. C., Eze, U. A., & Nwokedi, M. (2023). Violent crimes and insecurity on Nigerian highways: A tale of travelers' trauma, nightmares and state slumber. *Heliyon, 9*(10), e20489. https://doi.org/10.1016/j.heliyon.2023.e20489

UN. (2023, May 15). *Road safety week: African nations steer towards reducing deaths | UN News*. https://news.un.org/en/story/2023/05/1136627

UN Global Pulse. (2019, June 26). *Developing an ethical AI framework in Ghana • UN Global Pulse*. https://www.unglobalpulse.org/event/developing-an-ethical-ai-framework-in-ghana/

UNEP. (2016, December 6). *West African countries introduce emissions standards in fuels | News | SDG Knowledge Hub | IISD*. http://sdg.iisd.org/news/west-african-countries-introduce-emissions-standards-in-fuels/

UNEP. (2020a, October 26). *New UN report details environmental impacts of export of used vehicles to developing world*. UN Environment. http://www.unep.org/news-and-stories/press-release/new-un-report-details-environmental-impacts-export-used-vehicles

UNEP. (2020b, December 28). *Global trade in used vehicles report*. UNEP—UN Environment Programme. http://www.unep.org/resources/report/global-trade-used-vehicles-report

UNESCO. (2021). *Recommendation on the ethics of artificial intelligence—UNESCO digital library* (SHS/BIO/REC-AIETHICS/2021). https://unesdoc.unesco.org/ark:/48223/pf0000380455

Uzondu, C., Jamson, S., & Marsden, G. (2022). Road safety in Nigeria: Unravelling the challenges, measures, and strategies for improvement. *International Journal of Injury Control and Safety Promotion, 29*(4), 522–532. https://doi.org/10.1080/17457300.2022.2087230

Vargas, J., Alsweiss, S., Toker, O., Razdan, R., & Santos, J. (2021). An overview of autonomous vehicles sensors and their vulnerability to weather conditions. *Sensors*, *21*(16), Article 16. https://doi.org/10.3390/s21165397

Zachmann, K. (2014). Risk in historical perspective: Concepts, contexts, and conjunctions. In C. Klüppelberg, D. Straub, & I. M. Welpe (Eds.), *Risk—A multidisciplinary introduction* (pp. 3–35). Springer International Publishing. https://doi.org/10.1007/978-3-319-04486-6_1

CHAPTER 9

Trustworthy AI in Healthcare: Exploring Ethics in Digital Health Technologies in Nigeria

Ayomide Owoyemi, Eugeniah Arthur, Tope Ladi-Akinyemi, Yemisi Babalola, and Damian Okaibedi Eke

Background

There is an emerging and thriving ecosystem of digital health technologies in Africa, driven by technological advances, the increasing need for personalised healthcare, the lack of or limited access to sustainable healthcare systems, and the growing emphasis on preventive care (Kipruto et al., 2022). From telemedicine, generative artificial intelligence used as bots, and health tech insurance to technologies used for healthcare logistics, pharma, and primary and specialty care, digital technologies are increasingly becoming pervasive (Holst et al., 2020; Owoyemi et al., 2022). Indeed, digital health technologies have been recognised by the

A. Owoyemi
University of Illinois Chicago, Chicago, IL, USA
e-mail: aowoye3@uic.edu

E. Arthur
Bowling Green State University, Bowling Green, OH, USA

D. O. Eke et al. (eds.), *Trustworthy AI*,
https://doi.org/10.1007/978-3-031-75674-0_9

World Health Organisation (WHO) as crucial elements that will drive the achievement of the Sustainable Development Goals (SDGs) by the year 2030, as well as the Universal Health Coverage (UHC) (Kipruto et al., 2022). As Manyazewal et al. (2023) pointed out, "some of the most critical targets in SDG 3 could be addressed using digital health interventions where digital and mobile technologies".

In the last decade, investments in Africa's health tech startups have seen a noticeable increase. This new wave of innovation and growth in Africa's health tech ecosystem is revolutionising healthcare access. Founders Factory Africa reported that healthcare startups in Africa raised a record US$3.5 billion in the first half of 2022, a 131% increase in the same period in 2021 (Wakefield, 2024). This sector is estimated by the World Economic Forum (WEF) to be worth $259 billion by 2030 because 14% of business opportunities in global health are expected to be in Africa (Manlan, 2019). For Nigeria, the digital health market is estimated to increase significantly by over $1 m between 2023 and 2028 (Kipruto et al., 2022). These are critical developments considering the state of African healthcare systems.

The healthcare systems in many African countries face significant challenges that significantly undermine their ability to provide adequate care to their populations. One of the primary issues is the need for sufficient infrastructure, including hospitals, clinics, and essential medical equipment for diagnosis and treatment (Hsia et al., 2012; Osakede, 2022). Many facilities must be updated, better maintained, and equipped to handle the volume of patients or the complexity of health issues they encounter (Azevedo, 2017; Oleribe et al., 2019). The situation is even

T. Ladi-Akinyemi
Olabisi Onabanjo University, Ago-Iwoye, Nigeria
e-mail: twladi-akinyemi@cmul.edu.ng

Y. Babalola
Babcock University, Ilishan-Remo, Nigeria
e-mail: babalolay@babcock.edu.ng

D. O. Eke (✉)
School of Computer Science, University of Nottingham, Nottingham, UK
e-mail: damian.eke@nottingham.ac.uk

more dire in rural areas, with many communities lacking formal healthcare services, forcing residents to travel long distances to access care. This scarcity of infrastructure is compounded by frequent shortages of essential medical supplies and medications, further crippling the healthcare system's effectiveness.

Furthermore, there is a severe shortage of healthcare professionals, including doctors, nurses, and other specialists in many countries of Africa. Many trained healthcare professionals prefer to emigrate to other countries outside Africa for better opportunities and working conditions (Eastwood et al., 2005; Naicker et al., 2009). This exodus exacerbates the already dire situation, leaving behind an overburdened and under-resourced workforce. These challenges reflect wider systemic issues such as corruption, inadequate funding, and inefficient management that plague the healthcare systems in many African countries.

Digital health technologies hold significant promise for addressing some of these multifaceted challenges facing African healthcare systems. From improving access to medical services to providing health education and remote monitoring of chronic conditions to empowering patients to manage their health more effectively, digital health technologies can significantly change African healthcare systems. This aligns with the perception that AI systems developed in and for Africa should focus on providing solutions to specific and contextual African problems (Wakunuma & Eke, 2024).

Nigeria is at the forefront of this technological revolution, where digital technologies, particularly AI, are being used to provide services. In May 2023, Nigeria launched what is regarded as the first African national digital healthcare platform, 'NIGCOMHEALTH', a telehealth service platform. The platform is a product of the collaboration between the Nigerian Communications Satellite Limited (NIGCOMSAT), Ethnomet, and Sawtrax. According to Abosede (2024), this AI-powered innovation for telehealth 'would enhance the capacity of healthcare professionals and solve the challenges faced by the inadequacies and inequitable distribution of health service delivery'. In addition, many digital health startups in Nigeria use AI systems to create and deliver patient services. This represents a dynamic shift in the healthcare landscape, leveraging cutting-edge technologies to enhance healthcare services. However, as is often the case, the enthusiasm that comes with increasing technological innovation usually overshadows crucial ethical considerations that must be addressed to ensure these advancements are beneficial and equitable. This chapter explores how digital health startups are considering ethics in designing, developing, and deploying these technologies, especially AI. We provide empirical evidence of how ethical digital health technologies in Nigeria consider concerns through a web-based cross-sectional survey. These concerns border on ethical considerations in choosing, developing, testing, deploying, and evaluating these digital healthcare solutions. While ethical principles such as respect for persons, beneficence, non-maleficence, and justice are generally accepted in healthcare, putting these into practice for digital health use with the rapidly evolving landscape, significant data generation, novel approaches, and the absence of regulatory controls have created new challenges (Nebeker et al., 2019).

Our findings show the current state of the art, particularly on how ethics is considered in data processing activities, including at the collection and storage stages of the data lifecycle. The next section of this chapter will explore the meaning of ethics in digital technologies. The subsequent sections discuss the methodology employed to generate and analyse the data, critical discussions about the findings, and the diverse implications for different stakeholders, including designers, developers, policymakers, and people in academia.

Ethics and Digital Health Technologies

Digital health technologies in the context of this paper refer to digital devices, systems, and applications that facilitate digital health data generation, analysis, and application in clinical research and practice. This includes systems for collecting electronic patient records, remote patient recruitment and consent, real-time data monitoring and evidence generation, big data analytics, telemedicine and virtual consultations, AI, and clinical decision support systems. The World Health Organization's (WHO) Global Strategy on Digital Health 2020–2025 highlights the critical importance of digital health technologies to clinical research and practice (WHO, 2020). Several countries in sub-Saharan Africa (SSA) are already achieving essential milestones of integrating digital health technologies (such as health, electronic health records, telemedicine, cloud-based applications, and artificial intelligence) into healthcare systems.

Research has found that by expanding digital health technologies for healthcare purposes, African health systems could realise up to 15% efficiency gains in 2030 (Jousset et al., 2023). Digital technologies are pervasive in human societies and have critical roles in shaping societies

(Ihde, 1990). This distinctive feature of pervasiveness as well as their ubiquity, virtuality, and magnification, digital technologies raise several ethical issues. The design and use of digital health technologies give rise to diverse ethical and legal concerns (Brall et al., 2019; Shaw et al., 2024; Zarif, 2022).

These include privacy and data security, informed consent, safety, equity and accessibility, algorithmic bias and discrimination, accountability and liability, efficacy and ethical use of big data. Many of these concerns are still emerging and there needs to be a clear understanding of how exactly they will unfold or how best to engage with them. Thus, questions of balancing the promised benefits of new digital health technologies and mitigating the risks they raise are subject to intense research and debate (Vayena et al., 2018).

In the context of digital health technologies, we refer to aspects of ethics that focus on the moral implications of the design, development, and deployment of digital health technologies. It examines the fundamental challenges and considerations that arise in the context of digital technologies and its intersection with health systems. This is at the core of global advocacy for responsible innovation promoting principles of equity, accountability, transparency, trust, autonomy, privacy, justice and benevolence (Stahl et al., 2021). Many of these principles are being codified in laws such as data protection regulations (such as the EU GDPR), digital health laws and regulations (e.g. the EU Regulation [EU] 2021/2282 on health technology assessment [HTAR]) as well as regulations of technologies in general (e.g. EU AI Act) (Council of Europe, 2021).

However, in Africa, understanding the ethical issues digital health technologies raise still needs to be clarified and needs more evidence in literature. This is unlike in Europe where ethics is integral to the governance of digital technologies (Eke & Stahl, 2024). Thus, we hope to provide empirically sound insights on what ethical issues the design and use of digital health technologies, particularly AI, raise in the Nigerian context. This survey aims to explore how ethics is considered and addressed in digital health companies and projects to provide an understanding of the landscape, awareness, and practice of ethics in the development, deployment, and management of digital health solutions.

Trustworthy Innovation in Healthcare in Africa

While AI and other digital technologies can bridge identifiable gaps in many African countries by providing scalable, efficient, and cost-effective solutions for diagnostics, treatment, and disease management, it is essential to ensure that these technologies are trusted by relevant stakeholders (Eke et al., 2023). Acceptability and effectiveness of critical innovations in healthcare depends on the level of trustworthiness built into them. Trustworthy innovation is often characterised by transparency, accountability, robustness, fairness, ability to mitigate biases, and inclusivity. In African issues such as usability, affordability, and the ability to allow individuals and African countries the opportunity to own and control their data is of crucial importance. It is about ensuring that these technologies are developed and deployed in a manner that respects both individual and collective privacy, promotes equitable access to healthcare, and minimises biases that could exacerbate existing disparities. This is particularly important in Africa, where the trust between healthcare providers and communities is often not robust. Trustworthiness is paramount, and by fostering trust in AI systems, healthcare innovations can achieve greater acceptance and efficacy, ultimately improving health outcomes and quality of life across the continent.

Achieving trustworthy AI in healthcare in Africa is possible, including through robust regulatory frameworks, collaborative partnerships, and effective integration of ethical principles and values into the design and development. In the context of design and deployment in healthcare, consideration of ethics is important. In this chapter, we consider the application of responsible innovation principles, particularly in AI, as an effective approach in achieving trustworthiness. But how do health technology startups go about ethics in their operations? The following sections provide details of our methodological choices and the key findings from our empirical research in Nigeria.

Method

A web-based cross-sectional survey was conducted using Google Forms (a free questionnaire resource from Google LLC). Ethical clearance (BUHREC 659/23) was granted for this study by the Institutional Review Board (IRB) of Babcock University, Ililshan-Remo, Nigeria. Only participants who have managed health tech startups in Nigeria were selected. The eligibility criteria were (i) being aged 18 or older, (ii) owning or managing a digital health organisation at the executive level, (iii) digital health organisation is focused on Africa. We excluded individuals who (i) were just employees in the organisation and (ii) did not run health focused organisations. Participants were recruited using a convenient sampling technique. Questionnaires were shared through WhatsApp, Twitter, LinkedIn, and email. Descriptive statistical analysis was then conducted on the collected data. Collected data were coded and analysed using *R* (Jones et al., 2022). Descriptive statistics were used to summarise the information. Categorical variables and cross-tabulation results were presented in frequencies and percentages in tables.

Findings

This study analysed data from 16 digital health startups with an average operational tenure of 27 months. Most (56%) of these startups focus on care provision, followed by 31% specialising in health data analytics. Although all the startups target the Nigerian market, three are headquartered abroad. Concerning data utility and privacy, 56% of the startups employ anonymisation techniques for the data they collect. Meanwhile, 44% use this data for customer profiling, and 25% leverage it for predicting user behaviour (Table 9.1).

Regarding data storage, only a quarter (25%) of the startups opt for domestic storage solutions in Nigeria. Most store their data in international cloud services in the United States, the United Kingdom, and Spain. Eighteen per cent of the surveyed startups incorporate Artificial Intelligence or Machine Learning into their products. Additionally, 12% of the startups were found to collect non-healthcare-related data without users' consent.

Concerning transparency and ethics, 44% of startups disclosed using third-party services and apps for user behaviour monitoring. Only one startup reported selling data to third parties. Finally, half of the respondents indicated the presence of a designated individual or department responsible for overseeing ethical and legal aspects of data governance. However, only 56% showed high concern for moral considerations in their operations.

Our analysis produced notable findings on the ethical priorities, user engagement practices among digital health startups, and the structural presence of ethics and legal governance units in these organisations. From

Table 9.1 Startup characteristics and distribution

	Frequency	*Percentage*
Country (headquarters)		
Nigeria	13	82
Canada	1	6
United States	1	6
Spain	1	6
Country where data is stored		
United States	7	44
Nigeria	4	25
Canada	1	6
Spain	1	6
Cloud	1	6
Cloud—Not sure of the country	1	6
Cloud—United Kingdom	1	6
Age of startup		
Greater than 1 year	11	69
1 year or less	5	31
Area of focus		
Care provision	9	56
Health data	5	31
Others	2	13
Incorporation of AI/ML in their products?		
Yes	3	19
No	13	81
Collection of non-healthcare related data without user's consent		
Yes	2	12
No	12	88
Sell data to third parties?		
Yes	1	6
No	15	94
Has a department responsible for ethical/legal governance?		
Yes	5	62
No	10	31
NA	1	6
Data used in profiling of users		
Yes	7	44
No	7	44
NA	2	12
Level of concern for ethical considerations		
High	9	56
Low	7	44

Table 9.2 Crosstab of the level of ethical concern and user engagement during design and development

Ethics concern	*User engagement during design and development*
Prioritised ethics	(9) 69%
Did not prioritise ethics	(4) 31%

Table 9.3 Crosstab of designated ethics and legal governance unit and startups that prioritised ethics

Designated ethics and legal governance unit	*Prioritised ethics*
Yes	(4) 50%
No	(4) 50%

the data presented in Tables 9.2, *69%* of the startups that prioritised ethics actively engaged with users in these initial stages. However, interestingly, among those startups that did not emphasise ethics, 31% still recognised the importance of user engagement during design and development. Concerning formal ethical structures (Table 9.3), half of the startups surveyed have taken the step to establish designated units or assign specific personnel to oversee ethics and legal governance. On the other hand, the remaining 50% operate without such specialised units.

Discussion

Our analysis provides insights into how the sector is or considering embedding ethics and responsible data management into their operations. Aligned with the growing emphasis on digital health in Africa and globally to enhance care delivery, our findings reveal a primary focus on patient care provision by these startups, similar to trends identified in different studies (Holst et al., 2020; Kipruto et al., 2022). This likely reflects Nigeria's pressing healthcare needs. Additionally, the attention to health data analytics underscores data's pivotal role in enhancing health outcomes, especially in Artificial Intelligence-driven solutions (Musa et al., 2023; Owoyemi et al., 2022).

A significant observation from our study is that most startups store their data outside Nigeria, even as they cater predominantly to the Nigerian market. While using cloud services outside Nigeria exemplifies a globalised ecosystem, it brings up questions about data sovereignty and its impact on user privacy. Data protection regulatory provisions are different in different countries. For instance, many African countries, including Nigeria, have enacted laws that require data to be stored locally and forbid cross-border transfers of personal data unless authorised by the data protection authorities or other designated entities (CIPESA, 2022). This means that using non-Nigeria, non-Africa cloud services raises legal complexities.

The nuances of data utility and privacy among the analysed startups offer significant insights. Over half of the startups employing anonymisation methods highlight awareness of privacy considerations. Conversely, the accumulation of unrelated health data without user consent by certain startups, combined with often disclosing the data to third parties, raises ethical concerns demanding further examination and potentially regulatory action. Such approaches could compromise user trust and openness to digital health tools, which are vital factors for the effective acceptance and influence of these platforms, as shown by a study conducted by Dhagarra et al. (2020).

The adoption of Artificial Intelligence (AI) and Machine Learning (ML) by 18% of the startups indicates a tentative trend towards incorporating such cutting-edge technologies to augment healthcare offerings. As the Nigerian digital health environment evolves, more healthcare startups will explore opportunities across population health, individual care, health systems, and pharmaceuticals and medical technology to leverage AI, as highlighted in a review by Adejumo et al. (2023).

On the ethical front, the appointment of specific individuals or departments to supervise ethical and legal facets of data governance in 50% of the startups is a promising sign of prioritisation of ethics by these startups. Yet, the contrast between the concern for ethics and the percentage of startups with dedicated ethics or legal governance bodies points to a potential misalignment between ethical aspirations and practical implementations, which is similar to the outcomes of a scoping review conducted by Sekandi et al. (2022). However, the evident correlation between ethical prioritisation and user engagement in the design and development stages underscores the importance of robust ethical practices. In a culturally diverse setting like Nigeria, aligning with local values and cultural nuances can significantly enhance user trust, participation, and outcomes, resonating with the Prioritarian principles outlined by Winters et al. (2020).

Conclusion

In conclusion, this exploration sheds light on the operational dynamics and ethical considerations among digital health startups in Nigeria, highlighting areas of strength and potential challenges. It provides a landscape of how ethical issues are addressed, which can be used to assess the trustworthiness of these digital health innovations. The insights could inform policy formulation, regulatory frameworks, and entrepreneurial strategies to foster Nigeria's responsible and user-centric digital health ecosystem. Future research could delve deeper into the implications of international data storage and the evolving role of AI and ML in shaping the digital health landscape in Nigeria.

Final results summary

What was already known on the topic	• Digital health innovations including AI, and telemedicine are rapidly expanding across Africa, significantly influencing healthcare delivery • Ethical concerns regarding the use of digital health technologies have been raised, focusing on issues like privacy, data security, and equitable access
What this study added to our knowledge	• The study revealed a gap between the expressed ethical concerns of startups and the practical implementation of ethical governance structures, pointing to potential misalignments in the sector • The study underscored the importance of user engagement in the design and development of digital health technologies, indicating a shift towards more inclusive and ethically aware practices

References

Abosede, O. (2024). *Artificial intelligence for human capital development and start-up companies in Nigeria—ACRP*. https://africachinareporting.com/artificial-intelligence-for-human-capital-development-and-start-up-companies-in-nigeria/. Accessed 24 July 2024.

Adejumo, A. A., Alegbejo-Olarinoye, M. I., Akanbi, O. O., Ajamu, O. J., Akims, S. M., & Koroye, O. F. (2023). Artificial Intelligence in medical practice: Closing the gap for the present and creating opportunities for the future. *The Nigerian Health Journal, 23*(2), 580–586.

Azevedo, M. J. (2017). The state of health system(s) in Africa: Challenges and opportunities. *Historical Perspectives on the State of Health and Health Systems in Africa, II*, 1–73.

Brall, C., Schröder-Bäck, P., & Maeckelberghe, E. (2019) Ethical aspects of digital health from a justice point of view. *European Journal of Public Health, 29*(Supplement_3), 18–22.

CIPESA. (2022). *Which way for data localisation in Africa?*

Council of Europe. (2021). Regulation (EU) 2021/2282 of the European Parliament and of the Council of 15 December 2021 on health technology assessment and amending Directive 2011/24/EU. *Official Journal of European Union, 50*.

Dhagarra, D., Goswami, M., & Kumar, G. (2020). Impact of trust and privacy concerns on technology acceptance in healthcare: An Indian perspective. *International Journal of Medical Informatics, 141*, 104164.

Eastwood, J. B., Conroy, R. E., Naicker, S., West, P. A., Tutt, R. C., & Plange-Rhule, J. (2005). Loss of health professionals from sub-Saharan Africa: the pivotal role of the UK. *The Lancet, 365*(9474), 1893–1900.

Eke, D., & Stahl, B. (2024). Ethics in the governance of data and digital technology: An analysis of European data regulations and policies. *Digital Society, 3*(1), 11.

Eke, D.O., Wakunuma, K., & Akintoye, S. (2023). Introducing responsible AI in Africa. In *Responsible AI in Africa: Challenges and opportunities* (pp. 1–11). Springer International Publishing Cham.

Holst, C., Sukums, F., Radovanovic, D., Ngowi, B., Noll, J., & Winkler, A. S. (2020). Sub-Saharan Africa—The new breeding ground for global digital health. *The Lancet Digital Health, 2*(4), e160–e162.

Hsia, R. Y., Mbembati, N. A., Macfarlane, S., & Kruk, M. E. (2012). Access to emergency and surgical care in sub-Saharan Africa: the infrastructure gap. *Health Policy and Planning, 27*(3), 234–244.

Ihde, D. (1990). *Technology and the lifeworld: From garden to earth* [Online]. https://philpapers.org/rec/IHDTAT-3. Accessed 5 August 2024.

Jones, E., Harden, S., & Crawley, M. J. (2022). *The R book*. Wiley.

Jousset, O., Kimeu, M., Müller, T., Sforza, G., Sun, Y. S., Ustun, A., & Wilson, M. (2023). *How digital tools could boost efficiency in African health systems*. Mckinsey.

Kipruto, H., Muneene, D., Droti, B., Jepchumba, V., Okeibunor, C. J., Nabyonga-Orem, J., & Karamagi, H. C (2022). Use of digital health interventions in sub-Saharan Africa for health systems strengthening over the last 10 years: A scoping review protocol. *Frontiers in Digital Health, 4*, 874251.

Manlan, C. (2019). *This is the key to boosting economic growth in Africa*. [Online] World Economic Forum. https://www.weforum.org/agenda/2019/05/investing-in-africans-health/. Accessed 24 July 2024.

Manyazewal, T. et al. (2023) Mapping digital health ecosystems in Africa in the context of endemic infectious and non-communicable diseases. npj Digital Medicine, 6(1), pp. 1–12.

Musa, S. M., Haruna, U. A., Manirambona, E., Eshun, G., Ahmad, D. M., Dada, D. A., Gololo, A. A., Musa, S. S., Abdulkadir, A. K., & Lucero-Prisno, D. E. (2023). Paucity of health data in Africa: An obstacle to digital health implementation and evidence-based practice. *Public Health Reviews, 44*, 1605821.

Naicker, S., Plange-Rhule, J., Tutt, R. C., & Eastwood, J. B. (2009). Shortage of healthcare workers in developing countries—Africa. *Ethnicity & Disease, 19*, 60–64.

Nebeker, C., Torous, J., & Bartlett Ellis, R. J. (2019). Building the case for actionable ethics in digital health research supported by artificial intelligence. *BMC Medicine, 17*(1), 137.

Oleribe, O. O., Momoh, J., Uzochukwu, B. S., Mbofana, F., Adebiyi, A., Barbera, T., Williams, R., & Taylor-Robinson, S. D. (2019). Identifying key challenges facing healthcare systems in Africa and potential solutions. *International Journal of General Medicine, 12*, 395–403.

Osakede, U. (2022). Infrastructure and health system performance in Africa. *Managing Global Transitions, 20*(4) [Online]. https://ojs.upr.si/index.php/fm/article/view/53. Accessed 24 July 2024.

Owoyemi, A., Osuchukwu, J. I., Azubuike, C., Ikpe, R. K., Nwachukwu, B. C., Akinde, C. B., Biokoro, G. W., Ajose, A. B., Nwokoma, E. I., Mfon, N. E., & Benson, T. O. (2022). Digital solutions for community and primary health workers: Lessons from implementations in Africa. *Frontiers in Digital Health, 4*, 876957.

Sekandi, J. N., Murray, K., Berryman, C., Davis-Olwell, P., Hurst, C., Kakaire, R., Kiwanuka, N., Whalen, C. C., & Mwaka, E. S. (2022). Ethical, legal, and sociocultural issues in the use of mobile technologies and call detail records data for public health in the East African Region: Scoping review. *Interactive Journal of Medical Research, 11*(1), e35062.

Shaw, J., Ali, J., Atuire, C. A., Cheah, P. Y., Español, A. G., Gichoya, J. W., Hunt, A., Jjingo, D., Littler, K., Paolotti, D., & Vayena, E. (2024). Research ethics and artificial intelligence for global health: Perspectives from the global forum on bioethics in research. *BMC Medical Ethics, 25*, 46.

Stahl, B. C., Akintoye, S., Bitsch, L., Bringedal, B., Eke, D., Farisco, M., Grasenick, K., Guerrero, M., Knight, W., Leach, T., & Nyholm, S. (2021). From responsible research and innovation to responsibility by design. *Journal of Responsible Innovation, 8*(2), 175–198.

Vayena, E., Haeusermann, T., Adjekum, A., & Blasimme, A. (2018). Digital health: Meeting the ethical and policy challenges. *Swiss Medical Weekly, 148*, w14571.

Wakefield, A. (2024). *How Africa's health tech industry is stacking up in 2024*. https://www.foundersfactory.africa/blog/africas-health-tech-industry-stacking-up-2024. Accessed 24 July 2024.

Wakunuma, K., & Eke, D. (2024). Africa, ChatGPT, and generative AI systems: Ethical benefits, concerns, and the need for governance. *Philosophies*.

WHO. (2020). *WHO global report on trends in prevalence of tobacco use 2000–2025*. World Health Organization.

Winters, N., Venkatapuram, S., Geniets, A., & Wynne-Bannister, E. (2020). Prioritarian principles for digital health in low resource settings. *Journal of Medical Ethics, 46*(4), 259–264.

Zarif, A. (2022). The ethical challenges facing the widespread adoption of digital healthcare technology. *Health and Technology, 12*(1), 175–179.

CHAPTER 10

Artificial Intelligence (AI) Onto-Norms and Gender Equality: Unveiling the Invisible Gender Norms in AI Ecosystems in the Context of Africa

Angella K. Ndaka, Harriet A. M. Ratemo, Abigail Oppong, and Eucabeth B. O. Majiwa

Introduction

In Africa as elsewhere, the current overriding message of most digitization advice is the prioritization of AI in strategies, policies and business model for any company or individual that wants to remain relevant now and in the future. AI and big data is becoming sovereign with almost an immaculate position, being placed at the centre of every business decision-making (Bronson, 2018, 2022; Healy & Fourcade, 2017). Although permeating invisibly and sophisticatedly, AI is beginning to shape decisions in private

A. K. Ndaka (✉)
Centre for Epistemic Justice Foundation, Nairobi, Kenya
e-mail: katee.ndaka@gmail.com

H. A. M. Ratemo
Department of Computer Science, Daystar University, Nairobi, Kenya
e-mail: hratemo@daystar.ac.ke

D. O. Eke et al. (eds.), *Trustworthy AI*,
https://doi.org/10.1007/978-3-031-75674-0_10

lives in a manner that appears ordinary (Augusto, 2007; Aurigi, 2007; Diefenbach et al., 2022). Companies integrating AI in its business model are being considered to make good choices while entities not upskilling, reskilling and/or applying AI in their everyday lives being deemed to be missing out in a big way (Wamba-Taguimdje et al., 2020). On the contrary, there are many ways governments, organizations, companies and individuals are enacting different versions of AI, including taking into consideration the different effects of AI on their businesses and individual lives. Although AI strategies, models and policies exist, with over 60 countries globally publishing their AI national strategies in the past 5 years (Zhang et al., 2020), there are still no universally agreed upon standards geared towards making AI sustainable, beneficial and safe for everyone. Further, despite AI being a technology, its enactment, governance and what it intends to achieve remain often heavily shaped by situated social values especially in the African context (Robinson, 2020). This raises critical questions on the place of African values and principles in the current AI ethics discourse (Eke, 2023). African ethics and expertise are often neglected in what Ruttkamp-bloem (2023) called epistemic injustice. Furthermore, Africa's current response to AI is reactive, with existing strategies foregrounding technology growth, as opposed to frameworks that govern this socio-technical assemblage.

AI is perceived as more than a technology in social science research space since it is a socio-technical assemblage comprising politics, interests and virtual substructures that is tied to physical infrastructures and human entities elsewhere (Hasselbalch, 2021, 2022). AI combines both conscious and unconscious decisions, agencies that define impressions such as access, value and socio-economic categorizations with implications on socio-material in societies where they are enacted (Burch & Legun, 2021; Carolan, 2017; Fourcade & Healy, 2017). AI is a useful

A. Oppong
Language Technology Lab, University of Cambridge, Cambridge, UK
e-mail: ao578@cam.ac.uk

E. B. O. Majiwa
Department of Agricultural and Resource Economics, Jomo Kenyatta University of Agriculture and Technology [JKUAT], Nairobi, Kenya
e-mail: eucamajiwa@rpe.jkuat.ac.ke

tool for enacting political and corporate interests for those in power (Latour, 2011; Mclennan, 2015). In the African context for instance, AI systems will likely continue historical legacies and enforce dominant knowledge systems and norms (Ndaka et al., 2024). Thus, different populations will be impacted differently by AI for many reasons including privileges, or lack thereof, their socio-political positioning, their uber capital, missing voices in STEM and decision-making spaces (Fourcade & Healy, 2017; Rosendahl et al., 2015). Consequently, the way gender perspectives, norms and biases are presented through data and propagated by the AI algorithmic activity in different sites will differ significantly. For instance, AI is already entrenching different forms of microaggressions against women of colour in other parts of the world like US (Boulamwini & Gebru 2018; Benjamin, 2019; Eubanks, 2018; Noble, 2018; West et al., 2019b). AI systemic biases are thus expected to be worse for African women due to extant culture and patriarchy sponsored biases that may be (re)produced through design and/or data (OECD, 2018). In this chapter, we explore how AI and gender vulnerabilities are entrenched in AI design, training and use. The study focuses on how social ontologies facilitate AI design, training and use. The study examines how enacting and re-enacting AI in what we call AI onto-norms—is capable of aggravating the vulnerability of women within the digital spaces.

The chapter examines how onto-norms propagate certain gender practices in digital spaces through character and the norms of spaces that shape AI design, training, and use. Additionally, the different user behaviours and practices regarding whether, how, when, and why different gender groups engage in and with AI-driven spaces is explored. By examining how data and content can knowingly or unknowingly be used to drive certain social norms in the AI ecosystems, this study argues that onto-norms shape how AI engages with the content that relates to women. Onto-norms specifically shape the image, behaviour, and other media, including how gender identities and perspectives are intentionally or otherwise, included, missed, or misrepresented in building and training AI systems. To address these African women related AI biases, we propose a framework for building gender equality intentionality within the AI systems. The framework aims to ensure capturing of women's voices and abetting the use of personal data to perpetuate further gender biases in AI systems.

Extant Gender Biases in AI Design, Algorithms and Data

AI and ML algorithms have permeated all aspects of our everydayness thus impacting decision-making with far-reaching consequences on society (Ntoutsi et al., 2019). AI and ML algorithms shape our everyday digital experience, including recommending high-risk situations like loans, and hiring choices (Mehrabi et al., 2022). While algorithmic decision-making offers an opportunity to reduce work burden and has more aspects than humans, however, algorithms are susceptible to biases that induce unfairness in decision-making. Unfair algorithmic activity is defined as one whose decisions favour a specific group of people (Chouldechova & Roth, 2018; Mehrabi et al., 2022). They can also be defined as any systematic error in the design, conduct, or analysis of a study (Althubaiti, 2016). These biases can stem from predictions biases, biased objectives, and systematic bias in data and feedback loops (Gupta et al., 2022). In this section, we discuss biases that emanate from AI artefact design, algorithmic biases, and context transfer biases.

Design Biases

Lack of diversity in AI development teams may lead to homogeneous teams transferring their assumptions and cognitive biases in the development process, resulting in unbalanced and unfair outcomes (Hall & Ellis, 2023; Ndaka & Majiwa, 2024; Rosendahl et al., 2015). While text and voice-based conversational agents (CAs) have become increasingly popular (Feine et al., 2020), the design of most commercial voice-based CAs leans more towards specific gender as highlighted by UNESCO study(West et al., 2019a). Notably, majority of the voice-based CAs adopt a "female exclusively or female by default" names and/or voice (e.g., Alexa, Cortana, Siri). For example, in advertising, gendered sentences (e.g., "Alexa lost her voice") frequently infer to feminine gender associations resulting in the manifestation of gender stereotypes (Feine et al., 2020). These in most cases may be designed by workforces that are overwhelmingly male career dominated, with women domiciled as career assistants. Compared to other professional sectors, women remain underrepresented in the technology space (West et al., 2019a). Such gender-based career characterization often reinforces traditional gender stereotypes thus negatively impacting on everyday interaction (Feine et al., 2020). Especially where female voice-based CAs often act as personal assistants, it reinforces dominant power and expectations of simple, direct, and unsophisticated answers (Feine et al., 2020).

The male-dominated IT industry lacks gender diversity especially in AI developers and STEM workers, potentially reinforcing male dominance and controlling algorithms, leading to gender-biased outcomes, as seen in 2015's facial recognition software. Additionally, men's perception of STEM when designing career advertisements leads to fewer women applying (Nadeem et al., 2022). Thus, gender inclusion in AI technology development introduces diverse perspectives, reduces cognitive biases, and mitigates bias-related risk management concerns (Hall & Ellis, 2023; Saka, 2021). Users and developers should be aware of the potential impact of gender and racial stereotypes and endeavour to avoid, overcome, or eliminate them entirely (Wellner, 2020).

Algorithmic and Data Biases

The intersection of gender and AI raises questions about the participation of minority groups and how to respond to risky technologies, especially in this age of algorithmic commodification (Ndaka et al., 2024; Wellner, 2020). The integration of AI will thus need to address the challenge of algorithmic bias and discrimination against underrepresented groups (Gardezi et al., 2023; Hall & Ellis, 2023). Most AI algorithms need big datasets for training (Domingues et al., 2022; Norori et al., 2021), and may discriminate against vulnerable groups owing to implicit data bias and training (Gwagwa et al., 2021). This poses a risk due to inconsistencies in training data, security breaches, and flawed AI models (Galaz et al., 2021).

With data-driven bias, most fields of human research are heavily biased towards participants with a Western, Educated, Industrialized, Rich, Democratic—WEIRD—profile (Kanazawa, 2020), which is not representative of the whole human population. Although data from mobile devices and satellites offer vast opportunities to address social vulnerabilities like poverty, AI-analysis solutions can be skewed due to underrepresentation of disadvantaged people. AI systems designed with poor, limited, or biased data sets may lead to training data bias, potentially causing incorrect management recommendations (Jiménez et al., 2019). AI algorithms may specifically disfavour women and underrepresented minorities since they are trained on biased data, reflecting and amplifying existing inequities (Gwagwa et al., 2021).

The lack of datasets diversity, with bias in algorithms often stemming from societal inequalities and discriminatory attitudes, often excludes minority gender perspectives from the samplings (Saka, 2021). This bias can equally arise from incorrect data classification, often at the intersection of race and gender (Hall & Ellis, 2023).

The key concern is whether datasets exist that are fit or suitable for the purpose of the various applications, domains and tasks for which the AI system is being developed and deployed. This is because ML systems determined by the data have predictive behaviour and the data also largely defines the machine learning task itself. The suitability of a dataset depends on three factors: statistical methods to address representation issues, consideration of the socio-technical context, and understanding human interaction with AI systems (Schwartz et al., 2022).

Transfer Context Biases

AI systems are designed and developed for specific real-world settings, but are often tested in idealized scenarios (Schwartz et al., 2022). Thus, transfer context bias occurs when AI systems designed for one ecological, climate, or social-ecological context are incorrectly transferred to another, potentially leading to flawed results. Algorithm-based decision tools in discriminatory settings pose a risk as perceived ideas may differ by end users or those affected by systems' decisions (Schwartz et al., 2021). The bias in AI software usage can alter the application's original intent, idea, or impact assessment particularly when individuals or companies use off-the-shelf AI software (Chouldechova & Roth, 2018). AI systems may function as intended, but users may not understand their utility, leading not only to interpretation bias but also data misuse (Lajoie-O'Malley et al., 2020).

Theoretical Approach and Methods

In this chapter, we draw from the reflections of Annemarie Mol, a feminist Science and Technology Studies (STS) scholar who has published extensively on politics of ontologies (Mol, 1999, 2002, 2013). In her work, Mol (2013) conceptualizes onto-norms as the ways in which specific understandings of reality, or ontologies, shape and prescribe norms for thought and action. In her argument, norms are deeply embedded within the very fabric of how we perceive and make sense of the world around us. She further argues that "*an object cannot be removed from practices that sustain it*" (Mol, 2002, p. 31), and that reality does not exist in totality, rather it comprises actors, agencies, things, people and the words they use. This scenario is embedded in socio-political and socio-material contexts that link those realities to their conditions and political dimensions that shape them (Mol, 1999). Mol's concept of onto-norms helps us understand power and agency in relation to AI development and enactment. It highlights the ways in which ontological assumptions can shape and constrain possibilities for action and change. By making these onto-norms explicit, Mol (2013) encourages critical reflection on the taken-for-granted assumptions that underpin scientific and technological practices, thus opening up new avenues for questioning innovation, and their use cases.

This study captures the realities of AI and how the use cases are enacted, by focusing more on socio-material entanglement between the AI and the humans, agencies, things, and conditions that enact it. For instance, we ask questions such as what kinds of AI? Who is enacting this AI? What norms, practices, and conditions enable this enactment? And how do different enactions differently shape the enactors, and the outputs of the enactment? In asking these questions, this study unravels how different AI socio-materialities emerge (Mol, 2013), and how this shapes the lives of women and girls in their everyday interaction with AI. In this sense, ontology is seen as multiple, thus questioning multiple and sometimes contrasting realities, which are variously enacted as well as afforded to act in different ways (Mol, 2013).

In this chapter we treat AI enactment as a reality consisting of multiple bodies (Mol, 2002), and thus entangled in different socio-materialities that shape its emergence. We draw from Mol's theoretical reflections, to examine the elemental and invisible gender problems of AI and big data in the context of the African region. The study examines AI enactment through the lens of power and interests among the commonly used social media and search sites, specifically Facebook, Google, TikTok, Instagram, LinkedIn, and twitter, and their large language models. We use participant observation and digital content analysis to examine how gender norms shape and are shaped by different social actors and things. The study investigates which AI onto-norms emerge, and how they work with social actors in the entangled space to propagate certain gender norms and practices in different AI spaces through design, training, and use. Our research focused on 20 online participants whose digital activity was observed with their consent between June and September 2023. In this participant observation, we particularly focused on aspects such as what kind of post, the post frequencies, commentary and post engagement, and the common kind of posts that the participants engaged with, and/or received recommendation to engage in. To get insights about the design spaces, two of the authors focused their observation on the gender norms exemplified in data patterns in the large language models, the norms and practices of groups that designed AI as well as annotated and moderated AI data. By examining how different actors enacted AI, we were able to tell how, when, whether, and why different gender groups engage with and in AI-driven spaces. We also noticed how data and algorithmic activity knowingly or unknowingly drove certain gender within the AI ecosystems. For purposes of confidentiality, the results are presented as a generalized narrative, which withholds specific participant and site names. The study is cognizant that these AI realities happen in different sites but emerge differently.

Results

The results presented in this chapter are done in two cases conducted in totally different contexts but within African context. The first case focuses on design and data biases observed in NLP systems—with particular focus on machine translation from English to Twi and vice versa in Ghana. The second case focuses on how norms are algorithmically mediated in and through data in digital social spaces in Kenya.

Norms at Design-Scapes

Case Study 1: Design and Data Onto-norms—Examining Gender Bias in NLP Systems (Machine Translation from English—Twi)—Ghana

Machine Translation (MT) is a powerful tool in Natural Language Processing that is used to translate between two languages. In this narrative analysis, we will examine gender bias in an English-to-Twi machine translation, mainly focusing on biases that may be reflected in datasets. Just like how Prates, Avelar, & Lamb (2020) explored a list of comprehensive job positions from the U.S. Bureau of Labor Statistics, it was used to build sentences. The Google Translate API was used to translate and collect statistics on the frequency of female, male, and gender-neutral pronouns in the decoded output. There was an unbiased gender distribution towards the female gender for fields linked to STEM jobs. However, our data showed some gender representation bias within the STEM jobs. This is also referred to as allocation bias—where tools decide which gender to refer to and allocate to which role. They use embedded stereotypes in data to define what is feminine and what is masculine. For instance, a word like "cleaner" is more likely to be allocated to a female, as compared to a male. This shows us how AI tools tend to conform to the already extant stereotypes of being masculine or feminine. This was observed in a case where we analysed a machine translation of English to Twi Language (a commonly spoken language in Ghana). Zhao et al. (2018) pointing to detection and mitigation of gender bias from data sets argues that training data can include and/or amplify bias.

In our experiment, we performed a machine translation to show the bias in the evaluation of generated texts. Using an English-Twi parallel Corpus from (Azunre et al., 2021) and Google Collab as our sources of data for machine translation, we noticed four sources of gender bias in NLP systems namely input representation, data, models, and research design. The data was evaluated over a test set and our own generated data using two metrics: Bleu scores and our native speakers' judgement of how accurate the translation is in percentages as shown in Table 10.1. The results showed a critically skewed gender distribution in data as shown in Table 10.2.

During this analysis, an interesting observation was made on the original dataset curated by (Azunre et al., 2021). Most words were not only associated with the "he", but that the "he" was associated with higher-status professions as also observed by some studies (Kurita et al., 2019). Our work shows a continuation of the same gender bias in the way local languages are translated or represented in English. Take an example, the

Table 10.1 Distribution of dataset used in training the sequence-to-sequence machine translation model

Training	*Test*	*Validation*
24,728	1373	1373

Table 10.2 Distribution of masculine, feminine and multiple in the data

Set	*Other*	*Masculine*	*Feminine*	*Multiple*
Original Data	21,097	2972	1149	203
Percentage	83.0%	11.7%	4.5%	0.8%

pronoun He/She in Twi is Ɔ, which is normally gender neutral and hence represents both males and females. However, on translating this to English, this is how the sentences are translated as shown in Table 10.3.

Ideally, the correct translation—that reflects data inclusivity—should be read as shown in Table 10.4.

In another case, the translation amplified and/or 'superiorised' a male professional over a female professional. An instance is when the language model was prompted to translate from English to *twi*, and was fed with the phrases, "she is an engineer" and "he is an engineer". The results were as shown in Table 10.5.

We observed that the term 'nimdefo' was added after 'Ɔyɛ mfiri' signifying differentiated levels between male and female engineers. 'Nimdefo' means intelligent in Twi and this signifies the superior allocation and

Table 10.3 Gender bias in translation

English	*Twi*
He is a doctor	Ɔyɛ dɔkota
He is a lawyer	Ɔyɛ mmrahwɛfo

Table 10.4 Correct gender translation

English	*Twi*
He/She is a doctor	Ɔyɛ dɔkota
He/She is a lawyer	Ɔyɛ mmrahwɛfo

Table 10.5 Gender profession biases

Input Sentences	*Model Prediction*
She is an engineer	Ɔyɛ mfiri
He is an Engineer	Ɔyɛ mfiri nimdefo

attention paid by LLMs when 'he' is situated or associated with the profession "engineer". These observed trends show design-based biases that are entrenched by not only the 'who'(designers) is shaping AI models, but also by the 'what'(data) that is training those models. This is mostly compounded by the fact that most professionals that are training these local language models are male and hence carry their inherent biases when designing and training these models.

Norms at Use-Scapes

Case Study 2: Examining Misogyny in AI-Mediated Digital Social Sites(Kenya)

In this case study, we used participant observation to examine how 20 selected social actors consciously or unconsciously work with algorithms to enact some gender realities in social media spaces. The character of the content posted, frequency of such content, and content engagement was keenly observed for a period of 3 months. The participants were randomly selected and confidentially approached to give consent for this experiential observation to be done on their activity. For purposes of getting authentic data, the period within which this observation was done was not precisely communicated. Gender balance was ensured in selection of the observed participants.

a. The character of content

Within this particular period, we observed that Kenyan community has three key topics that every social media content oscillates around: relationships, money and politics. This particular period of observation, we focused on norms about relationships—which also tends to intersect with other topics owing to the African community life philosophy. Within this sphere, we observed that while over 50% of content posted on social spaces had some negative connotation about women and girls, the larger percentage was mostly posted by male participants. For instance, out of every 10 men that did a post, 9 of them presented the character of women negatively. While most of the content presented women as selfish, and opportunists as relates to money, other posts generalized women and girls as promiscuous, unpredictable, untrustworthy, complicated, and the extreme ones presenting women and girls as a form of danger to their male counterparts. Common catch phrases and hashtags that accompanied these posts were “fear women”, “Daughters of eve”, and “daughters of Delila”, “the other gender” etc. Within this space, women also posted about other women. 6 out of every 10 women had something negative, or a condemnation/victimization, or an expression of negative emotions like shame and regret about their fellow women. This sub-study observed three common kinds of content posted online.

The first kind of posts contained content that was driving agitation for men to be allowed to keep many intimate partners for their “peace of mind”. While the content applauded polygamy, it openly condemned the ‘second wife’ commonly referred to as “mpango wa kando” aka “side chick” as an infidel. This is regardless of whether the man in question initiated the relationship, and gave the other party the correct information about his marital status or not. Either way, the other woman involved is blamed by both men and women for infidelity and promiscuity, while the wife, commonly referred to as “the goat wife” is judged for her inability to keep the husband. Here we notice a society that places the sole responsibility of holding societal relationships together, not only according to the male gender unfettered privilege, but also requiring women and girls to take responsibility for issues that the male gender should address.

The second kind of posts seemed to amplify and justify the polygamy stunt. Despite Kenya having a population of 50% male and 50% female, the rhetoric in social media presents the population of women in Kenya as doubling that of men. And the key slogan that supports this narrative, which appeared in more than 10 posts observed within this period was “the concept of polygamy is about every woman having a husband, and not men having many secret wives”. Upon approaching one participant who keenly pushed this rhetoric with a question in social space discussion about polygamy, he declared that a man can have as many women as he can but he must never tell them about the existence of each other. Reason being the fear that the women will collude against the man, and may end up murdering the man. This kind of narrative was heavily supported by most male participants in those engagements and cultural acceptance was invoked to justify these norms.

The third kind of posts contained content that heavily supported practices that entrench the thriving of gender-based violence and the resulting currently hiking femicide. While not so many participants seemed religious and cultural in the deepest sense, in many posts there was a silent trend that almost expected every woman to stick and fight for her marriage, however abusive it is and this is deeply entrenched in the character of the social media narrative. In so many cases religion and culture were conveniently invoked when necessary to support this narrative. It was noted that every case of woman-initiated separation was directly stereotyped to the woman pursuing her husband's wealth, the woman being promiscuous, and/or the woman branded as being proud and rude (if they are economically endowed). In most of the cases, the male gender was presented as innocent or victims. Our results showed that there is almost an unspoken creed that before pursuing her happiness, career growth, or economic independence, the women should support their husbands to achieve his ends first. This was seen in posts that presented single and independent women who have stable income and are running successful careers as egoistic, proud, disrespectful, and unmarriageable.

Here we see certain norms that have historically marginalized women being re(produced) in the digital social sites in the most subtle, fast and accurate way. While such norms were situated within individuals and communities, and sometimes were never shared openly, digital social sites provide a thriving environment to spread these norms faster and wider. The reasons for such spread include the invisibility of digital space that curtails the essence of responsibility, algorithmic push and activity that catalyse the spread of the norms and unfettered access by digital companies to data—with minimal or zero accountability about their digital activities.

b. Algorithmic Role in Mediating Misogyny.

During the analysis of the content posted on social sites we noticed a very interesting activity happening with the post engagement. Those who had been in social media longer, noticed a new trend in posts engagement. While previously, posts in digital social spaces used to get engagement chronologically, with earlier posts receiving engagement before latter posts. Some posts got engagement faster, and seemed to move faster and get more likes than others. To test if algorithmic activity had any role in this trend, we decided to do intermittent posts, with posts applauding women, while others trying to fix and/or condemn women. Our results showed that the posts that contained content that presented women and girls as positively impacting the society received less likes and less engagement compared to content that presented women as badly behaved, or as lacking in one way or the other. Any form of posts that challenged power relations got engagement by a few like-minded women, otherwise it remained muted and unpopular in the social media.

For instance, our results showed that generally, posts that cast aspersions on the behaviour of women received 95% engagement compared to 5% engagement in the posts that appraised women. This shows that posts that were misogynistic in nature were likely to get engagement compared to the ones that adopted a feminist approach. The results also show that men were more likely to engage this content more than women, with comments that followed misogynistic posts being 60% and 40% from male and female respectively. On assessing the character of the content by those engaging the posts, the more misogynistic comments not only received more likes and support, but they also seemed to make the commenters more popular in the space. On observing this, we noticed a new activity, which was also supported by one of my participants in confidence. There emerged a new breed of fictional stories created using screen-shot WhatsApp chats, or own person content. The participant in question highlighted that online content creators were willing to do anything for 'likes'. This included creating sex scandals, fictional stories, staged sex or pornographic clips and stage short video plays driving certain gender norms. They also created scripted WhatsApp chats to draw online engagement to their content. And because sexist content got more visibility compared to non-sexist one, most male and female social media influencers chose to create content that was mainly objectifying women, negatively presenting women and sometimes victimizing real victims of GBV. In most of these posts while the male commenters castigated the fictional or non-fictional woman involved, they normalized the man's behaviour- mostly referring to it as a 'man's thing'. It was also observed that the female commenters reacted to the posts with disdain, disappointment, and mockery to their female 'victims'.

Discussion: Practices That Sustains AI Onto-Norms and Implications it Has on Women and Girls in Africa

The results show that while the embedded norms of the social actors designing, training, and using AI were in a co-evolving entanglement with each other and responsible in influencing the ideals, AI was learning and propagating thin the digital spaces. In the first set of data for instance, we see stereotypes embedded in data and algorithms heavily 'superiorising' the male professionals in STEM compared to female professionals. We also notice career role allocation from historical stereotyped male vs female roles. This is seen to be playing in the local language models which already confer roles like doctor, lawyer, and engineer a male character. In cases where our researchers tried to 'impose' the position of a female engineer, the male engineer is accorded an additional accolade like an intelligent engineer. In the second set of data, we see that while the norms and stereotypes of digital social users influenced the content that was preferred, AI algorithms in those spaces were working with these actors to amplify the virality of the discourses that were shaping gender norms in social spaces.

Efe (2022) argues that AI "*creates digital spaces that tend to be spaces of extraction and exploitation and thus digital-regional colonial sites*" (p. 253). While most of these digital sites consistently withhold vital information concerning their digital features and products as highlighted by Dieffenbach and Colleagues (2022), these features continue causing knowledge and actual harm to the society. This is because they produce new value areas that not only undermine existing knowledge and tramp on epistemic values of communities (Felt, 2017; Ndaka et al., 2024; Subramaniam et al., 2016), but also entrench historical structural and social marginalization of some knowledge groups especially among women and girls (Ndaka & Majiwa, 2024; Rosendahl et al., 2015). For instance, masked in complexified invisibility (Dieffenbach et al., 2022), is an algorithmic activity that amplifies sensational content in digital spaces. Our findings show that in the last few years the trend about what goes viral, and what gets engagement in digital spaces is shaped by both the character of the content and the algorithmic push happening in the invisibility of the internet. This also resonates with claims by Haugen, an Ex-Facebook employee and now a whistle-blower, who while testifying against Facebook claimed that an engagement-based formula was being used to help sensational content—such as posts that feature dis/misinformation, political rage, misogyny, and other forms of sexist posts—to move faster, far and wide in the society.[1]

[1] https://www.npr.org/2021/10/05/1043377310/facebook-whistleblower-frances-haugen-congress.

While it may be easier to identify hate speech in social media, using the globally accepted constructs of what is referred to as offensive (Waseem & Hovy, 2016), it is very easy to miss some types of social offences especially in cases where victims themselves seem to accept, interact comfortably and enjoy the flow of thought—treating this as a norm. Our results showed that in most misogynistic posts, women not only engaged with the post, but also supported the content of the posts by expressing emotions like shame, disappointment, and disgust to their fellow women victimized in the posts. This shows how historical norms embedded in everyday conversations are being transmitted in and through digital spaces. Worse is the way the algorithms are learning and picking these norms and practices that sustain the norms and amplifying them in the digital social spaces.

Some studies point that sexism is a characteristic that increases the interactive nature of social media posts, in fact sexists' posts are more interactive than racial posts Clarke and Grieve (2017). Misogyny particularly is a major and urgent problem in large social sites like Facebook, and twitter. It includes "*aspects, such as sexual harassment, the stereotypes associated with "stupid" women's behaviour against male, objectification of the female body and a lot of other problems*" (Shushkevich et al., 2020). Our results showed that sexism and misogyny was not only increasing the interactive nature, but that there was an invisible push that was making such posts move faster and get wider engagement. Some sites like twitter have features like high-speed propagation of tweets which not only makes them viral but creates the possibility of these tweets staying in the site for a long time and getting larger viewership through retweeting (Hewitt et al., 2016). Facebook on the other hand has features like algorithm reward engagement, which enables the post that receives comments and likes, and other interactions, spread more widely and quickly, being featured more prominently in feeds instead of posts following chronological order of posting.

The results of this study show that despite the society being misogynistic, the new algorithmic activity is not only urging this vice on but also amplifying it through post engagement reward systems and a pushed engagement. This has resulted in new values in digital spaces—with online content creators interested more in what content sells as opposed to the content that builds the society. Since sexism and misogyny increases that interactive nature of content, then such content becomes the practice that drives the new norms in the digital spaces. And these norms are directly driven by the AI algorithms entangled in such spaces. Since AI learns from the data that is fed to it every day, then the algorithms pick up these norms and spread them faster and wider, while learning to perfect this in digital spaces. As a result, new values are not only created, but we see new practices that are propagated by the society entangled in this space as we are going to discuss in the next section.

Impacts of the New AI Onto-Norms on Women and Girls

In the African context, posts that seem to drive negative gender norms e.g., misogyny and sexism have been prominent in some social sites, like Facebook and twitter, and have been used by those sites for economic gains. Some studies show that there has been an increase in the content that targets female leaders and influencers,[2] mostly presenting them in a negative way. This has not only been used to wash down the gains by female role-modelling, but has also lowered the perceptions of women and girls about their rights in relation to gender-based violence. A 2022 demographic and health survey conducted in Kenya shows that 43% of women aged 15–49 believe that a husband is justified to beat his wife. Several reasons are used to support this vice including but not limited to unfaithfulness, coming home late, burning food, going out without reporting to the husband, arguing with the husband, neglecting children and if she refuses to cook.[3] The top reason given for why husbands should beat their wife is unfaithfulness—which our research showed that it could be over-featured and exaggerated in social media, amplified by AI, while at the same time the authenticity of content may not be verified in the era of deep fakes and fictional content creators. While our focus was not necessarily on the posts themselves, and who they target, we argue that this kind of content that involves nudity of female influencers, objectification of the African female body, and amplification of women's 'bad behaviour' and other stereotypes, even in cases where actions or inactions committed involve a male actor—is creating a new oppressive digital spaces, and the data from the content is weaponizing AI to target women and girls unfairly in digital and physical spaces.

While this is happening, the digital companies in question are amassing massive data, which they use to classify their users as well as create new

[2] https://pollicy.org/wp-content/uploads/2023/05/Byte_Bullies_report.pdf.

[3] See: https://www.knbs.or.ke/kenya-demographic-and-health-survey-kdhs-2022/.

products that are used to drive their profits (Fourcade & Healy, 2017). Since sexist content sells more, this is increasingly attracting new forms of norms and practices among designers and the African digital users—which is further is mediating new forms of digitally gender-based violence, with the content emerging from these norms being used by the algorithm to drive profits up for some of the social media sites like twitter and Facebook.

Intentionality in Design, Training, and Use

Gender diversity is a very important aspect in technology development because of its ability to draw unique perspectives and knowledge from different genders, and articulate it into designs and other levels of technology development and deployment. It is noteworthy that different gender groups represent certain norms, and the way they do and receive things is different. Our results have not only shown how norms by dominant groups and things are driving new gender norms, but also show how the thriving algorithmic environments are subtly but effectively silencing and subordinating women further, exposing them to social injustices like GBV (whether digitally mediated or actual physical GBV) and other forms of marginalization. Furthermore, the results reveal critical exclusion of women perspectives in AI designs and data in large language models. This implies that AI development and use spaces are characterized by an asymmetrical cognitive environment where women are not deemed as knowledge peers—rather, they are reduced to data givers (lingual, media and behavioural) and just statistics. The concept of gender inclusion AI debates is conveniently being reduced to demographic disaggregation, with most solutions being mere tokenistic additions while muting some aspects of deeper gender perspectives. The norms propagated in these spaces are conveniently being reproduced in the technology itself further marginalizing women and girls in the digital space. This interplay of norms, practices, and material technology further entrenches the unequal power relations in the age where AI is being used to classify, commodify, and currencify human data for profits (Fourcade & Healy, 2017). The key questions are: in the current age of big data are women provided with a conducive environment to engage with AI technology as rational enquirers (Giladi, 2018) or they are being peripheralized, and always forced to seek for epistemic recognition and affirmation from their male peers (Koskinen & Rolin, 2021; Poliseli & Leite, 2021)? Is society busy fixing women using machines? Could that be the reason why the knowledge produced is so weak such that it reduces women to objects of technology (Koskinen & Ludwig, 2021; Ndaka et al., 2024)?. With the current activism against the current rise of GBV, which has been associated with digitally mediated GBV, women have also been subjected with unfair labour of identifying these injustices, and sometimes having to picket to seek for affirmation from dominant groups including the authorities.

We propose intentionality in ensuring inclusion of women and girls in critical spaces that shape how technology is designed, trained, mediated, deployed and governed. Women should not be seen as people who come to manage risk and consequences (Burch et al., 2023; Viseu, 2015) but as groups that carry knowledge contributions that can shape how technology impacts and is impacted by society. Intentionally bringing women into the design space ensures that they influence how and when norms are formed, how activities are done, which practices thrive, as well as ensuring that their strengths are utilized, and the knowledge they carry is acknowledged in a way that recognizes and articulates their needs and values (Felt, 2017). Bailey (2022) argues that diversity solves complex human problems, because it brings unique ways of thinking and seeing things—which is critically needed in AI design and use—not just aptitude. He further argues that representation can be a powerful tool that can inspire people conceptualizing AI to strive beyond capabilities and ways of seeing things. That way developed technology will be able to recognize the existence of other worlds (Higgins, 2021). This intentionality is not limited to technology design, but also in the way the laws that govern and regulate AI technology are crafted, accountability with individual data, and the algorithmic activities that are taking place in digital spaces. That way, the society will not participate in disgracing the marginalized groups while invisibly and unconsciously enriching powerful tech companies and players.

Conclusion

In conclusion, this chapter explores the complex effects of AI on various groups, highlighting the new gender norms in digital spaces. The chapter examines how AI algorithms reinforce biased gender norms, with a focus on African women in particular. It also addresses issues like the lack of gender-specific identities, and biased translations in local languages. The paper argues that AI onto-norms shape how AI engages with the content that relates to women in terms of image, behaviour, and other media, which includes how gender identities and perspectives are intentionally or otherwise, included, missed, or misrepresented in building and training AI systems. Drawing from Annemarie Mol's concept of onto-norms, the study uncovers the intricate dynamics between AI social actors, algorithms, and societal norms by studying the nuanced ways in which AI influences the lives of women and girls in Africa. The norms propagated in these spaces, that make male gender superior and demean female gender in professional and social spaces are conveniently being reproduced in the technology itself further marginalizing women and girls in digital and the society. This interplay of norms, practices, and material technology further entrenches the unequal power relations in the age where AI is being used to classify, commodify human data for profits. Thus this paper underlines the significance of understanding the norms and practices that shape how biases in AI are entrenched. It argues that understanding these norms helps in correcting biases in AI design, training, and application to advance gender equality and mitigate creation of new negative gender norms in and through AI. The paper proposes intentionality in order to ensure the inclusion of women and girls in critical spaces that shape how technology is designed, trained, mediated, and deployed, as well as the laws that govern and regulate AI technology, accountability with individual data, and the algorithmic activities that are taking place in digital spaces. That way, the society will not participate, driving the marginalization of already existing groups while invisibly and unconsciously enriching powerful tech companies and players.

References

Azunre, P., Osei, S., Addo, S.A., Adu-Gyamfi, L.A., Moore, S.E., Adabankah, B., Opoku, B., Asare-Nyarko, C., Nyarko, S., Amoaba, C., Appiah, E.D., Akwerh, F., Lawson, R.N., Budu, J., Debrah, E., Boateng, N.A., Ofori, W., Buabeng-Munkoh, E., Adjei, F., Ampomah, I.K., Otoo., J., Borkor, R.N., Mensah, S.B., Mensah, L., Marcel, M.A., Amponsah, A.A., & Hayfron-Acquah, J.B. (2021). English-Twi Parallel Corpus for Machine Translation. *ArXiv, abs/2103.15625*

Althubaiti, A. (2016). Information bias in health research: Definition, pitfalls, and adjustment methods. *Journal of Multidisciplinary Healthcare, 9*, 211–217. https://doi.org/10.2147/JMDH.S104807

Augusto, J. C. (2007). *1 Ambient intelligence: The confluence of ubiquitous/pervasive computing and Artificial Intelligence*.

Aurigi, A. (2007). *New technologies, same dilemmas: Policy and design issues for the augmented city*. https://doi.org/10.1080/10630730601145989

Bailey, L. D. (2022). Diversity in science, technology, engineering and mathematics: what does a scientist look like? *Bioanalysis, 14*(7), 401–403. https://doi.org/10.4155/BIO-2022-0033

Benjamin, R. (2019). *Race after technology: Abolitionist tools for the new Jim code*. Polity.

Bronson, K. (2018). Smart farming: Including rights holders for responsible agricultural innovation. *Technology Innovation Management Review, 8*(2).

Bronson, K. (2022). *The immaculate conception of data : agribusiness, activists, and their shared politics of the future* [Book]. McGill-Queen's University Press.

Buolamwini, J., & Gebru, T. (2018). Gender shades: Intersectional accuracy disparities in commercial gender classification. In *Proceedings of the 1st Conference on Fairness, Accountability, and Transparency* (Vol. 81, pp. 1–15). PMLR. https://proceedings.mlr.press/v81/buolamwini18a.html

Burch, K. A., & Legun, K. (2021). *Overcoming barriers to including agricultural workers in the co-design of new AgTech: Lessons from a COVID-19-present world*. https://doi.org/10.1111/cuag.12277

Burch, K. A., Nafus, D., Legun, K., & Klerkx, L. (2022). *Intellectual property meets transdisciplinary co-design: Prioritizing responsiveness in the production of new AgTech through located response-ability 1*, 3. https://doi.org/10.1007/s10460-022-10378-3

Burch, K., Guthman, J., Gugganig, M., Bronson, K., Comi, M., Legun, K., Biltekoff, C., Broad, G., Brock, S., Freidberg, S., Baur, P., & Mincyte, D. (2023). Social science—STEM collaborations in agriculture, food and beyond: An STSFAN manifesto. *Agriculture and Human Values*. https://doi.org/10.1007/s10460-023-10438-2

Carolan, M. (2017). Agro-Digital governance and life itself: Food politics at the intersection of code and affect. *Sociologia Ruralis, 57*(November), 816–835. https://doi.org/10.1111/soru.12153

Chouldechova, A., & Roth, A. (2018). The frontiers of fairness in machine learning. arXiv. http://arxiv.org/abs/1810.08810

Clarke, I., & Grieve, J. (2017, August). Dimensions of abusive language on Twitter. In *Proceedings of the first workshop on abusive language online* (pp. 1–10).

Diefenbach, S., Christoforakos, L., Ullrich, D., & Butz, A. (2022). Invisible but understandable: In Search of the sweet spot between technology invisibility and transparency in smart spaces and beyond. *Multimodal Technologies and Interaction, 6*(10). https://doi.org/10.3390/mti6100095

Domingues, T., Brandão, T., & Ferreira, J. C. (2022). Machine learning for detection and prediction of crop diseases and pests: A comprehensive survey. *Agriculture (Switzerland), 12*(9), 1–23. https://doi.org/10.3390/agriculture12091350

Efe, A. (2022). *The Impact of AI on Social Problems and Solutions: An Analysis on the Context of Digital Divide and Exploitation, 1*(13), 247–264.

Eke, D.O. (2023). ChatGPT and the rise of generative AI: Threat to academic intergrity? *Journal of Responsible Technology. 13,* 100060. https://doi.org/10.1016/.jrt.2023.100060

Eke, D. O., Wakunuma, K., & Akintoye, S. (2023). Introducing responsible AI in Africa. In *Responsible AI in Africa: Challenges and Opportunities* (pp. 1–11). Springer International Publishing.

Eubanks, V. (2018). *Automating inequality: How high-tech tools profile, police, and punish the poor.* Martin's Press.

Feine, J., Gnewuch, U., Morana, S., & Maedche, A. (2020). Gender bias in chatbot design. In *Lecture notes in computer science* (including subseries lecture notes in artificial intelligence and lecture notes in bioinformatics). (Vol. 11970). LNCS (Issue January). Springer International Publishing. https://doi.org/10.1007/978-3-030-39540-7_6

Felt, U. (2017). *The handbook of science and technology studies* (4th ed.). The MIT Press.

Fourcade, M., & Healy, K. (2017). Seeing like a market. *Socio-Economic Review, 15*(1), 9–29. https://doi.org/10.1093/ser/mww033

Galaz, V., Centeno, M. A., Callahan, P. W., Causevic, A., Patterson, T., Brass, I., Baum, S., Farber, D., Fischer, J., Garcia, D., McPhearson, T., Jimenez, D., King, B., Larcey, P., & Levy, K. (2021). Artificial intelligence, systemic risks, and sustainability. *Technology in Society, 67*(May), 101741. https://doi.org/10.1016/j.techsoc.2021.101741

Gardezi, M., Joshi, B., Rizzo, D. M., Ryan, M., Prutzer, E., Brugler, S., & Dadkhah, A. (2023, January). Artificial intelligence in farming: Challenges and opportunities for building trust. *Agronomy Journal*, 1–12. https://doi.org/10.1002/agj2.21353

Giladi, P. (2018). Epistemic injustice: A role for recognition? *Philosophy and Social Criticism, 44*(2), 141–158. https://doi.org/10.1177/0191453717707237

Gupta, M., Parra, C. M., & Dennehy, D. (2022). Questioning racial and gender bias in AI-based recommendations: Do espoused national cultural values matter? *Information Systems Frontiers, 24*(5), 1465–1481. https://doi.org/10.1007/s10796-021-10156-2

Gwagwa, A., Kazim, E., Kachidza, P., Hilliard, A., Siminyu, K., Smith, M., & Shawe-Taylor, J. (2021). Road map for research on responsible artificial intelligence for development (AI4D) in African countries: The case study of agriculture. *Patterns, 2*(12), 100381. https://doi.org/10.1016/j.patter.2021.100381

Hall, P., & Ellis, D. (2023). A systematic review of socio-technical gender bias in AI algorithms. *Online Information Review, 47*(7), 1264–1279. https://doi.org/10.1108/OIR-08-2021-0452

Hasselbalch, G. (2021). Data Ethics of Power. *In Data Ethics of Power*. https://doi.org/10.4337/9781802203110

Hasselbalch, G. (2022). *Data pollution & power: White paper for a global sustainable development agenda on AI.*

Hewitt, S., Tiropanis, T., & Bokhove, C. (2016, May). The problem of identifying misogynist language on Twitter (and other online social spaces). In *Proceedings of the 8th ACM Conference on Web Science* (pp. 333–335).

Higgins, M. (2021). Response-ability Revisited: Towards Re(con)figuring Scientific Literacy. In *Unsettling Responsibility in Science Education. Palgrave Studies in Educational Futures*. Palgrave Macmillan. https://doi.org/10.1007/978-3-030-61299-3_7

Jiménez, D., Delerce, S., Dorado, H., Cock, J., Muñoz, L. A., Agamez, A., & Jarvis, A. (2019). A scalable scheme to implement data-driven agriculture for small-scale farmers. *Global Food Security, 23*(May), 256–266. https://doi.org/10.1016/j.gfs.2019.08.004

Kanazawa, S. (2020). What do we do with the WEIRD problem? *Evolutionary Behavioral Sciences, 14*(4), 342–346. https://doi.org/10.1037/ebs0000222

Koskinen, I., & Ludwig, D. (2021). Philosophy or philosophies? Epistemology or epistemologies? *Global Epistemologies and Philosophies of Science*, 15–25.

Koskinen, I., & Rolin, K. (2021). Structural epistemic (in)justice in global contexts. *Global Epistemologies and Philosophies of Science*, 115–125. https://doi.org/10.4324/9781003027140-12

Kurita, K., Vyas, N., Pareek, A., Black, A. W., & Tsvetkov, Y. (2019). Measuring bias in contextualized word representations. In M. R. Costa-jussà, C. Hardmeier, W. Radford, & K. Webster (Eds.), *Proceedings of the First Workshop on Gender Bias in Natural Language Processing* (pp. 166–172). Association for Computational Linguistics. https://doi.org/10.18653/v1/W19-3823

Lajoie-O'Malley, A., Bronson, K., van der Burg, S., & Klerkx, L. (2020). The future(s) of digital agriculture and sustainable food systems: An analysis of high-level policy documents. *Ecosystem Services, 45*, 101183. https://doi.org/10.1016/j.ecoser.2020.101183

Lambrecht, A., & Tucker, C. (2019). Algorithmic bias? An empirical study of apparent gender-based discrimination in the display of STEM career ads. *Management Science, 65*(7), 2966–2981. https://doi.org/10.1287/mnsc.2018.3093

Latour, B. (2011). Drawing things together. In *The map reader: Theories of mapping practice and cartographic representation* (pp. 65–72). John Wiley and Sons. https://doi.org/10.1002/9780470979587.ch9

Mclennan, S. J. (2015). *Information technology for development techno-optimism or information imperialism: Paradoxes in online networking, social media and development techno-optimism or information imperialism: Paradoxes in online networking, social media and development*. https://doi.org/10.1080/02681102.2015.1044490

Mehrabi, N., Morstatter, F., Saxena, N., & Jan, L. G. (2022). A survey on bias and fairness in machine learning. arXiv.

Mol, A. (1999). Ontological politics. A word and some questions. *The Sociological Review*, *47*(S1), 74–89. https://doi.org/10.1111/J.1467-954X.1999.TB03483.X

Mol, A. (2002). *The body multiple : Ontology in medical practice* [Book]. Duke University Press.

Mol, A. (2013). *Special Issue: A turn to ontology in science and technology studies?* *43*(3), 379–396. https://doi.org/10.2307/48646314

Nadeem, A., Marjanovic, O., & Abedin, B. (2022). Gender bias in AI-based decision-making systems: A systematic literature review. *Australasian Journal of Information Systems, 26*, 1–34. https://doi.org/10.3127/AJIS.V26I0.3835

Ndaka, A., Lassou, P. J. C., Kan, K. A. S., & Fosso-Wamba, S. (2024). Toward response-able AI: A decolonial perspective to AI-enabled accounting systems in Africa. *Critical Perspectives on Accounting*, *99*. https://doi.org/10.1016/j.cpa.2024.102736

Noble, S. U. (2018). *Algorithms of oppression: How search engines reinforce racism*. NYU Press.

Norori, N., Hu, Q., Aellen, F. M., Faraci, F. D., & Tzovara, A. (2021). Addressing bias in big data and AI for health care: A call for open science. *Patterns, 2*(10), 100347. https://doi.org/10.1016/j.patter.2021.100347

Ntoutsi, E., Fafalios, P., Gadiraju, U., & Iosifidis, V. (2019). *Bias in data-driven artificial intelligence systems: An introductory survey*.

Organisation for Economic Co-operation and Development (OECD). (2018). *Bridging the digital gender divide: Include, upskill, innovate*. OECD.

Poliseli, L., & Leite, C. M. P. (2021). Developing transdisciplinary practices: An interplay between disagreement and trust. In *Global Epistemologies and Philosophies of Science* (pp. 77–91).

Prates, M. O. R., Avelar, P. H. & Lamb, L. C. (2020). Assessing gender bias in machine translation: a case study with Google Translate. *Neural Computing & Applications, 32*, 6363–6381. https://doi.org/10.1007/s00521-019-04144-6

Robinson, S. C. (2020, October). Trust, transparency, and openness: How inclusion of cultural values shapes Nordic national public policy strategies for artificial intelligence (AI). *Technology in Society, 63*. https://doi.org/10.1016/j.techsoc.2020.101421

Rosendahl, J., Zanella, M. A., Rist, S., & Weigelt, J. (2015). Scientists' situated knowledge: Strong objectivity in transdisciplinarity. *Futures, 65*, 17–27. https://doi.org/10.1016/j.futures.2014.10.011

Ruttkamp-bloem, E. (2023). Epistemic just and dynamic AI ethics in Africa. *Springer International Publishing*. https://doi.org/10.1007/978-3-031-08215-3

Saka, E. (2021). Big data and gender-biased algorithms.

Schwartz, R., Down, L., Jonas, A., & Tabassi, E. (2021). *A proposal for identifying and managing bias in artificial intelligence*. National Institute of Standards and Technology.

Schwartz, R., Vassilev, A., Greene, K., Perine, L., Burt, A., Hall, P., & Greene, K. (2022). *Towards a standard for identifying and managing bias in artificial intelligence*. NIST Special Publication 1270. https://nvlpubs.nist.gov/nistpubs/SpecialPublications/NIST.SP.1270.pdf

Shushkevich, E., Cardiff, J., Rosso, P., & Akhtyamova, L. (2020). Offensive Language Recognition in Social Media. *Computación y Sistemas, 24*(2), 523–532.

Subramaniam, B., Foster, L., Harding, S., Roy, D., & TallBear, K. (2016). Feminism, postcolonialism, technoscience. In U. Felt, R. Fouche, C. A. Miller, & L. Smith-Doerr (Eds.), *The handbook of science and technology studies* (4th ed., pp. 407–433). MIT Press.

Viseu, A. (2015). Integration of social science into research is crucial. *Nature, 525*(7569), 291–291. https://doi.org/10.1038/525291a

Wamba-Taguimdje, S. L., Wamba, S. F., Kamdjoug, J. R. K., & Wanko, C. E. T. (2020). Influence of artificial intelligence (AI) on firm performance: The business value of AI-based transformation projects. *Business Process Management Journal, 26*(7), 1893–1924.

Waseem, Z., & Hovy, D. (2016, June). Hateful symbols or hateful people? predictive features for hate speech detection on twitter. In *Proceedings of the NAACL student research workshop* (pp. 88–93).

Wellner, G. P. (2020). When AI is gender-biased: The effects of biased AI on the everyday experiences of women. *Humana Mente, 13*(37), 127–150.

West, M., Kraut, R., & Han, E. C. (2019a). I'd blush if I could: Closing gender divides in digital skills through education. https://doi.org/10.54675/RAPC9356

West, S. M., Whittaker, M., & Crawford, K. (2019b). *Discriminating systems: Gender, race, and power in AI. AI Now Institute*. https://ainowinstitute.org/discriminatingsystems.html

Zhang, Y., Xiong, F., Xie, Y., Fan, X., & Gu, H. (2020). The impact of artificial intelligence and blockchain on the accounting profession. *IEEE Access, 8*, 110461–110477.

Zhao, J., Wang, T., Yatskar, M., Ordonez, V., & Chang, K.-W. (2018). Gender bias in coreference resolution: Evaluation and debiasing methods. In M. Walker, H. Ji, & A. Stent (Eds.), *Proceedings of the 2018 Conference of the North American Chapter of the Association for Computational Linguistics: Human Language Technologies*, Volume 2 (Short Papers) (pp. 15–20). Association for Computational Linguistics. https://doi.org/10.18653/v1/N18-2003

CHAPTER 11

Relationality and Data Justice for Trustworthy AI Practices in Africa

Emma Ruttkamp-Bloem

Introduction

The aim of this chapter is to unpack what is needed to ensure the trustworthiness of AI (artificial intelligence) *practices* in Africa through the lens of social justice considerations. In this sense, this chapter offers a societal perspective on trustworthiness, a view of trustworthiness from the human side, bottom-up from the viewpoint of communities. The chapter is a call for a strategy for building a sustainable equitable AI ecosystem in Africa, supported through trustworthy AI practices focused on public and communal benefit, rather than enriching Big Tech companies on the other side of the world. The idea is thus that this strategy will be informed by social justice concerns. I will introduce the notion of 'AI justice', which is justice for every inhabitant of the African continent who engages with AI technology at any stage of its lifecycle, and which is a notion embedded in a relational ethic and emerging from a combination of data and design

E. Ruttkamp-Bloem (✉)
Department of Philosophy, University of Pretoria, Pretoria, South Africa
e-mail: emma.ruttkamp-bloem@up.ac.za

Centre for AI Research (CAIR), DSI, Pretoria, South Africa

D. O. Eke et al. (eds.), *Trustworthy AI*,
https://doi.org/10.1007/978-3-031-75674-0_11

justice approaches as elements of social justice in the domain of AI. In this sense, an AI practice will be trustworthy when it protects rights and benefits of the communities whose data it uses. In this sense I will speak of trustworthy AI practices 'serving' communities.

The motivation for this approach can be found in the works of scholars such as Abeba Birhane, Sasha Costanza-Chock, Lina Dencik, and Kate Crawford, who have been warning for some time that AI is a "registry of power" (Crawford, 2022) and a discipline that is "socially and politically loaded … prioritizing and promoting the concentration of resources, tools, knowledge, and power in the hands of already powerful actors" (Birhane et al., 2022, p. 182). Moshe Vardi (2022) recently juxtaposed the AI business model of surveillance capitalism with the ACM Code of Professional Ethics, flagging the business aim of Big Tech in relation to the commodification of data for profit. There is more behind this business model however—what drives this business model is power and the monopolisation of power (e.g., Birhane, 2020; Buolamwini, 2023; Crawford, 2022; Eke et al., 2023; Greene & Joseph, 2015; Thatcher et al., 2017, Mezzadra & Neilson, 2017). In Africa, this business model is concretised as data colonisation (Couldry & Meijas, 2019) or algorithmic colonisation (Birhane, 2020), exclusion fed by digital poverty (Goralski & Tan, 2022; Mhlanga, 2021), intersectionality (Ulnicane, 2024), and geopolitical realities that allow Big Tech to continue practices flying in the face of international law, such as their exploitation of gig workers in Africa (Gray & Suri, 2019; Kwet, 2019; Muldoon et al., 2023).

This chapter is a challenge to all AI actors in Africa—the researchers, designers, developers, deployers, and users—to claim their collective ownership of the domain of AI and stand together to build social resilience against this business model. The reality is that Africa cannot become a global role player in terms of AI technology if the African ecosystem does not ensure a voice for Africa on equal grounds. If this does not happen, AI in Africa will not be sustainable AI technology, as it won't be responsible AI technology. This means that it is imperative that the Big Tech business model should be boycotted in Africa and upended such that power remains in the hands of the inhabitants of the continent, while ensuring bottom-up control of AI practices so that trustworthy AI practices are practices that promote data and design justice. The only ethical system that can support such an effort is a relational ethic, as will be explained in § 3.

This might seem a daunting task given crucial practical facts such as the unevenness of connectivity and Internet penetration in Africa, representativity of data sets, lack of quality STEM education across the continent, political leaders more interested in their own survival and riches than in the benefit of the communities they serve, lack of sufficient and efficient data infrastructure, and of course access to the kind of computing power needed to power the newest AI technologies such as generative AI. It is precisely because of the practical socio-political-economic nature of many of these concerns that I call for a bottom-up, community-informed, and -led social justice strategy for building a sustainable equitable AI ecosystem in Africa. I suggest this strategy to be informed by data and design justice principles (e.g., Costanza-Chock, 2020; Dencik et al., 2019; Dencik & Sanchez-Monedero, 2022; Taylor, 2017) based on an ethics that is relational and concrete (Birhane, 2021), ensuring a focus on communities and historical injustices, and enabling structures that can help build social resilience to potential harm from AI technology though trustworthy AI practices.

Africa should not miss the opportunity to make itself heard and settle itself on the frontline of AI innovation and development. By 2030 African youth will make up 42% of global youth.[1] This prediction, together with the fact that AI technology changes the world in which near-future generations will live on a daily basis, makes the case for the urgency of building just and beneficial AI technology through trustworthy AI practices in Africa. Picking up this challenge means, however, that Africa should wake up to the colonial undertones of the business model that allows promises made by Big Tech companies (for instance, to 'empower' "unbanked women" [Birhane, 2020, p. 393] in Africa) to go unchallenged, and to even be welcomed by some (Kimani, 2019). It is not AI technology that is the danger to African independence and flourishing, it is algorithmic and data colonialism in the guise of technological solutionism (Birhane, 2020) that is swallowing up Africa.

In the next section I explain my understanding of algorithmic colonisation and its effects and dangers. This form of colonisation is the main obstacle to establishing trustworthy AI practices in Africa as it is fed by the Big Tech business model, which, in its turn, is fed by current geopolitical power balances, digital poverty, and uneven access to connectivity

[1] https://www.weforum.org/agenda/2022/09/why-africa-youth-key-development-potential/.

across Africa. In § 3, I explain that a relational ethic enables reflection on historic injustice and oppression in a way that would assist the boycotting of the Big Tech business model. I demonstrate that from a relational perspective, a data and design justice approach is necessary to ensure that inhabitants of the African continent do not become 'digital refugees' but are instead empowered to drive their own AI ecosystem for the benefit of their communities through trustworthy AI practices. In §4, based on the previous sections, I conclude with some recommendations in terms of governance practices that will support a social justice perspective on trustworthy AI practices in Africa.

Algorithmic Colonialism and the Loss of African Voices

Algorithmic colonialism is the reason why we have to speak of building social resilience against harm from AI technology in Africa. Algorithmic colonialism disempowers Africans to effectively participate in global AI technology research, design, and development, and its unjust practices target and exploit vulnerable groups and amplify inequality and structural and epistemic injustice, ultimately making it impossible to speak of trust, and trustworthy AI practices.

Abeba Birhane (2020, p. 390) explains that there is a strong overlap behind the drivers of Western tech monopolies and "traditional colonialism". Both are driven by a "desire to dominate, control and influence social, political, and cultural discourse", and I will argue towards the end of § 3, also by the race for geo-political power. The difference between these approaches is that traditional colonialism is shaped by political forces, while 'algorithmic colonialism' is driven by "corporate agendas" (Birhane, 2020, p. 390).

Rather than physical invasion, algorithmic colonialism comes in the form of "'state-of-the-art algorithms' and 'AI driven solutions' to social problems" (Birhane, 2020, p. 390). Building on the work of Greene and Joseph (2015) and Thatcher et al. (2017), Cloudy and Mejias (2019, p. 338), speak of this technological push for power as a form of "fundamental appropriation", while Mezzadra and Neilson (2017) speak of it in terms of extraction of resources. Birhane (2020, p. 391) illustrates this when she writes that "[a]lgorithmic colonialism, driven by profit maximization at any cost, assumes that the human soul, behaviour, and action [are] raw material free for the taking. Knowledge, authority, and power to sort, categorize, and order human activity rests with the technologist, for whom we are merely data producing 'human natural resources'".

Couldry and Meijas (2019, p. 337) came up with the notion of 'data colonialism' to give context to the social processes of surveillance capitalism, heralded by writers such as Dyer-Witheford (1999) and explained by writers such as Zuboff (2019) as the commodification of data for profit; and to explain how Big Data is viewed from the perspective of the Global South. Broadly, the concern is that previously colonised countries find themselves at the mercy of Big Tech companies in the Global North much along the lines that characterised the 'race for Africa' in the mid-eighteenth century. Again, citizens of such countries face the possibility of their rights being disrespected, their humanity being ignored, and their culture being erased in the race for geo-political power that comes with the commodification of data in the context of AI technology (e.g., Noble, 2018; Whittaker, 2021). In the words of Couldry and Meijas (2019, pp. 337–338), "[d]ata colonialism combines the predatory extractive practices of historical colonialism with the abstract quantification methods of computing. Understanding Big Data from the Global South means understanding capitalism's current dependence on this new type of appropriation that works at every point in space where people or things are attached to today's infrastructures of connection".

In her turn, Karen Hao (2022) describes 'AI colonialism'[2] as the result of the fact that "[g]lobal AI development ... is impoverishing communities and countries that don't have a say in its development—the same communities and countries already impoverished by former colonial empires". Birhane (2020, p. 389) echoes this when she writes that "[n]ot only is Western developed AI unfit for African problems, the West's algorithmic invasion simultaneously impoverishes development of local products while also leaving the continent dependent on Western software and infrastructure". Two main drivers of such impoverishment and dependence to my mind are a misapplication of the notion of data sovereignty by some African leaders and the digital divide spurred by unequal access to connectivity.

The issue of data ownership in Africa comes up whenever there is collaboration in the digital domain with external entities. Data benefits should always be distributed in favour of Africans, if it is their data that

[2] I prefer the term 'algorithmic colonialism' but will use the terms interchangeably.

is at issue. This means that also in terms of data infrastructure development, the African focus should always be on ownership of data as potential benefit for Africans from AI technology surely is a core motivation to engage with AI. These thoughts relate to the more encompassing concept of digital sovereignty, which "is an orientation and strategic position that aims to reaffirm the authority of state actors over cyberspace, including over the development of digital technology" (Rainie et al., 2019, p. 301). More specifically, data sovereignty in the context of algorithmic colonialism refers to the right of African people "to govern the collection, ownership, and application of data about [their] communities, peoples, lands, and resources" (Rainie et al., 2019, p. 301), which obviously speaks to the right to self-determination, which implies at least to some extent, protection of vulnerable communities.

As such, "this vision requires recognition of the rights of individual countries to develop and use the policy instruments necessary to govern cyber activities within their legal territory" (Soulé, 2023).[3] In terms of geo-political power conflicts and resisting data and algorithmic colonialism, safeguarding data sovereignty is core to ensuring African states remain in the digital running as it were. However, of course there are two sides to this story as the rights to freedom of opinion and freedom of thought, and even the rights to freedom of movement and association, might be violated under certain regimes in the name of digital and data sovereignty. In this sense, there is a real danger in the African context in terms of how data sovereignty is understood or unpacked by governments of African states.

This danger relates to conflating digital sovereignty with data localisation (Soulé, 2023, p. 2) in Africa. Advocates of data localisation, "... which include some African governments, seek on the one hand to emphasize the nation-state as the main vector of cyberspace governance, while on the other hand taking advantage of companies and private investment to promote digital development" (Soulé, 2023, p. 3). The problem is that this view of data localisation does not take sufficiently into account the structural elements needed for data localisation to inform data sovereignty. These elements include "... the financial resources and technical capabilities required to deploy the data centres that would be needed to meet this requirement" (Soulé, 2023, p. 3). Against this background,

[3] See also Musoni et al (2023).

Soulé (2023, p. 3) warns that the 700 + data centres envisaged to see the light in Africa in the next decade, might in fact not make for data sovereignty but rather, ironically, for a form of "data capitalism", because of a lack of comprehensive regional data protection laws and a "general lack of widespread, systematic data collection across the continent".

There is a core tension here that needs to be unpacked in the context of fostering trustworthy AI practices in Africa: On the one hand, the motivation for building new African-owned (or at least African-driven) data centres is to address digital inequalities by ensuring "reciprocal and equitable access, use and benefits from ... data" (Soulé, 2023, p. 3). On the other hand, infrastructure, and structural challenges, such as access to electricity and connectivity, mean that most African investors cannot fund such data centres, and as such, African governments often turn to Big Tech or foreign investors such as China. Soulé (2023, p. 3) makes the crucial point that "[t]his disparity raises questions about true digital sovereignty and local data ownership in Africa", as data sovereignty is supposed to prevent misuse of data and ensure "trustful and respectful relationships" (Cocq, 2022) among governments, researchers, and data communities.

The other driver of impoverishment of African data processes is connectivity as impetus of the digital divide and ultimate exclusion of Africans in the AI space. Addressing this issue is crucial to building trustworthy AI practices characterised by data justice objectives (see the next section), as uneven connectivity hinders AI research, design, and development and, as such, it enables the painting of Africa as a mere consumer of AI technology rather than a producer, which, in its turn, suits the AI business model and current geo-political and algocratic[4] narratives. An illustration of this unevenness are comments such as this one by Roche et al., (2022, p. 1096), who write that perhaps the overbalance towards

[4] The concept of an 'algocracy' is defined by Danaher (2016) as the practice in which "algorithms structure, nudge, influence, constrain, control ... the behaviour of its human subjects". The three main concerns relating to this notion are automation, data analysis, and adaptability. As far as automation goes, the concern is whether humans are in/on/out of the loop. As far as data analysis goes, the issue is that data mining algorithms are logic producing systems "that are [as such supposedly] technical, objective, impartial, commonsensical, pragmatic, and reliable" (Kitchin, 2014). This creates an illusion of impartiality that may instil false trust in these systems. Thirdly, adaptability relates to the fact that the logic of machine learning algorithms is adaptable as the way in which algorithms solve problems is not pre-determined (e.g., Burrell, 2016).

the North is not surprising, "... given the prominence of these countries in the development of such advanced technologies and the greater availability of resources for policy work in the Global North". The digital divide ensures that this labelling seems appropriate, and this feeds the Big Tech business plan. If the Global North is portrayed as the benefactor of the Global South in global AI conversations, Africa has effectively lost the challenge to resist algorithmic colonialism.

Much more than that, however, is that this exclusion and portrayal of Africans as mere AI consumers with their hands out for the benefits that the North will bestow on them, also to a notable extent, ensures both the continued exploitation of African communities for their data and the existence and extension of the exploitation of gig workers in Africa by Big Tech (e.g., Gray & Suri, 2019; Irani, 2015; Kwet, 2019), without which Big Tech companies cannot advance. So, crucial to understand is that inequality in fact feeds the business plan of Big Tech companies, which is the best motivation for viewing the right to connectivity as universal access to AI technology as a basic human and digital right from the perspective of the Global South.

Digital poverty driven by lack of connectivity in Africa is an important cause of Africa's exclusion from the AI production space and, as stated, provides fertile ground for algorithmic colonisation practices. There are various aspects to digital poverty which should be taken into account when we speak of fostering trustworthy AI practices. Firstly, AI technology, especially in its generative guise, relies upon huge amounts of data and massive computing power. This means loss of agency in building such technology in digital poor countries. Secondly, as such, poorer economies have minimal or limited digital presence online, and so, do not exist as data points and are not part of answers generated by generative AI chatbots. This means allocation harm in terms of decisions relating to allocation of economic resources (see Crawford, 2017), while it also points to a slow but certain erasure of cultural diversity and an overall risk of data-poor countries being colonised by the standards embedded in AI models.[5] There is here again a tension that will have to be navigated in trustworthy AI practices: On the one hand there is the role AI technologies that might play in opening up and democratising information and

[5] See for instance, the UNESCO document, 'Guidance for the Use of Generative AI in Education and Research' (https://unesdoc.unesco.org/ark:/48223/pf0000386693).

knowledge, while on the other hand, there is the potential for reinforcing and entrenching existing inequalities at global and local levels.

In trustworthy AI practices it would thus be essential to constantly reflect on the value orientations, cultural standards, and social customs embedded in training models, and to foster a culture in which neither the information provided by generative AI applications nor outcomes of autonomous decision-making algorithms are accepted at face value. There should always be reflections relating to data provenance, to the social impact of any implementation of AI-generated decisions or predictions, to potential human rights violations, and ultimately, to the potential of such outcomes feeding inequality by cementing Northern values and power. This implies the need for a bottom-up, community-led approach to establishing trustworthy AI practices, as the grassroots impact and needs of AI actors will be prioritised in such reflections, especially if such practices aspire to promote data justice. Let us then now consider in more detail how to counter the dangers to African ownership and leadership in AI technology discussed above, with the building of trustworthy AI practices based on data justice objectives, supported by design justice principles, and made possible by embeddedness in a relational ethic.

AI Justice, Relationality, and Trustworthy AI Practices

Before continuing, it is necessary to reflect a moment on the notion of 'trustworthy AI practices'. In this chapter, 'trustworthy' refers to practices that are trusted because they have the flourishing of the communities who trust them at heart. The diversity of societies across the African continent and even within its regions and countries means that there is also a diversity of economic and societal needs and a diversity of ways in which benefits, and harm, can play out. For this reason, the essential feature of trustworthy AI practices in Africa is that these practices should be driven from the bottom up, informed by the communities supplying the data to fuel AI systems and impacted by the decisions these systems generate. The hope of building AI technology by Africans for Africans (see, e.g. the values of the Masakhane NLP group[6]) can be positively realised only in an environment that is genuinely focused on the benefit of all, starting with

[6] https://www.masakhane.io/.

the most vulnerable, and informed from the ground up. In this sense, trustworthy AI practices are practices that empower communities[7] and protect their rights, while ensuring that they benefit from engagement with AI technology.

Let us now unpack what 'bottom up' means in terms of Big Tech hype and resultant manipulation, and the issue of digital poverty. To start this discussion, we have to rethink the kind of ethics that would underlie a drive to overcome algorithmic colonialism and the inequality gap exacerbated and exploited as it is by the Big Tech business model. This ethic must be relational in the sense advocated for by Abeba Birhane, because the aim in establishing trustworthy AI practices is to move away from structural and resulting algorithmic injustice by latching onto concepts of justice that are community focused. Birhane (2021, p. 1) writes that "[o]utlining the idea of ethics built on the foundations of relationality, … calls for a rethinking of justice". She explains that "[r]elational ethics, at its core, is an attempt to unravel our assumptions and presuppositions and to rethink ethics in a broader manner via engaged epistemology in a way that puts the needs and welfare of the most impacted and marginalized at the centre" (Birhane, 2021, p. 2). Thus, for her, rethinking ethics must be driven by "concrete knowledge of the lived experience of marginalized communities" (Birhane, 2021, p. 2).

She continues to argue that it is not possible to understand such lived experiences without taking into account historical injustices combined with the impact of AI systems on vulnerable communities (Birhane, 2021, p. 2). She concludes that relational ethics in this sense is "a framework that necessitates we re-examine our underlying working assumptions, compels us to interrogate hierarchical power asymmetries, and stimulates us to consider the broader, contingent, and interconnected background that algorithmic systems emerge from (and are deployed to) in the process of protecting the welfare of the most vulnerable" (Birhane, 2021, p. 2). Relational frameworks cannot view human existence and experience

[7] Note that in this sense the communities referred to in this chapter are 'data communities' rather than communities only in the cultural or language sense, but that these can overlap. One individual can therefore be a member of more than one data community (e.g., in terms of roles such as being a client of a bank, a patient applying for access to healthcare, a person being surveilled by authorities, a person speaking Tshivenda, etc.). The point is that every individual by virtue of being a member of a given data community should benefit from that membership in ways to be determined by the individuals making up the community in question.

outside of a "web of relations" (Birhane, 2021, p. 3), as it is precisely the "primacy of relations and dependencies" (Birhane, 2021, p. 4) through which we come into being (Mbiti, 1969).

Situating bottom-up approaches to establishing trustworthy AI practices in Africa within a relational ethic is then an obvious move in the quest for an equitable African AI ecosystem, as vulnerable individuals and groups are at the centre of such an ethic in Birhane's (2021) terms, because their only epistemic privilege is to "recognize harm and injustice" (Birhane, 2021,p. 4). To enable the establishment of trustworthy AI practices, the tech community supported by AI ethicists thus have to "zoom out and draw the bigger picture: A shift from asking 'how can we make a certain dataset representative?' to examine 'what is the product or tool being used for? Who benefits? Who is harmed?'" (Birhane, 2021, p. 4).

Birhane (2021, pp. 4–5) further links a relational AI ethics to participatory design (Slavin, 2016), given that humans are in the centre of reflection. Following on to this, in the rest of the chapter, I explain my reasons for claiming that a bottom-up account of trustworthy AI practices, apart from being embedded in a relational ethic, should, in addition, be driven by a call for data justice, enriched by design justice principles. The notion of data justice comes from a long tradition of social justice engagement with the nature of information and communication systems (see, e.g., Kitchin & Lauriault, 2014). The data justice focus is specifically on Big Data and the framing of its impact on society. Dencik and Sanchez-Monedero (2022, p. 2) write that "[d]ata justice has emerged as a key framework for engaging with [inequality] challenges in a way that privileges an explicit concern for social justice. Privileging social justice concerns in the analysis of information and communication systems is not in itself new, but the concept of data justice has been used to pave a way for a shift in understanding of what is at stake with datafication beyond digital rights". This shift is a focus on *how* algorithms determine benefit or harm to communities impacted by AI-driven decisions and predictions through their classification mechanisms, rather than exclusively on the outcome of these decisions themselves.

Specifically, I suggest data justice is an apt approach to drive African AI strategies as it provides a foil to algorithmic colonialism given that it analyses data through the lens of structural inequality, "highlighting the unevenness of implications and experiences of data across different groups and communities in society" (Dencik & Sanchez-Monedero, 2022, p. 3). Dencik and Sanchez-Monedero (2022, p. 3) write that data justice debates focus on how data-centric systems work as "sorting mechanisms", specifically aiming to understand "what their relationship is to historical contexts, social structures and dominant agendas as not just a question of individual privacy, but one of justice". Thus, "[t]o speak of data justice is … to recognise not only how data, its collection and use, increasingly impact on society, but also that datafication is enabled by particular forms of political and economic organisation that advance a normative vision of how social issues should be understood and resolved. That is, data is both a matter in and of justice" (Dencik & Sanchez-Monedero, 2022, p. 3).

I am locating my discussion of data justice in the context of thinking of AI technology as a "registry of power" (Crawford, 2022), entrenched in a complex matrix of political and economic power, and in the context of AI methods such a machine learning from the point of view of a classification ethics (Crawford, 2017), because a relational ethics focus calls for a 'zooming out' (Birhane, 2020) to focus on the power relations driving classification practices. Noteworthy, is that the question of who decides how to classify data can only be answered if Satya Mohanty's (1993) warning that "interpreting the world accurately requires knowing what it would take to change it" is taken to heart. My claim is that only a bottom-up relational data justice approach can take up this challenge, as it is focused on identifying the "relationships of power and privilege that sustains injustice" which Mohanty (1993) calls for and which are playing out at community level, and aims to use this knowledge to upset the business model driving data colonialism and AI technology, ultimately making for trustworthy AI practices.

Speaking of relationships of power brings us back to the business model driving AI technology, based as it is on AI technology as "socially and politically loaded" (Birhane et al., 2022, p. 182). A core spin-off of this business model, which needs to be noted and highlighted in terms of African AI, and which has been alluded to often in the above, is the allocation of geo-political power to *private entities* located in the North. This point is not made clear enough in current AI ethics literature broadly speaking. In fact, it seems to me that the geo-political power play behind AI technology is an integral part of Big Tech's business plan. The surveillance capitalism business plan speaks of commodification of data for profit (Vardi, 2022), but I think it is safe to say that profit is in fact a by-product of the business plan, which is at its core aimed at gathering information, ultimately, in order to inform political power.

This kind of geo-strategic technological power feeds off the potential of AI technology to offer solutions to social and economic problems, which makes technological solutionism a danger to never underestimate (Birhane, 2020, p. 391). This is particularly pertinent from an African point of view, as AI technology on this continent is viewed firstly as a mechanism to leap-frog solutions to core socio-economic problems, and secondly, as a way into the global digital economy. To ensure they are not pawns in Big Tech's geo-strategic thinking, Africans should therefore always ask 'who speaks', 'who decides', and 'who benefits'.

Within the context of data colonialism, this geo-strategic aspect of the AI business model together with the concerns around data poverty briefly touched on above, may easily turn citizens in Africa into digital refugees. I mean this in at least two senses: Firstly, many citizens of African countries do not have the connectivity needed to really engage with AI technology more than perhaps fleeting social media interactions and resultant commercial manipulation. Such people barely exist in terms of algocratic decision-making and, the tragedy is, that if they do, if tech companies do get a hold of their data, they are typically not well-protected against potential harm, given their geographic and economic situations and the way in which the algorithmic colonialism machinery works. Secondly, given the massive amounts of data and compute power needed to power foundation models, entire countries and regions are pushed out to the boundaries of the AI domain as mere consumers, and, as such, their rights are not front and centre in the research, design, development, and deployment of AI technology.

The vulnerability of data-poor communities, combined with potential allocation and representation harm[8] as results of structural bias in training data (Crawford, 2017), and solidified by algorithmic colonialism, calls for a more hands-on blueprint for trustworthy AI practices in Africa. To make the approach I am suggesting should be followed to establish trustworthy AI practices even more concrete and hands-on, I want to move back to Birhane (2021) and in addition to data justice, also invoke

[8] Allocation harm is immediate and transactional in the sense that it is related to the allocation of resources based on human patterns in training data. It is fed by representation harm, which is more subtle as it relates to identity prejudice and stereotyping dormant in training data, brought to life by the generation of automated decisions impacting the lives of the very data subjects that offered the fuel to power these decisions. (See Crawford and Calo (2016) as well as the Crawford's keynote at the opening of the 2017 NIPS conference (Crawford, 2017).).

the wisdom of design justice as a focus on "community-led practices to build the worlds we need" (Costanza-Chock, 2020). Design justice as such is "a call for us to heed the growing critiques of the ways that design (of images, objects, software, algorithms, sociotechnical systems, the built environment, indeed, everything we make) too often contributes to the reproduction of systemic oppression. Most of all, it is an invitation to build a better world, a world where many worlds fit; linked worlds of collective liberation and ecological sustainability" (Costanza-Chock, 2020, p. xvi).

The focus for design justice grounds "our understanding of design, technology, and social change in the daily practices of activists and community organizers" (Costanza-Chock, 2020, p. xvi). This bottom-up focus is clear from the ten design justice network principles,[9] especially Principle 1: We use design to sustain, heal, and empower our communities, as well as to seek liberation from exploitative and oppressive systems; Principle 2: We centre the voices of those who are directly impacted by the outcomes of the design process; Principle 3: We prioritise design's impact on the community over the intentions of the designer; Principle 8: We work towards sustainable, community-led and -controlled outcomes; Principle 9: We work towards non-exploitative solutions that reconnect us to the earth and to each other; and Principle 10: Before seeking new design solutions, we look for what is already working at the community level. We honour and uplift traditional, indigenous, and local knowledge and practices.

To counter the homogenisation of algorithmic design that "philosophically and economically finds itself at odds with cultural philosophies and interests of the Global South" (Roche et al., 2022), we thus need trustworthy AI practices that are driven bottom-up by the communities they emerge from and serve. In this way structural inequality will be constrained as the main driver of data colonialism, as trustworthy AI practices embedded in a relational ethic will identify relationships of power that sustains injustice. This, in its turn, will inform thinking about change (Mohanty, 1993) and building epistemologies other than the algorithmic colonialist one of oppression and harm. This kind of change thinking will be aimed at realising 'AI justice', which is justice for every inhabitant of the African continent who engages with AI technology at any stage of its

[9] https://designjustice.org/read-the-principles

lifecycle. AI justice is a notion that emerges from data and design justice and is therefore also embedded in a relational ethic. It is the promise of AI justice in this sense that will make AI practices trustworthy, as the focus would always be on communities and their benefits and social resilience. This, then brings us to the final section of this chapter that is focused on what is needed to ensure this kind of relational and socially just approach to trustworthy AI.

Establishing Trustworthy AI Practices in Africa

All that remains perhaps now in a sense, is to recap why and how a data and design justice approach, embedded in a relational ethic, would counter algorithmic colonialism and make for trustworthy AI practices. Birhane in fact gives the beginning of the answer already in her 2021 article. She (2021, p. 7) writes that "[t]hinking in relational terms about ethics begins with reconceptualizing data science and machine learning as practices that create, sustain, and alter the social world. The very declaration of a taxonomy brings some things into existence while rendering others invisible. For any individual person, community, or situation, algorithmic classifications and predictions give either an advantage or they hinder".

Thus, firstly, embedding trustworthy AI practices in a relational ethic means focusing on how AI practices change and influence societies and the communities that they consist of. If such a focus is driven by data and design justice aspirations of benefit to, protection of, and respect for communities impacted by AI technology, the neutralisation of one of the core enablers of algorithmic colonialism can commence. This enabler is the combination of the vulnerability of communities that are not connected and invisible to AI algorithms, the oppression of communities that are exploited by Big Tech because they live in certain geo-economic circumstances, and the geo-political and economic power that comes from exploiting such communities and selling them the empty promises of technological solutionism. This potential neutralisation will result from the community-led and -informed nature of data justice and design justice practices.

Relational ethics thus encourages us to view the establishment of trustworthy AI practices as a counter to the "practice of creating and reinforcing existing and historical inequalities and structural injustices" (Birhane, 2021, p. 8). To recap, an AI practice will be trustworthy when it protects and benefits the communities whose data it uses, and this is the sense in which trustworthy AI practices 'serve' communities. To ensure that trustworthy AI practices will be practices that uphold the rights of the communities they serve, it is imperative for every AI actor—researchers, designers, developers, deployers, users, and those involved in end-of-use—to understand their responsibility to think and act relationally, aiming to ensure that every digital citizen has what they need to build a life of value, a dignified life, in tandem with AI technology.

In addition, in terms of hype from Big Tech, it is crucial that alternative epistemologies and discourses are encouraged and formulated so that the information on the advances of AI technology and the capabilities of such technology the ordinary person in the street receives, does not originate solely in the messages of Big Tech leaders in popular media. The fear-of-missing-out approach and the blowing up of Big Tech advancements towards artificial general intelligence (AGI) all play into the profit and power these companies are amassing, as buying into their discourse means guaranteed data sources as well as a revenue stream for them (Goodlad & Baker, 2023). We need African AI discourses as counter to these hyped ones, so that we ensure AI actors on this continent are literate about the working and scope of current and future AI technology, as well as aware of their own rights and responsibilities when interacting with such technology. Building such alternative discourses is part of a bottom-up approach to trustworthy AI practices as such practices belong to every AI actor in every community. Future research in linking epistemic justice to data and design justice is urgently needed in this regard.

The motivation behind this view of what trustworthy AI practices could look like in Africa, is to ensure that Africa's voice is heard in AI spaces. This view is not driven by economic gain or political power. Rather, it is driven by firm beliefs that Africa deserves to be heard, and that Africa has a core contribution to make to AI technology and its trajectory. These beliefs are appropriate also in intergenerational justice terms, given that AI technology belongs to Africa perhaps more so than to any other region, given the African continent's young population, mentioned before, and the power of AI technology to shape future worlds. Of course, there are many points of critique against such an approach. The most important critique is a practical one related to how exactly to drive a bottom-up strategy such as the one I am proposing. The biggest obstacle is political will, and the main practical challenges are AI literacy in terms of social impact and rights on the one hand, and lack of connectivity and data poverty on the other hand. The Northern business model seems the chosen way to many leaders, and the reason for this choice relates to the urgency in Africa to be viewed as a global role player in the AI domain in order to access the economic (and political) gain related to this status. The best way to address this problem and to make clear the gain from a bottom-up approach, its potential to make for sustainable AI technology and to bring even more stability than the immediate economic gain the Northern business model is supposed by some to bring, is to call for alternative technological epistemologies, in which for instance 'success' means benefit to data communities, rather than simply a high confidence interval (see, e.g., Birhane et al (2022)), and to ensure connectivity is treated as a basic digital right.

In terms of governance to ensure trustworthy AI practices of this kind, the following are core points to keep in mind. African AI strategies should have as a departure point the upending of Big Tech power relations and their business plan. This does not mean no collaboration with the North, but it does mean that there should be certain bottom lines to such collaboration, such as data ownership. Regional collaboration should also seriously be pursued. Secondly, connectivity as universal access to AI technology should be the first and most crucial element of any African AI strategy and should be given the status of a basic digital right. Thirdly, regulation should be developed taking into account the power and cost of algorithmic colonialism and should thus always be developed bottom-up, led by the communities that are exploited and discriminated against due to inequality and uneven access to connectivity. (One way to realise this bottom-up approach is through redesigned community impact assessments - accompanying ethical impact assessments - that should be completed right though the AI system lifecycle.) This has important implications for competition and support to start-ups and SME's.

In addition, apart from investment in cybersecurity, serious investment in basic education and higher education and training and promoting digital literacy should be a priority. Digital literacy should in fact be understood as digital literacies as literacy efforts should not only be focused on technical training, but also on social justice issues in the AI domain and digital sphere in general. Above all, digital literacy should be informed by communities more than by government, as the main aim would be to empower communities to build social resilience against potential harm from AI technology.

This chapter is thus a call for establishing real concrete grassroots bottom-up multi-stakeholder approaches to trustworthy AI practices. All AI actors are responsible for building sustainable AI technology in every stage of the AI lifecycle. This responsibility should be driven by a relational ethic that is focused on ending the impact of previous injustices and allowing communities to inform reflection on how to prevent harm, ensure benefit to the community, and ensure social resilience of communities through data justice objectives. Africans should be in control of their AI space and participate globally as owners of their data and as core role players in the future of the world. This means that it is imperative that the Big Tech business model should be boycotted in Africa. African data, and the power that it brings, should always remain in the hands of the inhabitants of the continent, while ensuring bottom-up formulation and control of AI practices. Africa should not miss this opportunity to make itself heard, to build just and, therefore trustworthy and sustainable, AI practices, and prove its leadership in AI innovation and development.

References

Birhane, A. (2021). Algorithmic injustice: A relational ethics approach. *Patterns, 2*(2), 100205. https://doi.org/10.1016/j.patter

Birhane, A. (2020). Algorithmic colonisation of Africa. *Scripted, 17*(2), 398–409.

Birhane, A., Kalluri, P., Card, D., Agnew, W., Dotan, R., & Bao, M. (2022). The values encoded in machine learning research. *FAccT '22: Proceedings of the 2022 ACM Conference on fairness, accountability and transparency* (pp. 173–184). https://doi.org/10.1145/3531146.3533083

Buolamwini, J. (2023). *Unmasking. A story of hope and justice in a world of algorithms*. Random House.

Burrell, J. (2016). How the machine 'Thinks': Understanding opacity in machine learning algorithms. *Big Data & Society*, 2016, 1–12, 5. http://journals.sagepub.com/doi/abs/10.1177/2053951715622512

Cocq, C. (2022). Revisiting the digital humanities through the lens of indigenous studies—Or how to question the cultural blindness of our technologies and practices. *Journal of the Association for Information Science and Technology, 73*(2), 333–344.

Costanza-Chock, S. (2020). *Design justice: Community-led practices to build the worlds we need*. The MIT Press.

Couldry, N., & Mejias, U. A. (2019). Data colonialism: Rethinking big data's relation to the contemporary subject. *Television & New Media, 20*(4), 336–349. https://doi.org/10.1177/1527476418796632

Crawford, K. (2022). *The atlas of AI. Power, politics, and the planetary costs of artificial intelligence*. Yale University Press.

Crawford, K. (2017). The trouble with bias. NIPS 2017 Keynote. https://www.youtube.com/watch?v=fMym_BKWQzk

Crawford, K., & Calo, R. (2016). There is a blind spot in AI research. *National News, 538*(7625), 311–313.

Dencik, L., & Sanchez-Monedero, J. (2022). Data justice. *Internet Policy Review, 11*(1). https://doi.org/10.14763/2022.1.1615

Dencik, L., Hintz, A., & Cable, J. (2019). Towards data justice. Bridging anti-surveillance and social justice activism. In D. Bigo, E. Isin & E. Ruppert (Eds.), *Data politics*. Creative Commons (pp. 167–186), CC BY-NC-ND.

Danaher, J. (2016). The threat of algocracy: Reality, resistance and accommodation. *Philosophy and Technology, 29*, 245–269. https://doi.org/10.1007/s13347-015-0211-1

Dyer-Witheford, N. (1999). *Cyber-marx: Cycles and circuits of struggle in high technology capitalism*. University of Illinois Press.

Eke, D. O., Wakunuma, K., & Akintoye, S. (2023). *Responsible AI in Africa: Challenges and Opportunities*. Cham: Springer Nature.

Goodlad, L. M. E., & Baker, S. (2023, February 20). Now the humanities can disrupt AI. *Public books*. Last accessed July 28, 2024, Available at https://www.NowtheHumanitiesCanDisrupt“A”PublicBooks.

Gray, M. L., & Suri, S. (2019). *Ghost work: How to stop silicon valley from building a new global underclass*. Harper Business.

Greene, D. M., & Joseph, D. (2015). The digital spatial fix. *Triple C, 13*(2), 223–247.

Goralski, M. A., & Tan, T. K. (2022). Artificial intelligence and poverty alleviation: Emerging innovations and their implications for management education and sustainable development. *The International Journal of Management Education, 20*(3), 100662. https://doi.org/10.1016/j.ijme.2022.100662

Hao, K. (2022, April 19). AI colonialism. *MIT technology review*. Accessed on July 28, 2024. https://www.technologyreview.com/2022/04/19/1049592/artificial-intelligence-colonialism/

Irani, L. (2015). Difference and dependence among digital workers: The case of amazon mechanical Turk. *South Atlantic Quarterly, 114*(1), 225–234. https://doi.org/10.1215/00382876-2831665. https://escholarship.org/uc/item/6xk920pj

Kimani, M. (2019, June 28). 5 reasons why Facebook’s new cryptocurrency ‘Libra’ is bad news for Africa. *Kioneki*. Accessed on July 28, 2024. Available at https://kioneki.com/2019/06/28/5-reasons-whyfacebooks-new-cryptocurrency-libra-is-bad-news-for-africa/

Kitchin, R. (2014, April–June). Big data, new epistemologies and paradigm shifts, *Big Data & Society*, 1–12. http://journals.sagepub.com/doi/abs/10.1177/2053951714528481

Kitchin, R., & Lauriault, T. (2014). *Towards critical data studies: Charting and unpacking data assemblages and their work the programmable city working paper 2*; pre-print version of chapter to be published. In J. Eckert, A. Shears & J. Thatcher (Eds.), *Geoweb and big data*. University of Nebraska Press. Available at SSRN. https://ssrn.com/abstract=2474112

Kwet, M. (2019, March 13). Digital colonialism is threatening the global south. *Al Jazeera*. Last accessed July 28, 2024. Available at https://www.aljazeera.com/indepth/opinion/digital-colonialismthreatening-global-south-190129140828809.html

Mbiti, J. S. (1969). *African religions and philosophy* (Heinemann).

Mezzadra, S., & Neilson, B. (2017). On the multiple frontiers of extraction: Excavating contemporary capitalism. *Cultural Studies, 31*(2–3), 185–204. https://doi.org/10.1080/09502386.2017.1303425

Mhlanga, D. (2021). Artificial Intelligence in the industry 4.0, and its impact on poverty, innovation, infrastructure development, and the sustainable development goals: Lessons from emerging economies? *Sustainability, 13*(11), 5788. https://doi.org/10.3390/su13115788

Mohanty, S. P. (1993). The epistemic status of cultural identity: On "Beloved" and the postcolonial condition. *Cultural Critique, 1993*, 41–80.

Muldoon, J., Cant, C., Graham, M., et al. (2023). The poverty of ethical AI: Impact sourcing and AI supply chains. *AI & Society*. https://doi.org/10.1007/s00146-023-01824-9

Musoni, M., Karkare, P., Chloe, T., & Domingo, E. (2023, May). *Global Approaches to Digital Sovereignty: Competing Definitions and Contrasting Policy* (ECDPM Discussion Paper No. 344). https://ecdpm.org/work/global-approaches-digital-sovereignty-competing-definitions-and-contrasting-policy

Noble, S. U. (2018). *Algorithms of oppression: How search engines reinforce racism*. NYU Press.

Rainie, S. C., Kukutai, T., Walter, M., Figueroa-Rodrígez, O. L., Walker, J., & Axelsson, P. (2019). Issues in open data: Indigenous data sovereignty. In T. Davies & B. Walker (Eds.), *The state of open data: Histories and horizons* (pp. 300–319). African Minds.

Slavin, K. (2016). Design as participation. *Journal of Design and Science*. https://doi.org/10.21428/a39a747c

Roche, C., Wall, P. J., & Lewis, D. (2022). Ethics and diversity in artificial intelligence policies, strategies and initiatives. *AI and Ethics, 3*(3). https://doi.org/10.1007/s43681-022-00218-9

Soulé, F. (2023). *Navigating Africa's digital partnerships in a context of global Rivalry*. CIGI Policy Brief No. 180. Waterloo, ON: CIGI. www.cigionline.org/publications/navigating-africas-digital-partnerships-in-a-context-of-global-rivalry/

Thatcher, J., O'Sullivan, D., & Mahmoudi, D. (2017). Data colonialism through accumulation by dispossession: New metaphors for daily data. *Environment and Planning D: Society and Space, 34*(6), 990–1006.

Taylor, L. (2017). What is data justice? The case for connecting digital rights and freedoms globally. *Big Data & Society, 4*(2), 2053951717736335.

Ulnicane, I. (2024). Intersectionality in AI: Framing concerns and recommendations for action. *Social Inclusion, 12*. https://doi.org/10.17645/si.i236

Vardi, M. Y. (2022). ACM, ethics, and corporate behaviour. *Communications of the ACM, 65*(3), 5.

Whittaker, M. (2021). The steep cost of capture. *Interactions, 28*(6), 50–55. https://doi.org/10.1145/3488666

Zuboff, S. (2019). *The age of surveillance capitalism: The fight for a human future at the frontier of power*. Public Affairs.

CHAPTER 12

Decoloniality as an Essential Trustworthy AI Requirement

Kutoma Wakunuma, George Ogoh, Simisola Akintoye, and Damian Okaibedi Eke

Introduction

In our recently edited book, titled *Responsible AI in Africa: Challenges and Opportunities,* we made a strong case for AI systems developed in and for Africa to be embedded with African values, principles, needs, contexts,

K. Wakunuma
Centre for Computing and Social Responsibility, De Montfort University, Leicester, UK
e-mail: kutoma@dmu.ac.uk

G. Ogoh · D. O. Eke (✉)
School of Computer Science, University of Nottingham, Nottingham, UK
e-mail: damian.eke@nottingham.ac.uk

G. Ogoh
e-mail: George.Ogoh@nottingham.ac.uk

S. Akintoye
Northumbria Law School, Northumbria University, Newcastle Upon Tyne, UK
e-mail: simi.akintoye@northumbria.ac.uk

D. O. Eke et al. (eds.), *Trustworthy AI*,
https://doi.org/10.1007/978-3-031-75674-0_12

and realities (Eke et al., 2023a). This book provided foundational theoretical approaches for responsible AI in Africa. In realisation that trustworthy AI approaches provide practical and technical approaches to achieving responsible AI, we present a critical requirement for trustworthy AI in Africa. We make the argument that *decoloniality* is an essential requirement for ensuring trustworthy AI in Africa. This is because it addresses the deep-seated colonial biases and power imbalances that often permeate technological development and deployment (Mohamed et al., 2020). Trustworthy AI is characterised by requirements defined by socio-cultural and contextual expectations and often include the need to respect human autonomy and individual privacy, fairness, accountability, transparency, and robustness (Li et al., 2023). Expectations for trustworthiness are different in different regions and we argue that decoloniality ought to be a requirement for African societies living with the scars of colonialism and continued coloniality. Incorporating decolonial principles ensures that AI systems do not perpetuate historical injustices but instead contribute to a more balanced, inclusive, equitable, and just society. Decoloniality therefore aims to dismantle the legacies of colonialism or coloniality that continue to shape global power dynamics and knowledge production and in this case AI. As such, in the context of AI, this involves critically examining and addressing the ways in which coloniality influences data collection, algorithm design, and the deployment of AI technologies. For example, the entrenchment of colonial biases in AI systems often stems from the data on which these systems are trained. Data-sets that primarily originate from non-African contexts can lead to AI systems that fail to accurately represent or address the realities of African societies (Buolamwini & Gebru, 2018).

This chapter explores identifiable colonial tendencies embedded within AI which perpetuate biases, inequalities, and systemic discrimination rooted in historical colonialism. By examining how AI technologies often reflect and reinforce these colonial legacies, the chapter highlights the urgent need for a decolonial approach to AI design, development, and deployment. The discussion then shifts to the decoloniality of AI, emphasising strategies and practices that prioritise the voices, experiences, and needs of African communities. This involves rethinking AI from a perspective that values local knowledge systems, promotes inclusive participation, and ensures equitable benefits for all stakeholders.

Additionally, the chapter explores the concept of trustworthy AI within the African context, addressing how AI can be designed and implemented to respect and consider African values, embrace African cultural values, foster transparency, and build trust among the diverse African populace. In addition to trustworthy AI requirements found in literature (Ferrer et al., 2021; Miller, 2020), we introduce decoloniality as a critical requirement for AI systems, particularly ones built in and for Africa and other regions with long histories of colonialism and coloniality. Our aim is to provide clarity on how to achieve decoloniality as a requirement for trustworthy AI in and for Africa. By providing a clear idea of how decoloniality can be achieved, we believe that policymakers, designers as well as deployers can become more aware of how to effectively implement and assess this requirement.

We hope that the arguments we put forward here will help policy makers in formulating regulations that protect cultural identities and promote fairness, avoiding the imposition of foreign values that could marginalise local communities. It can also encourage AI designers and developers to create AI systems that are contextually relevant and sensitive to African cultural and social dynamics, improving user acceptance and effectiveness. Additionally, it can promote the design of AI systems that address the real needs and challenges of African communities, enhancing the technology's impact and usefulness, while fostering collaboration with local communities. In other words, it can help in avoiding exploitation or harm to local populations; empowering citizens with AI tools that respect and reflect their cultural identities and values, promoting digital inclusion.

Coloniality in AI Systems

There is sufficient evidence from literature to show that AI systems often perpetuate and exacerbate historical patterns of domination, exploitation, hierarchies of power, and inequality/marginalising that are reminiscent of colonial practices (Arora et al., 2020; Mollema, 2024). These are legacies of colonialism that persist in contemporary globalised structures which are referred to as *coloniality* (Quijano, 2007). Hao (2020) pointedly declared that AI is creating a new colonial world order. What does this 'order' look like and what specific colonial tendencies are evident in the AI lifecycle?

There are so many ways AI reflects coloniality. One of those ways is in what has been termed *data colonialism* (Couldry & Mejias, 2019). Similar to colonial practices of resource extraction, AI and digital capitalism in general rely strongly on the extraction of large datasets collected from individuals and communities globally. This data often originates from users in Africa but is monetised and controlled by companies based in the Global North. These datasets are harvested, more often than not, without adequate informed consent (informed consent here means where users are provided with comprehensive and unambiguous information that they comprehend before voluntarily giving consent) (Gravett, 2023). The level of data extraction mainly by big tech companies (e.g. from online platforms) parallels historical resource extraction patterns that never benefited the locals.

Furthermore, the collected datasets from the internet often do not reflect the exact narratives from Africa but reflect perspectives that mirror experiences of people in the Global North (Eke & Ogoh, 2022). Relevant datasets that strongly reflect the needs and contexts of Africans are mostly missing in existing AI models. When these exact narratives, contexts, and needs are not included in the datasets, the developed systems are not effective for the non-represented or underrepresented communities. This reinforces existing inequalities and biases in ways that fail to address the specific needs of the people. A good example here is facial recognition technologies that have been shown to have higher error rates for people with darker skin tones, which can lead to discriminatory practices in surveillance and law enforcement (Buolamwini & Gebru, 2018; Raji et al., 2020).

Another way colonial tendencies in AI manifests is in the fact that the majority of AI research and development is conducted in a few countries and by a handful of large corporations, mainly based in the United States, Europe, and China. With very strict intellectual property laws and practices, the ability of developing countries in the Global South to innovate and adapt AI technologies to local needs is hindered in many ways. This helps to maintain a dependency on technologies developed in the Global North, limiting local growth and technological sovereignty. This is what Birhane (2020) called *algorithmic colonialism* which is the "desire to dominate, monitor, and influence social, political, and cultural discourse through the control of core communication and infrastructure mediums". It is our belief that whoever controls the data and the algorithm for AI controls the power. The concentration of this power in the hands of powerful corporations and countries mirrors colonial economic structures where wealth (in this case data and mineral resources for AI) was extracted from colonies to benefit colonial powers; and colonies prevented from self-empowerment via unfair regulations.

Other exploitative tendencies are evident in the global outsourcing of some aspects of development and maintenance that rely on low-wage labour such as data labelling and content moderation (Ludec et al., 2023). It is evident that this perpetuates labour exploitation similar to colonial labour practices where the benefits of technological advancements are concentrated in the wealthy countries, while the labour costs are borne by cheap labourers in the Global South (Williams, 2022). The case of exploitation of data labellers in Kenya has been widely reported (Rowe, 2023). Additionally, AI hardware, such as semiconductors, batteries, and sensors, often requires minerals that are exploitatively extracted (Crawford, 2021). These include rare earth minerals, lithium and cobalt that Africa is rich in. For instance, the extraction of lithium and cobalt has been associated with labour exploitation, particularly in regions like the Democratic Republic of Congo, where child labour and unsafe working conditions are prevalent (Calvão et al., 2021; Tsurukawa et al., 2011).

Colonial tendencies are also evident in the Global North-focused ethical standards developed for AI systems (Eke et al., 2023b). AI is a value-laden technology that reflects cultural norms, values and principles. Existing AI ethics frameworks are developed in the Global North and do not often take into account the socio-cultural values, perspectives, and contexts from Africa. This reflects the colonial tendency to ignore epistemological and ethical frameworks that existed in the colonies pre-colonisation. This perpetuates power imbalances and leads to the exploitation of the underrepresented communities or regions. It is safe to say that any AI system developed to reflect these colonial tendencies will not be considered trustworthy in the African context. A non-decolonised AI system will not and should not be considered trustworthy for any context in Africa. That is why we are introducing decoloniality as a critical trustworthy AI principle. But what does decoloniality of AI mean?

Decoloniality of AI

Historically, *colonialism* was characterised by territorial appropriation, exploitation of the natural environment and of human labour, direct control of social structures (Mohamed et al., 2020). *Decolonisation* is a movement that involves the challenging, undoing, or dismantling of colonialism and its identified structures and systems (Darwin, 1988). Historically in politics, this movement focused mainly on the transfer of power and governance from colonial administrators to indigenous sovereign nations. However, colonial effects endure to the present day and wherever this is identified, the concept of ***coloniality*** is introduced (Maldonado-Torres, 2007; Mignolo, 2013; Mohamed et al., 2020; Quijano, 2000). Mohamed et al. (2020) stated that coloniality means the continuity of established patterns of power between coloniser and colonised—and the contemporary remnants of these relationships—and how that power shapes our understanding of culture, labour, intersubjectivity, and knowledge production. Decoloniality is therefore an *active process* that seeks to address and dismantle the deep-seated impacts of coloniality on knowledge systems, technologies, cultures, identities, and social structures. Decoloniality is an *active, transformative, and interventional process* as opposed to a passive or descriptive concept like 'postcolonial' or nationalistic concept like 'anti-colonial'. This is a restorative process that involves identifying and addressing current colonial tendencies. It is a concept that recognises that achieving political independence is not enough and that emphasises the recovery and validation of knowledge systems, values, contexts, and practices of underrepresented voices. Decoloniality is about restoring what was suppressed; creating new, equitable systems and practices.

As pointed out in the previous section, colonial systems of thought, power, dominance, and control often remain embedded in institutions, education, and societal norms as coloniality. Decoloniality works to build more just and equitable structures by providing a framework for dismantling colonial tendencies. Using a simple analogy, decolonisation is ensuring that the stranger in our house leaves, while decoloniality is the process of cleaning the house in the aftermath of the stranger leaving; including repairing the damages, renovating the house to our needs, taste, context, and ensuring that whenever the stranger comes again, it will only be a 'visit' and similar damages will not occur again.

Having said that, we have identified reflections of colonial tendencies or coloniality in the AI lifecycle which shows that AI can perpetuate historical patterns of control, domination, and exclusion. Therefore, AI requires active interrogation. It requires decoloniality to ensure the decentralisation or balance of power, epistemic justice and that AI systems promote fairness, equity and are contextually aware. Decoloniality here encompasses critical theoretical and practical frameworks for understanding and addressing the enduring effects of colonial tendencies in AI. It is not enough to identify the presence of colonial structures of domination and power imbalance in AI. Decoloniality involves developing practical approaches to address them and to shape the understanding, design, development, and use of AI in ways that will centre the perspectives, voices, needs, and contexts of underrepresented communities. The vision of decoloniality of AI is to ensure that AI systems created in and for underrepresented communities, such as Africa, reflect their interests and needs. That is why we introduce decoloniality as an essential requirement of trustworthy AI, particularly in Africa. In the next section, we explain what decoloniality as a requirement looks like.

Decoloniality here should not be confused with nationalist and Marxist thought. Grosfoguel, (2007) put it this way: "this is not an essentialist, fundamentalist, anti-European critique. It is a perspective that is critical of both Eurocentric and Third World fundamentalisms, colonialism, and nationalism. What all fundamentalisms share (including the Eurocentric one) is the premise that there is only one sole epistemic tradition from which to achieve Truth and Universality". In this sense, decoloniality does not deny the validity of epistemologies from the Global North but it is an attempt to prioritise the African contexts, needs, languages, narratives, and values in the design and use of AI.

Decoloniality as a Trustworthy AI Requirement in Africa

According to the US National Institute of Standards and Technology, the building blocks of AI trustworthiness include ensuring; *validity and reliability, safety, security and resiliency, accountability and transparency, explainability and Interpretability, privacy, fairness with mitigation of harmful bias* (NIST, 2022). The EU-independent High Level Expert Group (HLEG) provided fundamental components of trustworthy AI as *lawful* (AI systems comply with all applicable laws), *ethical* (they should adhere to ethical principles and values), and *robustness* (they should be technically and socially robust. These components work in harmony and overlap in theory and practice (HLEG, 2019). The HLEG went further to list seven key requirements that AI systems should meet for trustworthy AI to be realised. These include; *human agency and oversight, technical robustness and safety, privacy and data governance, transparency, diversity, non-discrimination and fairness, environmental and societal well-being and accountability.* These key requirements for trustworthy AI in the United States and Europe share several commonalities but also exhibit distinct differences due to variations in regulatory environments, cultural values and societal priorities. Common requirements include the emphasis on ethical principles (such as fairness, accountability, and transparency), bias mitigation, security and safety, and human-centric design. However, the EU's requirements emphasise the protection of human rights with established regulations (such as EU AI Act and the GDPR) and the US requirements lean on innovation-friendly approaches. While the EU requirements are basically based on the precautionary principles and the need to prioritise collective well-being, the US requirements are founded on market-driven approaches and strong emphasis on individual rights.

From the above, one can see that requirements for trustworthiness of AI are different (in conceptualisation and in operations) in different countries and regions. These differences are inherent in the nature of the concept of trustworthiness. Requirements for trustworthiness differ significantly across different cultural and political contexts, needs, values, principles. Different factors influence the perception of trust and trustworthiness. For instance, in a region that leans more to collectivist or communal principles, AI systems may need to demonstrate benefits for the community to achieve trustworthiness. AI's role in supporting communal harmony, collective privacy and addressing collective needs will be paramount. On the other hand, for individualistic cultures, trustworthiness might focus on personal benefits, individual privacy and rights, and respect for autonomy will be critical.

Although we are not proposing a fully formed framework for trustworthiness of AI in Africa, we argue that considering Africa's colonial history and the continued influence of coloniality in the design, development, and deployment of AI systems, decoloniality *should* be an essential requirement for AI to achieve trustworthiness in Africa. Our argument is based on the fact that AI systems must be aware of and sensitive to historical contexts to avoid perpetuating colonial biases. Trustworthy AI should aim to reverse coloniality by promoting economic justice and benefiting local communities. It should be focused on addressing structural inequities through access, inclusion, and representation. The integration of local knowledge systems should be critical, ensuring that technologies are relevant and respectful of relevant needs, contexts, and traditions. The support for local languages and dialects and enabling broader accessibility and usability should be prioritised given that many AI systems are designed primarily for Western languages and communication styles. The emphasis on the importance of cultural sovereignty, where African communities control and define their cultural expressions to avoid cultural imperialism, should be prominent. Africans should be intentional in the promotion of ethical frameworks grounded in African philosophies and values, such as *Ubuntu, umunna, and ujamaa* which emphasise community, mutual respect, and interconnectedness (Eke et al., 2023b; Wakunuma et al., 2022).

Additionally, trustworthiness must also be linked to how African countries can control their data, ensuring it is used ethically and benefits local populations rather than being exploited by foreign entities. As an essential requirement for trustworthiness, decoloniality should provide an assessment mechanism to address data and algorithmic colonialism and existing power imbalances. Ensuring that Africans own and or control their data empowers citizens and nations to make decisions that best reflect their needs and priorities. It supports the right to self-determination, allowing communities to leverage data for their own development goals. This can help prevent exploitation from external entities and ensure that AI systems are not driven by external priorities. Given that most underlying infrastructures for AI are non-African owned, trustworthiness should also be about how AI should support local economic development, creating opportunities for innovation, entrepreneurship, and job creation within African countries. It should ensure that AI technologies are developed and deployed in ways that are culturally relevant, ethically sound, and supportive of local socio-economic development. The focus will be on addressing historical and structural inequities, promoting cultural sensitivity, and fostering global equity. It is also about providing fair distribution of benefits as it relates to the mining of natural resources in Africa used for AI systems or infrastructure. Decoloniality works towards addressing the exploitative nature of mining these resources by non-African entities in a way that local communities and countries get fair benefits from resources they own.

Also, it is recognised that while science is a product of epistemic values, contextual values which reflect moral, societal, or personal concerns are also reflected in the application of scientific knowledge (Mohamed et al., 2020). Decoloniality ensures that AI systems are designed with a deep understanding of the cultural, social, and economic realities of the communities they serve, which is essential for trustworthiness. This involves not only recognising and addressing colonial tendencies in AI, but also actively ensuring that AI systems reflect the needs, values, and contexts of African communities. Decoloniality will minimise the risks of harm that can arise from cultural insensitivity or ignorance. This is crucial for maintaining the trust of users and ensuring that AI applications are beneficial rather than detrimental.

How Decoloniality can be Realised and Assessed

Realising decoloniality as a requirement for trustworthy AI should involve the use of both technical and non-technical methods. Some non-technical methods include education and awareness programmes for designers, developers, deployers, policymakers, and the public. This can involve the integration of decoloniality in existing curriculum or via workshops and seminars. It can also involve the inclusion of decoloniality in policies and regulatory frameworks. Participatory design approaches that involve local communities in the design and implementation process can help to ensure that critical needs are met, and cultural contexts are respected. It can also involve the identification and integration of indigenous expertise, language and knowledge systems, and practices into the design and use of AI. Clear pathways for investments in local economies and establishment of fair-trade practices can also contribute to achieving decoloniality. Technical approaches to realise decoloniality can include the development and use of datasets that are representative of diverse African populations; development of collaborative and non-exploitative platforms that can facilitate collaboration between global and local developers in a way that knowledge transfer and mutual benefits are ensured. Building systems to ensure that data collected within a country or community are stored, processed, and owned in that country. This can ensure data sovereignty. Decoloniality can also be realised through capacity building including but not limited to training programmes to build local expertise. This multifaceted approach combines education, policy development and reforms, community engagement, economic empowerment, inclusive datasets, and capacity building in the realisation of decoloniality as an essential requirement for trustworthiness.

Likewise, the deployment of AI in Africa must consider the unique socio-economic and cultural landscapes of the continent. AI solutions must be tailored to address local challenges and opportunities as well as utilise indigenous knowledge and community-driven approaches. For instance, AI applications in agriculture can significantly enhance food security by providing farmers with predictive analytics for crop management, while respecting traditional farming practices and knowledge (Adewusi et al., 2024).

From the above points, key criteria for assessing decoloniality can thus be *representation and inclusion* (how representative are the datasets and the development team?), *community involvement* (level of meaningful involvement of local communities), *cultural sensitivity* (how are local contexts, needs, languages, values, and principles are embedded in the systems), *economic and social impact* (impact on local economic development and social empowerment) and *data sovereignty* (who owns or controls the data collected in Africa?). These can be assessed through established methods such as *impact assessments* (EIA ethical impact assessment and social impact assessment) (Brey, 2012; Brey et al., 2022; Stahl & Eke, 2024), *audits and reviews* (third-party audits or internal reviews) (LaBrie & Steinke, 2019). Developing some sort of *diversity metrics* (Mitchell et al., 2020) to track metrics such as diversity of datasets, development teams, and stakeholder involvement can also help. Although this can possibly become a tick box exercise, it will contribute to understanding how decoloniality is being achieved. Another thing that can be done is to develop *standards and certification programmes* for decolonial AI, providing benchmarks for decolonial AI development and deployment. Community feedback mechanisms such as *surveys, interviews, and public consultations* can also be critical assessment approaches for decoloniality as a requirement for trustworthy AI (Table 12.1).

Challenges to Decolonising AI in Africa

Decoloniality is not a new concept. What is new is its application in the context of AI. As Ndlovu-Gatsheni (2013) observed, it is "not only a long-standing political and epistemological movement aimed at liberation of (ex-) colonised peoples from global coloniality but also a way of thinking, knowing, and doing". He went further in another work (2015) to posit that he believes that decoloniality is the future of Africa. For us, it is a requirement that demonstrates the need to appreciate a pluriversal approach rather than a universal approach to AI design, development, and deployment. However, we identify a number of challenges or barriers to achieving decoloniality of AI in Africa.

Table 12.1 Critical Questions of decoloniality as a requirement for Trustworthy AI

a. Have the AI system's design, development and deployment considered integrating relevant local languages and dialects, religious beliefs and other belief systems and cultural values (such as ideas of interconnectedness, solidarity, and shared/collective responsibility)
b. Have the AI system's design, development and deployment considered integrating relevant local data and are datasets used for the AI system owned and controlled by locals (citizens and local institutions)?
c. Was the AI system developed or deployed using relevant local expertise and where there is none, have the designers and developers contributed to capacity development or education of local voices/experts?
d. If you are mining local resources relevant to the design and development of AI systems, are you ensuring fair distribution of profits/benefits?
e. Did the development and deployment of the AI system include community voices and representation in the AI lifecycle?
f. Are local experts or workers fairly remunerated?

The first challenge is the significant dependency on big tech companies. This dependency manifests in several ways and has far-reaching implications. Many underlying infrastructure for AI are developed, owned, and controlled by big tech companies. From hardware infrastructure such as computing power Central Processing Units (CPUs) and Graphics Processing Units (GPUs), Tensor Processing Units (TPUs), edge devices to software infrastructure like operating systems, frameworks and libraries, development environments, and cloud platforms. African countries and companies heavily rely on them. This reliance on proprietary technologies limits local innovation and creates a form of technological dependency. In the same vein, many AI applications depend on cloud storage services provided by major tech companies such as Amazon Web Services (AWS), Google Cloud, and Microsoft Azure. This reliance can be costly and limits local data sovereignty. This makes efforts to keep data within national borders complicated.

Furthermore, profits from AI-related activities often flow back to Big Tech companies who are headquartered outside of Africa, rather than benefiting local economies. More often than not, these companies prioritise investments that serve their interests, which may not align with the needs and priorities of African communities. In the absence of regulations in Africa, these tech companies often impose their own ethical standards, which may not reflect the ethical considerations and priorities of African societies. The evident gaps in local governance frameworks to effectively regulate and oversee the activities of these companies are significant to ensuring accountability and transparency. And there is an increasing trend of these companies funding policy and regulatory discussions in Africa in order to have significant influence over local regulatory frameworks, which can result in regulations that favour their interests over those of local communities.

Another challenge is the lack of a defined way of achieving decoloniality in AI in Africa as it makes it difficult to create coherent strategies, measure progress, and mobilise resources effectively. Decoloniality is a complex and multifaceted concept with various interpretations. This can lead to confusion about what decoloniality in AI specifically entails and what goals and benchmarks should be set. The interests of local and international actors may sometimes conflict, complicating the development of a unified approach to decoloniality in AI. This is a gap this chapter is attempting to fill.

In addition to the above, another challenge arises from the lack of enhanced digital literacy on AI Technologies. Digital literacy goes beyond basic computer skills; it includes understanding the implications of AI, being aware of data rights and privacy issues, and having the ability to critically evaluate the impact of AI technologies. This lack of critical awareness deprives the continent of an opportunity to empower individuals and communities to recognise and resist colonial influences and challenge the colonial aspects embedded in these systems including questioning the intentions behind certain technologies and advocating for more culturally relevant and equitable and inclusive alternatives in how AI systems are designed, developed, and deployed. Lack of enhanced digital literacy also contributes to stifled local innovation across Africa due to unavailability of skills to develop AI solutions that address local needs, that also contributes to an imbalanced global technology ecosystem where Africa is considered as a consumer rather than developer of AI technologies.

Recommendations

As the AI landscape in Africa continues to evolve, it is imperative to recognise the critical role of decoloniality in establishing trustworthiness of AI as discussed above. Decoloniality is our way of challenging the entrenched power dynamics and biases embedded in coloniality of AI, advocating for a more equitable and inclusive approach to AI development. By embedding decolonial principles into AI systems, we ensure that these technologies will not only be innovative but also fair, inclusive, and reflective of the diverse cultural and social realities of Africa and the wider global population. This requires intentional efforts to reimagine and restructure AI practices, policies, and collaborations. We therefore make the following recommendations to Africa's national government institutions and AI developers as essential steps to achieve decoloniality AI, thereby fostering systems that serve all humanity equitably and ethically.

Strengthening Policy and Regulatory Frameworks

To achieve decoloniality and foster trustworthy AI, it is imperative to strengthen policy and regulatory frameworks by making decoloniality an essential requirement in AI governance. Although there are numerous policy recommendations such as UNESCO's recommendation on the ethics of AI (UNESCO, 2021) or the EU AI Act of 2024 (Council of Europe, 2021), none of them cover the aspect of decoloniality. As such, any policy and regulatory framework on AI in Africa ought to involve the development of policies that explicitly address and rectify the historical and systemic biases rooted in colonial legacies, ensuring that AI technologies do not perpetuate existing inequalities. Regulatory frameworks must enforce standards for ethical AI practices, mandating transparency, accountability, and fairness in AI development and deployment. These policies should be created through inclusive, participatory processes that engage diverse stakeholders, including marginalised communities, to ensure their voices and perspectives shape the regulatory landscape. Additionally, frameworks should support local innovation and the integration of indigenous knowledge systems, promoting a more diverse and representative AI ecosystem. Through the integration of this concept in regulations, a trustworthy AI environment that upholds human rights, fosters social justice, and aligns with the principles of decoloniality can emerge.

Promoting Inclusive Data Practices

Decoloniality within the context of trustworthy AI calls for the promotion of inclusive data practices that encompass the diverse experiences and perspectives of all communities. This involves collecting and curating datasets that are representative of different cultural, social, and economic backgrounds, thereby avoiding the perpetuation of colonial biases and ensuring a fairer, more accurate reflection of global populations. Inclusive data practices require engaging with local communities to understand their unique contexts and needs, integrating indigenous knowledge systems, languages, and respecting cultural sensitivities in data collection and usage. Furthermore, transparency in data sourcing, consent, and handling are essential to build trust and accountability. By focusing on inclusivity in data practices, AI systems that are more equitable, culturally aware, and effective in addressing the needs of diverse populations can be developed, ultimately fostering a more just and decolonised AI technological landscape.

Developing Local Capacity and Community Engagement

The achievement of decoloniality and trustworthy AI, it is essential to develop local capacity and engage communities by actively involving them in the AI development process, thereby ensuring local needs and perspectives are not only considered but prioritised. Decoloniality needs locals with appropriate expertise and knowledge to provide guidance on the practical and theoretical approaches of achieving decoloniality. This entails promoting community-driven research and development, where local voices guide the design and implementation of AI solutions. Building local technical expertise through accessible education and training programmes is vital, as it will empower African communities to take ownership of AI innovations. Collaborative partnerships with local governments, Civil Society Organisations, academia, and private sector entities are crucial to creating a supportive AI ecosystem that respects and integrates indigenous knowledge systems and cultural contexts. Smith (2021) has argued for the importance of indigenous knowledge in her call for decolonising methodologies. Equally, indigenous knowledge has an important role to play in AI innovation within local and community capacities. Ethical and responsible AI practices must be at the forefront, with transparency and accountability measures ensuring that communities are continuously informed and involved in the development process. By supporting community-led initiatives and enhancing the accessibility and usability of AI technologies, local community innovations that align with local values and needs can result. Continuous monitoring and evaluation, with active community feedback, will also ensure that AI applications remain equitable, inclusive, and beneficial, ultimately fostering a more just and trustworthy technological landscape.

Developing and Implementing Culturally Sensitive AI Design

The willingness to develop and implement culturally sensitive AI systems is critical to achieving decoloniality in AI. Designers, developers, and deployers of AI must recognise and appreciate the value proposition inherent in achieving decoloniality. From increased acceptability of technology, equity and inclusion, bias mitigation, empowerment, cultural preservation, and respect to global solidarity, there are real incentives for decoloniality as a requirement for trustworthiness. This approach requires actively involving indigenous and marginalised voices in the AI development process, ensuring that their perspectives and knowledge systems are central to the design and implementation of AI technologies. Culturally sensitive AI design entails the creation of algorithms and datasets that accurately reflect the socio-cultural diversity of the populations they serve, avoiding the replication of colonial biases and stereotypes. Noble (2018) has critically examined how algorithms can oppress and therefore perpetuate inequalities and societal biases because of who creates them which is determined by their values. As such, an inclusive and culturally sensitive design process becomes imperative in avoidance of bias and inequalities. Additionally, this involves designing user interfaces and functionalities that are accessible and relevant to different cultural groups, promoting inclusivity and equity. By prioritising culturally sensitive AI design, AI systems that are not only technically robust but also ethically sound and socially just can be created which foster trust. Costanza-Chock (2020) discusses the concept of design justice and makes the case for reimagining design processes through the inclusion of needs of marginalised communities, something which the decoloniality concept is keen on.

Encouraging Local Innovation

Decoloniality also calls for the encouragement of local innovation by empowering communities to develop AI technologies that reflect their unique cultural contexts, needs, and values. This entails providing robust support for local entrepreneurs, researchers, and developers through funding, resources, and access to state-of-the-art technology and infrastructure. By fostering an environment where local talent can thrive. The dominance of global tech giants can slowly begin to be challenged; lead to a reduction in dependency on foreign technologies that may not align with local realities. In addition, encouraging local innovation also involves creating collaborative networks that connect local innovators with global experts, ensuring knowledge exchange while maintaining respect for indigenous knowledge systems. Policies should therefore prioritise the protection of intellectual property rights for local creators and facilitate the commercialisation of homegrown AI solutions. Through these measures, a diverse and inclusive AI landscape that honours decolonial principles, promotes self-reliance, and ensures that AI technologies are trustworthy, ethical, and beneficial for all communities can be cultivated.

Fostering Equitable International Collaboration

For AI to be truly inclusive, equitable, and without colonial tendencies, equitable and inclusive international collaboration is crucial. This involves creating partnerships where knowledge exchange and technological development are balanced, ensuring that all parties benefit equally and that power dynamics do not replicate colonial hierarchies. Such collaborations should consider the voices and needs of historically marginalised communities, integrating their perspectives into global AI initiatives. This requires transparent and fair agreements that protect the intellectual property and cultural heritage of local communities, ensuring they receive proper recognition and benefits. These collaborations should focus on empowering local researchers and developers, enabling them to contribute meaningfully to the global AI discourse. Additionally, collaborative AI projects should be guided by ethical standards that emphasise social justice, inclusivity, and respect for diverse cultural contexts. By fostering truly equitable international collaboration, a more inclusive and decolonised AI ecosystem that is globally interconnected yet deeply respectful of local nuances and needs can be built.

This chapter underscores the importance of a decolonial approach to AI, which not only aligns technological advancement with the principles of social justice and equity but also empowers African nations to harness AI for sustainable and inclusive development. Achieving decoloniality in AI development is crucial for creating systems that are reflective of diverse cultural and social needs. These measures collectively lead to empowered communities, ensuring AI systems uplift rather than oppress, and fostering a global AI ecosystem rooted in justice and inclusivity.

Conclusion

The chapter has explored various elements related to decoloniality, including the concept of coloniality or colonial tendencies in AI. It further explored the decoloniality of AI, examining critical elements necessary for transforming AI technologies into tools of empowerment rather than exploitation. We have emphasised the importance of culturally aware algorithmic design, ensuring that AI systems are sensitive to and respectful of different cultural contexts and values. Decoloniality in AI is fundamentally about restoring what was suppressed to creating new, equitable systems and practices that respect and elevate all voices. Furthermore, our chapter provides clarity on why and how to achieve this essential requirement. As we have noted above, decoloniality is an active, transformative, and interventional process that calls for equal access to AI resources and participation in the AI lifecycle as well as to empower marginalised communities. We have also presented decoloniality as a trustworthy AI requirement in Africa. This is important because it ensures that AI technologies are developed and deployed in ways that align with African values, knowledge, needs, and socio-economic contexts. As we alluded to, trustworthiness is influenced by different factors which may be based on collectivist or communal principles for others while, on the other hand, it may be based on personal benefits for others. Presented too was an exploration of the challenges to decolonising AI in Africa. These challenges include the dominance of Western technological paradigms and the lack of local expertise and infrastructure. To conclude, this chapter has highlighted some critical elements to address and rectify the historical and systemic biases embedded within AI technologies. Emphasising the importance of diverse and inclusive datasets, the chapter underscored the necessity for AI systems to accurately reflect the multifaceted nature of its user's experiences including those from the African continent. It also stressed the significance of culturally aware algorithmic design, ensuring AI systems are sensitive to and respectful of various cultural contexts and values. Thus, our recommendations include promoting capacity building to empower communities with the skills and resources needed to develop and control their AI technologies, enhancing community engagement to ensure AI solutions are aligned with local needs and perspectives, and encouraging equitable international collaboration to balance power dynamics and share benefits fairly.

References

Adewusi, A. O., et al. (2024). AI in precision agriculture: A review of technologies for sustainable farming practices. *World Journal of Advanced Research and Reviews, 21*(1), 2276–2285.

Arora, S., et al. (2020). Improving malignancy prediction in AUS/FLUS pediatric thyroid nodules with the aid of ultrasound. *Hormone Research in Paediatrics, 93*(4), 239–244.

Birhane, A. (2020). Algorithmic colonization of Africa. *Scripted, 17*, 389.

Brey, P. et al. (2022). SIENNA D6. 1: Generalised methodology for ethical assessment of emerging technologies [Online]. Accessed on August 07, 2024, from https://research.utwente.nl/files/303706744/SIENNA_D6.1_Generalised_methodology_for_ethical_assessment_of_emerging_technologies.pdf

Brey, P. A. (2012). Anticipatory ethics for emerging technologies. *NanoEthics, 6*(1), 1–13.

Buolamwini, J., & Gebru, T. (2018). Gender Shades: Intersectional accuracy disparities in commercial gender classification. In *Proceedings of Machine Learning Research* (pp. 1–15). Conference on Fairness, Accountability, and Transparency.

Calvão, F., Mcdonald, C. E. A., & Bolay, M. (2021). Cobalt mining and the corporate outsourcing of responsibility in the Democratic Republic of Congo. *The Extractive Industries and Society, 8*(4), 100884.

Costanza-Chock, S. (2020). *Design justice: Community-led practices to build the worlds we need*. The MIT Press.

Couldry, N., & Mejias, U. A. (2019). Data colonialism: Rethinking big data's relation to the contemporary subject. *Television & New Media, 20*(4), 336–349.

Council of Europe. (2021). Regulation (EU) 2021/2282 of the European Parliament and of the Council of 15 December 2021 on health technology assessment and amending Directive 2011/24/EU. *Official Journal of the European Union, 50*.

Crawford, K. (2021). *The atlas of AI: Power, politics, and the planetary costs of artificial intelligence*. Yale University Press.

Darwin, J. (1988). Decolonisation. *Britain and decolonisation* (pp. 3–33). Macmillan Education UK.

Eke, D., & Ogoh, G. (2022) Forgotten African AI narratives and the future of AI in Africa. *The International Review of Information Ethics*, *31*(1). https://doi.org/10.29173/irie482

Eke, D.O., Chintu, S. S., & Wakunuma, K. (2023b). Towards shaping the future of responsible AI in Africa. In *Responsible AI in Africa: Challenges and opportunities* (pp. 169–193). Springer International Publishing Cham.

Eke, D.O., Wakunuma, K., & Akintoye, S. (2023a). *Responsible AI in Africa: challenges and opportunities*. Springer Nature.

Ferrer, X., et al. (2021). Bias and discrimination in AI: A cross-disciplinary perspective. *IEEE Technology and Society Magazine, 40*(2), 72–80.

Gravett, W.H. (2023). Digital coloniser? China and artificial intelligence in Africa. In *Survival December 2020–January 2021: A world after Trump* (pp. 153–177). Routledge.

Grosfoguel, R. (2007). The Epistemic Decolonial Turn: Beyond political-economy paradigms. *Cultural Studies, 21*(2–3), 211–223.

Hao, K. (2020). *The problems AI has today go back centuries* [Online]. MIT Technology Review. Accessed on May 26, 2024, from https://www.technologyreview.com/2020/07/31/1005824/decolonial-ai-for-everyone/

HLEG. (2019). High-level expert group on artificial intelligence. *Ethics guidelines for trustworthy AI*, 6 [Online]. Accessed on August 06, 2024, from https://www.aepd.es/sites/default/files/2019-09/ai-definition.pdf

LaBrie, R. C., & Steinke, G. (2019). Towards a framework for ethical audits of AI algorithms [Online]. Accessed on August 07, 2024, from https://scholar.archive.org/work/wv7pfbs3uve5xegh336ffeeuta/access/wayback/https://aisel.aisnet.org/cgi/viewcontent.cgi?article=1398&context=amcis2019

Le Ludec, C., Cornet, M., & Casilli, A. A. (2023). The problem with annotation. Human labour and outsourcing between France and Madagascar. *Big Data & Society*, *10*(2), 20539517231188724.

Li, B., et al. (2023). Trustworthy AI: From principles to practices. *ACM Computing Surveys, 55*(9), 1–46.

Maldonado-Torres, N. (2007). On the coloniality of being: Contributions to the development of a concept. *Cultural Studies*, *21*(2–3), 240–270.

Mignolo, W. D. (2013). Introduction: Coloniality of power and de-colonial thinking. In *Globalization and the decolonial option* (pp. 1–21).

Miller, K. (2020). A matter of perspective: Discrimination, bias, and inequality in AI. In *Legal regulations, implications, and issues surrounding digital data* (pp. 182–202). IGI Global.

Mitchell, M. et al. (2020). Diversity and inclusion metrics in subset selection. In *Proceedings of the AAAI/ACM Conference on AI, Ethics, and Society*. AIES '20: AAAI/ACM Conference on AI, Ethics, and Society, (pp. 117–123). ACM.

Mohamed, S., Png, M.-T., & Isaac, W. (2020). Decolonial AI: Decolonial theory as sociotechnical foresight in Artificial Intelligence. *Philosophy & Technology, 33*(4), 659–684.

Mollema, W. J. T. (2024). Decolonial AI as disenclosure. *Open Journal of Social Sciences, 12*(2), 574–603.

Ndlovu-Gatsheni, S. J. (2015). Decoloniality as the future of Africa. *History Compass, 13*(10), 485–496.

Ndlovu-Gatsheni, S. J. (2013). Why decoloniality in the 21st century. *The Thinker, 48*(10), 5–9.

NIST. (2022). Trustworthy and responsible AI. *NIST* [Online]. Accessed on August 07, 2024, from https://www.nist.gov/trustworthy-and-responsible-ai

Noble, S. U. (2018). *Algorithms of Oppression: How Search Engines Reinforce Racism*. NYU Press.

Quijano, A. (2007). Coloniality and modernity/rationality. *Cultural Studies, 21*(2–3), 168–178.

Quijano, A. (2000). Coloniality of power and Eurocentrism in Latin America. *International Sociology, 15*(2), 215–232.

Raji, I. D. et al. (2020). Saving face: Investigating the ethical concerns of facial recognition auditing. In: *Proceedings of the AAAI/ACM Conference on AI, Ethics, and Society*, 145–151.

Rowe, N. (2023, August 2). 'It's destroyed me completely': Kenyan moderators decry toll of training of AI models. *The Guardian*.

Smith, L. T. (2021). *Decolonizing methodologies: Research and indigenous peoples*. Bloomsbury Publishing.

Stahl, B. C., & Eke, D. (2024) The ethics of ChatGPT—Exploring the ethical issues of an emerging technology. *International Journal of Information Management*.

Tsurukawa, N., Prakash, S., & Manhart, A. (2011). Social impacts of artisanal cobalt mining in Katanga, Democratic Republic of Congo. *Öko-Institut eV, Freiburg*, [Online] Accessed on August 07, 2024, from http://resourcefever.com/publications/reports/OEKO_2011_cobalt_mining_congo.pdf

UNESCO, C. (2021). Recommendation on the ethics of Artificial Intelligence.

Wakunuma, K. et al. (2022). *Responsible AI, SDGs, and AI Governance in Africa*. Institute of Electrical and Electronics Engineers.

Williams, A. (2022). The exploited labor behind Artificial Intelligence [Online]. Accessed on August 07, 2024, from https://www.noemamag.com/the-exploited-labor-behind-artificial-intelligence

Correction to: Trustworthy AI

Damian Okaibedi Eke, Kutoma Wakunuma,
Simisola Akintoye, and George Ogoh

Correction to:
D. O. Eke et al. (eds.), *Trustworthy AI*,
https://doi.org/10.1007/978-3-031-75674-0

The original version of this book was inadvertently published without the funding details in the copyright page, which have now been included. The book has been updated with the changes.

The updated version of this book can be found at
https://doi.org/10.1007/978-3-031-75674-0

D. O. Eke et al. (eds.), *Trustworthy AI*,
https://doi.org/10.1007/978-3-031-75674-0_13

Epilogue

As we bring this book to a close, it is crucial to reflect on the transformative journey explored across the chapters. The narrative has delved into the critical themes of trustworthy Artificial Intelligence (AI), the African context, and the intersection of ethics, governance, and socio-cultural values. The editors and the contributors have made it clear that AI in Africa cannot be approached in the same way it is in the Global North. Instead, Africa must assert its voice and presence in global AI development, embracing an Afrocentric approach that champions inclusivity, fairness, and social justice.

The chapters have woven a powerful narrative about the need for decoloniality, highlighting how AI systems, like many other technologies, can perpetuate historical power imbalances if left unchecked. It is not enough to adopt AI solutions developed elsewhere; Africa must co-create its technological future. This means designing AI frameworks that align with the continent's diverse cultural landscapes, uphold ethical integrity, and prioritise the welfare of its communities. The notion of "trustworthiness" in AI must encompass not just technical robustness but also a deep commitment to the socio-economic upliftment of African societies.

Through the various lenses explored in this book—be it in healthcare, gender equality, or governance—the message is clear: Africa has the potential to lead in shaping an AI future that reflects its unique needs and aspirations. However, this can only be achieved through a concerted effort from policymakers, researchers, technologists, and civil

D. O. Eke et al. (eds.), *Trustworthy AI*,
https://doi.org/10.1007/978-3-031-75674-0

society, working together to build resilient AI systems that serve the public good.

The journey towards building trustworthy AI in Africa is just beginning, and the road ahead is filled with both challenges and opportunities. Yet, as the book demonstrates, Africa is well-positioned to harness the power of AI in ways that foster sustainable development, ethical governance, and inclusive growth. By focusing on relationality, justice, and the empowerment of local communities, Africa can create a digital future that is not only technologically advanced but also deeply human-centred.

This work calls on all stakeholders to take action, invest in African AI research and infrastructure, and ensure that AI technologies benefit the many, not just the few. This investment is crucial for building the necessary capacity and expertise to develop and deploy AI solutions that are tailored to Africa's unique context. In doing so, we will not only ensure Africa's rightful place in the global AI narrative but also create a legacy of innovation that empowers future generations.

Barbara Glover

Programme Officer-African Union High-Level Panel on Emerging. Technologies (APET) AUDA-NEPAD

Index

D. O. Eke et al. (eds.), *Trustworthy AI*,
https://doi.org/10.1007/978-3-031-75674-0

FSC
www.fsc.org
MIX
Papier | Fördert
gute Waldnutzung
FSC® C083411

Kolibri 360 GmbH
Ferdinand-Jühlke-Straße 7
99095 Erfurt, Deutschland
produktsicherheit@kolibri360.de